DEDICATION

I dedicate this book to the Lord (Jesus), for His grace in allowing me the time and health necessary to complete this project, to my loving wife (Marialis) for her continual sacrificial support, and to my son (Daniel Ariel) who is a gift from above.

KILLING JESUS

IS HE ALIVE TODAY?

RENÉ A. LÓPEZ

Author of *The Jesus Family Tomb Examined*

Foreword by Daniel B. Wallace, Author and Greek Scholar

KILLING JESUS

21st Century Press is a publisher dedicated to publishing books with high family values. We believe the vision for 21st Century Press is to provide families and individuals with user-friendly materials that will help them in their daily lives and experiences.

It is our hope that this book will help you discover truths for your own life and help you meet the needs of others. May you be richly blessed.

21st Century Press
2131 W. Republic Rd. PMB 211
Springfield, MO 65807
800-658-0284
www.21stcenturypress.com

ISBN: 978-0-9894317-2-9
Cover illustration: Lee Fredrickson
Book Design: Lee Fredrickson

21stCENTURY
P R E S S
READING YOU LOUD AND CLEAR.

CONTENTS

FOREWORD

Book forewords often take on many shapes and sizes. Some are mere endorsements of the work, while others give details of its contents, urging the reader with their informed Tolle lege! This foreword is of the latter sort. The reason for this is that the chapter titles, as helpful as they are, may not always be clear to the reader who wants to get a bird's eye view of the contents of the work.

But first, for some preliminaries. I am happy to both endorse this volume and write its foreword. I learned a great deal reading through the draft and found that Dr. López really did his homework and seemingly answered all conceivable objections to the resurrection of Jesus. Dr. López has produced a very useful resource on the resurrection of Jesus. He takes the interesting angle that many have "killed" Jesus—both literally in the Gospels, and through various philosophies and approaches that have denied the Gospels any historical credibility about the resurrection. The best approach for the reader is to simply read through each chapter seriatim. However, the book is written in such a way that someone could just as easily pick up at any chapter and begin reading. Each chapter, in other words, is essentially self-contained. Below is a description of each unit.

The first chapter, "Killing Jesus: A Chronology" is simply quotations from the NT on the passion narrative. He lets scripture speak for itself.

Chapter two, "Killing Jesus Throughout the Centuries," reveals ten different philosophies that have been utilized since the Reformation to mitigate the Bible's testimony. López helpfully yet succinctly critiques each of these views.

Chapter three, "Killing the Document that Validates Jesus Rising," takes on a variety of views regarding Jesus' resurrection, especially modern skepticism about the text of the NT, recently uncovered evidence from ossuaries, and the notion that the early Christians must have embraced a spiritual, rather than bodily, resurrection. This chapter alone is worth the price of this book.

In the fourth chapter, "Killing Jesus Before Rising," the author lays out convincing reasons for belief in death by crucifixion in Jesus' case.

Although some have held to a "swoon theory," all of the evidence is over-whelmingly against it. No bona fide NT scholar, whether conservative, liberal, or somewhere in between, disagrees with this fact.

"Killing the Concept of Physical Resurrection" is the title for the fifth chapter. Here is discussed the evidence in the OT and NT that bodily resurrection is part and parcel of the Jewish understanding of the afterlife. Spiritual resurrection is simply not envisioned. In chapter six, "Killing the Evidence that He Rose Physically," López deals with the overwhelming evidence in the NT that Jesus' resurrection was a bodily resurrection. He offers a close reading of the texts, replete with exegetical backing (though most is reserved for the endnotes).

In the seventh chapter, the author addresses "Killing Prophecies of OT and NT Resurrection." Again, he offers a close reading of two key OT passages (Psalm 16:8–11 and Isaiah 53:10–12) that indirectly speak of the Messiah's resurrection.

The spiritual and pragmatic results of belief in the resurrection are the focus in chapter eight, "Killing the Resurrection that Transforms Lives." Here the author not only speaks of the eyewitnesses to the resurrected Christ, many of whom later suffering martyrdom for their faith, but also of his own life. López's testimony of a transformed life speaks volumes to today's postmodern world. The New Atheists are attacking the Christian faith not because they claim it is not true (though they of course claim this), but primarily because, according to them, it is not good. Dr. López's life stands as a glowing contradiction of that supposition. It is indeed sad commentary that all too many Christians do not realize that they are wit-nesses to the resurrected Christ and that their lives are often the only Bible that many unbelievers will ever read. If this book accomplishes nothing else, it should spur on believers to live out their faith in such a way that shuts up the accusations of hypocrisy within the church.

López concludes the body of his work with "Killing Jesus: Answers to Objections," his ninth chapter. Here the author interacts specifically with the recent book by Charles Pellegrino and Simcha Jacobovici, *The Jesus Family Tomb*.

The last section of the book, the Endnotes, is not to be overlooked. Nearly one fourth of the whole work is the documentation found in the Endnotes. Rather than clutter each page with footnotes, the author has wisely chosen to place the notes at the end. But don't ignore this section! There is much rich material here, both of the ancient literature and modern discussions. López has left virtually no stone unturned in his investigation.

This volume is a creative and inviting approach to the greatest miracle in world history. It lays out in fresh ways how we should regard the death and resurrection of Jesus, both historically and theologically. López is to be thanked for his fine contribution to the discussion. I believe that the single most important question you can ask yourself today is, "What am I going to do with Jesus?" This, of course, presupposes that there is something to do with Jesus, in particular to wrestle with whether he really was raised from the dead. I will now turn people to *Killing Jesus: Is He Alive Today?* as an excellent place to find the answer.

Daniel B. Wallace

INTRODUCTION

KILLING JESUS:

Is He Alive Today?

I believe it is easier to follow a historical and chronological account of the killing of Jesus by putting together the sequential reports of the last week of Jesus' life from all the Gospels. This way the reader gets the entire sense and straightforward chronological order of where, when and what events took place and be able to get a holistic sense of the incidents leading up to the killing of Jesus. Although much could be embellished when writing about the last week of Jesus leading up to his death, nothing, however, can really surpass the archaeological and historical documents recorded of the killing of Jesus in the four Gospels. Some scholars may critique the authenticity of some of the events as being authentic (see chapter 3), but in the final analysis the burden of proof is on the one saying otherwise.

The killing of Jesus by the hands of Pontius Pilate is one of the best-documented events in history (see chapter 4). However, the killing of Jesus did not appear to have ceased at the hands of the fifth Prefect of the Roman province of Judaea (AD 26-36), since many throughout the last two thousand years have attempted to kill the biblical Jesus by trying to disprove what the Gospels recorded about him. Hence, the killing of the biblical Jesus that occurred two thousand years ago continues to thrive today. And although many have tried redefining and killing Jesus anew from the portrait painted in the first-century A.D. New Testament documents, the real upsurge of this attempt came after the Reformation, as seen in the ten philosophical approaches (inductivism, materialism, rationalism, deism, skepticism, agnosticism, romanticism, idealism, evolution, and existentialism). A number of books today have adopted one or more of these philosophies and seek to redefine and kill the biblical Jesus through bizarre and radical theories void of any scholarly evidence.

One should not really begin to discuss or investigate the killing and rising of Jesus from the dead before looking at the document (the Bible) that testifies of Jesus' resurrection. The evidence shown in chapter 3 will demonstrate that the Bible can be trusted as a historical document, and thereby give credence to the resurrection accounts of Jesus of Nazareth.

Furthermore, many believe that even if Jesus could be alive today, he did not rise physically but spiritually. Once the reader carefully looks at all the available support shown in the Hebrew Scriptures, Judaic external documents and their view on this issue, the New Testament documents, and specifically the Gospel accounts, and the church fathers, they will be ready to conclude one thing from the evidence. That the view that people would rise bodily from the dead was the predominant understanding and background of the period when the witnesses of Jesus' resurrection recorded the NT.

Unfortunately, some have taken other avenues to argue that Jesus was not killed since he *really* did not die. It was all a hoax that was planned by Jesus' close acquaintances and friends. Of course, this is problematic to the Christian message. For, if there's no death (a necessary precursor to rising), then there can be no physical Resurrection and therefore no forgiveness of sins (Heb. 9:22; 1 Cor. 15:16-20). The biblical record verify Jesus' death on the cross, and extrabiblical sources do so as well. Josephus, Cicero, Tacitus, Lucian of Samosata, Mara Bar-Serapion, the Talmud, and even critical scholars, all testify of Jesus' death.

Also, the evidence from the OT and NT passages is overwhelming in giving a "preview of the oncoming attraction" of Jesus' physical resurrection. Numerous passages show that people were raised physically. Thus, one has no logical, textual and cultural (Jewish thought) basis to interpret the evidence any other way than to suggest that if Jesus, or anyone else before and after him, rose, they rose physically. In fact, all the witnesses in the NT clearly believed and give evidence that they saw Jesus. They claimed to have touched, ate, and conversed with him after he rose bodily from the dead. Believers were able to examine Jesus with their five senses. Hence no doubt should remain in concluding that Jesus possessed a physical body.

One must also consider at least two clear OT passages that specifically predict the resurrection of Jesus of Nazareth that were verified as fulfilled in the NT. There are other passages that implicitly or explicitly refer to the Jewish expectation of physical resurrection. However, even taking a conservative approach, these two passages show that the OT did predict the physical resurrection of Jesus of Nazareth, which are fulfilled in the NT.

Another problem arises, especially when discussing religion, occurs by not understanding how to distinguish scientific and circumstantial legal evidence. Once someone correctly approaches the data in an unbiased manner and knows how to properly define each of these disciplines and how they work, one can then arrive at an informed conviction about the resurrection of Jesus in a more objective manner.

After one has looked at the evidence in the book *Killing Jesus*, the following points will be clear. Enemies of the Resurrection actually helped solidify the testimony that validates its authenticity. For example, the empty tomb, the broken seal, the removal of the large stone, and the silence of Rome in not producing a body can only be logically and historically explained by the physical resurrection of Jesus.

That is not all. The disciples' transformed lives validate Jesus' resurrection. From running scared to proclaiming boldly the Resurrection that resulted in most of them being martyred argues for the authenticity of their having seen the risen Jesus.

If that was not enough, this author's life is a living testimony of the power of the Resurrection. May everyone reading this book be fortunate and blessed enough as I've been to experience the power to live, which was made possible through the death and resurrection of Jesus Christ. Hence, my prayer to you who reads *Killing Jesus: Is He Alive Today?* is that the Lord would enlighten you to see the truth that by simply believing in Jesus alone for eternal life (see John 1:12; 3:16-18; 5:24; 6:40-47; 11:25-27; 20:30-31; Rom. 3:21–4:25; Eph. 2:8-9; Rev. 22:17) you will be forever set free from the pains of being eternally separated from your creator and begin to experience this life right now!

CHAPTER 1

KILLING JESUS: A CHRONOLOGY

Friday:

The Anointing at Bethany

And when Jesus was in Bethany at the house of Simon the leper, a woman came to Him having an alabaster flask of very costly fragrant oil, and she poured it on His head as He sat at the table. But when His disciples saw it, they were indignant, saying, "Why this waste? For this fragrant oil might have been sold for much and given to the poor."

But when Jesus was aware of it, He said to them, "Why do you trouble the woman? For she has done a good work for Me. For you have the poor with you always, but Me you do not have always. For in pouring this fragrant oil on My body, she did it for My burial. Assuredly, I say to you, wherever this gospel is preached in the whole world, what this woman has done will also be told as a memorial to her.

Sunday:

The Triumphal Entry

Now when they drew near Jerusalem, and came to Bethphage, at the Mount of Olives, then Jesus sent two disciples, saying to them, "Go into the village opposite you, and immediately you will find a donkey tied, and a colt with her. Loose them and bring them to Me. And if anyone says anything to you, you shall say, 'The Lord has need of them,' and immediately he will send them."

All this was done that it might be fulfilled which was spoken by the prophet, saying:

"Tell the daughter of Zion, 'Behold, your King is coming to you, Lowly, and sitting on a donkey, A colt, the foal of a donkey.'"

So the disciples went and did as Jesus commanded them. They brought the donkey and the colt, laid their clothes on them, and set Him on them. And a very great multitude spread their clothes on the road; others cut down branches from the trees and spread them on the road. Then the multitudes who went before and those who followed cried out, saying:

"Hosanna to the Son of David! 'Blessed is He who comes in the name of the Lord!' Hosanna in the highest!"

And when He had come into Jerusalem, all the city was moved, saying, "Who is this?"

So the multitudes said, "This is Jesus, the prophet from Nazareth of Galilee."

Monday:

Jesus Cleanses the Temple

Then Jesus went into the temple of God and drove out all those who bought and sold in the temple, and overturned the tables of the money changers and the seats of those who sold doves. And He said to them, "It is written, 'My house shall be called a house of prayer,' but you have made it a 'den of thieves.'"

Then the blind and the lame came to Him in the temple, and He healed them. But when the chief priests and scribes saw the wonderful things that He did, and the children crying out in the temple and saying, "Hosanna to the Son of David!" they were indignant and said to Him, "Do You hear what these are saying?"

And Jesus said to them, "Yes. Have you never read,

'Out of the mouth of babes and nursing infants You have perfected praise'?"

Then He left them and went out of the city to Bethany, and He lodged there.

The Plot to Kill Jesus

Now it came to pass, when Jesus had finished all these sayings, that He said to His disciples, "You know that after two days is the Passover, and the Son of Man will be delivered up to be crucified."

Then the chief priests, the scribes, and the elders of the people assembled at the palace of the high priest, who was called Caiaphas, and plotted to take Jesus by trickery and kill Him. But they said, "Not during the feast, lest there be an uproar among the people."

Judas Agrees to Betray Jesus

Then one of the twelve, called Judas Iscariot, went to the chief priests and said, "What are you willing to give me if I deliver Him to you?" And they counted out to him thirty pieces of silver. So from that time he sought opportunity to betray Him.

Thursday:

Jesus Celebrates Passover with His Disciples

Now on the first day of the Feast of Unleavened Bread the disciples came to Jesus, saying to Him, "Where do You want us to prepare for You to eat the Passover?"

And He said, "Go into the city to a certain man, and say to him, 'The Teacher says, "My time is at hand; I will keep the Passover at your house with My disciples."'"

So the disciples did as Jesus had directed them; and they prepared the Passover.

When evening had come, He sat down with the twelve. Now as they were eating, He said, "Assuredly, I say to you, one of you will betray Me."

And they were exceedingly sorrowful, and each of them began to say to Him, "Lord, is it I?"

He answered and said, "He who dipped his hand with Me in the dish will betray Me. The Son of Man indeed goes just as it is written of Him, but woe to that man by whom the Son of Man is betrayed! It would have been good for that man if he had not been born."

Then Judas, who was betraying Him, answered and said, "Rabbi, is it I?"

He said to him, "You have said it."

Jesus Institutes the Lord's Supper

And as they were eating, Jesus took bread, blessed and broke it, and gave it to the disciples and said, "Take, eat; this is My body."

Then He took the cup, and gave thanks, and gave it to them, saying, "Drink from it, all of you. For this is My blood of the new covenant, which is shed for many for the remission of sins. But I say to you, I will not drink of this fruit of the vine from now on until that day when I drink it new with you in My Father's kingdom."

And when they had sung a hymn, they went out to the Mount of Olives.

Jesus Predicts Peter's Denial

Then Jesus said to them, "All of you will be made to stumble because of Me this night, for it is written:

'I will strike the Shepherd, And the sheep of the flock will be scattered.'

But after I have been raised, I will go before you to Galilee."

Peter answered and said to Him, "Even if all are made to stumble because of You, I will never be made to stumble."

Jesus said to him, "Assuredly, I say to you that this night, before the rooster crows, you will deny Me three times."

Peter said to Him, "Even if I have to die with You, I will not deny You!"

And so said all the disciples.

Jesus Washes the Disciples' Feet

Now before the Feast of the Passover, when Jesus knew that His hour had come that He should depart from this world to the Father, having loved His own who were in the world, He loved them to the end.

And supper being ended, the devil having already put it into the heart of Judas Iscariot, Simon's son, to betray Him, Jesus, knowing that the Father had given all things into His hands, and that He had come from God and was going to God, rose from supper and laid aside His garments, took a towel and girded Himself. After that, He poured water into a basin and began to wash the disciples' feet, and to wipe them with the towel with which He was girded. Then He came to Simon Peter. And Peter said to Him, "Lord, are You washing my feet?"

Jesus answered and said to him, "What I am doing you do not understand now, but you will know after this."

Peter said to Him, "You shall never wash my feet!"

Jesus answered him, "If I do not wash you, you have no part with Me."

Simon Peter said to Him, "Lord, not my feet only, but also my hands and my head!"

Jesus said to him, "He who is bathed needs only to wash his feet, but is completely clean; and you are clean, but not all of you." For He knew who would betray Him; therefore He said, "You are not all clean."

So when He had washed their feet, taken His garments, and sat down again, He said to them, "Do you know what I have done to you? You call Me Teacher and Lord, and you say well, for so I am. If I then, your Lord and Teacher, have washed your feet, you also ought to wash one another's feet. For I have given you an example, that you should do as I have done to you. Most assuredly, I say to you, a servant is not greater than his master; nor is he who is sent greater than he who sent him. If you know these things, blessed are you if you do them.

Jesus Identifies His Betrayer

"I do not speak concerning all of you. I know whom I have chosen; but that the Scripture may be fulfilled, 'He who eats bread with Me has lifted up his heel against Me.' Now I tell you before it comes, that when it does come to pass, you may believe that I am He. Most assuredly, I say to you, he who receives whomever I send receives Me; and he who receives Me receives Him who sent Me."

Now as they were eating, He said, "Assuredly, I say to you, one of you will betray Me."

And they were exceedingly sorrowful, and each of them began to say to Him, "Lord, is it I?"

He answered and said, "He who dipped his hand with Me in the dish will betray Me. The Son of Man indeed goes just as it is written

---

The order of the last supper is in 13 steps [some books show more steps, others fewer steps, so this is a general guideline]

1. The head of the company, Jesus in this case, opens with a prayer and
2. Gives the 1st cup of wine for everyone in the company to drink.
3. The head of the company washes his hands. This is where, it is believed, Jesus washed the disciples' feet.
4. The head of the company dips some of the bitter herbs into the salt water or vinegar and speaks a blessing, eats some of the herbs and hands them to the others.
5. The unleavened bread is broken into pieces, reserving half to be eaten after the supper, called the after dish.
6. The 2nd cup is filled and the youngest in the company (John) is instructed to ask questions about the significance of the Passover.
7. Psalms 113 and 114 are sung.
8. The 3rd cup of wine is filled, followed by prayer, and they all drink the cup.
9. Everyone washes his hands.
10. Supper begins by eating the unleavened bread and bitter herbs and the lamb. Everyone in the group must eat at least an olive size portion of the lamb. All of the lamb is to be consumed or destroyed. No bones of the lamb are to be broken.
11. The after dish of the bread broken earlier is eaten. It is believed this is where Jesus said, "Take eat, this is my body."
12. The 4th cup of wine is the point when Jesus told them to all drink of it, this was his blood.
13. Conclude with hymns and prayers. Psalms 115-118 and the Great Hallel – Psalm 136.

Taken from: http://www.biblewise.com/overview/chronology.htm

of Him, but woe to that man by whom the Son of Man is betrayed! It would have been good for that man if he had not been born."

Then Judas, who was betraying Him, answered and said, "Rabbi, is it I?"

He said to him, "You have said it."

The Prayer in the Garden

Then Jesus came with them to a place called Gethsemane, and said to the disciples, "Sit here while I go and pray over there." And He took with Him Peter and the two sons of Zebedee, and He began to be sorrowful and deeply distressed. Then He said to them, "My soul is exceedingly sorrowful, even to death. Stay here and watch with Me."

He went a little farther and fell on His face, and prayed, saying, "O My Father, if it is possible, let this cup pass from Me; nevertheless, not as I will, but as You will."

Then He came to the disciples and found them sleeping, and said to Peter, "What! Could you not watch with Me one hour? Watch and pray, lest you enter into temptation. The spirit indeed is willing, but the flesh is weak."

Again, a second time, He went away and prayed, saying, "O My Father, if this cup cannot pass away from Me unless I drink it, Your will be done." And He came and found them asleep again, for their eyes were heavy.

So He left them, went away again, and prayed the third time, saying the same words. Then He came to His disciples and said to them, "Are you still sleeping and resting? Behold, the hour is at hand, and the Son of Man is being betrayed into the hands of sinners. Rise, let us be going. See, My betrayer is at hand."

Betrayal and Arrest in Gethsemane

And while He was still speaking, behold, Judas, one of the twelve, with a great multitude with swords and clubs, came from the chief priests and elders of the people.

Now His betrayer had given them a sign, saying, "Whomever I kiss, He is the One; seize Him." Immediately he went up to Jesus and said, "Greetings, Rabbi!" and kissed Him.

But Jesus said to him, "Friend, why have you come?"

Then they came and laid hands on Jesus and took Him. And suddenly, one of those who were with Jesus stretched out his hand and drew his sword, struck the servant of the high priest, and cut off his ear.

But Jesus said to him, "Put your sword in its place, for all who take the sword will perish by the sword. Or do you think that I cannot now pray to My Father, and He will provide Me with more than twelve legions of angels? How then could the Scriptures be fulfilled, that it must happen thus?"

In that hour Jesus said to the multitudes, "Have you come out, as against a robber, with swords and clubs to take Me? I sat daily with you, teaching in the temple, and you did not seize Me. But all this was done that the Scriptures of the prophets might be fulfilled."

Then all the disciples forsook Him and fled.

Before the High Priest

Then the detachment of troops and the captain and the officers of the Jews arrested Jesus and bound Him. And they led Him away to Annas first, for he was the father-in-law of Caiaphas who was high priest that year. Now it was Caiaphas who advised the Jews that it was expedient that one man should die for the people.

Jesus Questioned by the High Priest

The high priest then asked Jesus about His disciples and His doctrine.

Jesus answered him, "I spoke openly to the world. I always taught in synagogues and in the temple, where the Jews always meet, and in secret I have said nothing. Why do you ask Me? Ask those who have heard Me what I said to them. Indeed they know what I said."

And when He had said these things, one of the officers who stood by struck Jesus with the palm of his hand, saying, "Do You answer the high priest like that?"

Jesus answered him, "If I have spoken evil, bear witness of the evil; but if well, why do you strike Me?"

Then Annas sent Him bound to Caiaphas the high priest.

Jesus Faces the Sanhedrin

And those who had laid hold of Jesus led Him away to Caiaphas the high priest, where the scribes and the elders were assembled. But

Peter followed Him at a distance to the high priest's courtyard. And he went in and sat with the servants to see the end.

Now the chief priests, the elders, and all the council sought false testimony against Jesus to put Him to death, but found none. Even though many false witnesses came forward, they found none. But at last two false witnesses came forward and said, "This fellow said, 'I am able to destroy the temple of God and to build it in three days.'"

And the high priest arose and said to Him, "Do You answer nothing? What is it these men testify against You?" But Jesus kept silent. And the high priest answered and said to Him, "I put You under oath by the living God: Tell us if You are the Christ, the Son of God!"

Jesus said to him, "It is as you said. Nevertheless, I say to you, hereafter you will see the Son of Man sitting at the right hand of the Power, and coming on the clouds of heaven."

Then the high priest tore his clothes, saying, "He has spoken blasphemy! What further need do we have of witnesses? Look, now you have heard His blasphemy! What do you think?"

They answered and said, "He is deserving of death."

Then they spat in His face and beat Him; and others struck Him with the palms of their hands, saying, "Prophesy to us, Christ! Who is the one who struck You?"

Friday:

Peter Denies Jesus, and Weeps Bitterly

Now Peter sat outside in the courtyard. And a servant girl came to him, saying, "You also were with Jesus of Galilee."

But he denied it before them all, saying, "I do not know what you are saying."

And when he had gone out to the gateway, another girl saw him and said to those who were there, "This fellow also was with Jesus of Nazareth."

But again he denied with an oath, "I do not know the Man!"

And a little later those who stood by came up and said to Peter, "Surely you also are one of them, for your speech betrays you."

Then he began to curse and swear, saying, "I do not know the Man!"

Immediately a rooster crowed. And Peter remembered the word of

Jesus who had said to him, "Before the rooster crows, you will deny Me three times." So he went out and wept bitterly.

Jesus Handed Over to Pontius Pilate

When morning came, all the chief priests and elders of the people plotted against Jesus to put Him to death. And when they had bound Him, they led Him away and delivered Him to Pontius Pilate the governor.

Judas Hangs Himself

Then Judas, His betrayer, seeing that He had been condemned, was remorseful and brought back the thirty pieces of silver to the chief priests and elders, saying, "I have sinned by betraying innocent blood."

And they said, "What is that to us? You see to it!"

Then he threw down the pieces of silver in the temple and departed, and went and hanged himself.

But the chief priests took the silver pieces and said, "It is not lawful to put them into the treasury, because they are the price of blood." And they consulted together and bought with them the potter's field, to bury strangers in. Therefore that field has been called the Field of Blood to this day.

Then was fulfilled what was spoken by Jeremiah the prophet, saying, "And they took the thirty pieces of silver, the value of Him who was priced, whom they of the children of Israel priced, and gave them for the potter's field, as the Lord directed me."

Jesus Faces Pilate

Now Jesus stood before the governor. And the governor asked Him, saying, "Are You the King of the Jews?"

Jesus said to him, "It is as you say." And while He was being accused by the chief priests and elders, He answered nothing.

Then Pilate said to Him, "Do You not hear how many things they testify against You?" But He answered him not one word, so that the governor marveled greatly.

Jesus Faces Herod

When Pilate heard of Galilee, he asked if the Man were a Galilean. And as soon as he knew that He belonged to Herod's jurisdiction, he sent Him to Herod, who was also in Jerusalem at that time. Now when Herod saw Jesus, he was exceedingly glad; for he had desired for a long time to see Him, because he had heard many things about Him, and he hoped to see some miracle done by Him. Then he questioned Him with many words, but He answered him nothing. And the chief priests and scribes stood and vehemently accused Him. Then Herod, with his men of war, treated Him with contempt and mocked Him, arrayed Him in a gorgeous robe, and sent Him back to Pilate. That very day Pilate and Herod became friends with each other, for previously they had been at enmity with each other.

Taking the Place of Barabbas

Now at the feast the governor was accustomed to releasing to the multitude one prisoner whom they wished. And at that time they had a notorious prisoner called Barabbas. Therefore, when they had gathered together, Pilate said to them, "Whom do you want me to release to you? Barabbas, or Jesus who is called Christ?" For he knew that they had handed Him over because of envy.

While he was sitting on the judgment seat, his wife sent to him, saying, "Have nothing to do with that just Man, for I have suffered many things today in a dream because of Him."

But the chief priests and elders persuaded the multitudes that they should ask for Barabbas and destroy Jesus. The governor answered and said to them, "Which of the two do you want me to release to you?"

They said, "Barabbas!"

Pilate said to them, "What then shall I do with Jesus who is called Christ?"

They all said to him, "Let Him be crucified!"

Then the governor said, "Why, what evil has He done?"

But they cried out all the more, saying, "Let Him be crucified!"

When Pilate saw that he could not prevail at all, but rather that a tumult was rising, he took water and washed his hands before the multitude, saying, "I am innocent of the blood of this just Person. You see to it."

And all the people answered and said, "His blood be on us and on our children."

Then he released Barabbas to them; and when he had scourged

Jesus, he delivered Him to be crucified.

The Soldiers Mock Jesus

Then the soldiers of the governor took Jesus into the Praetorium and gathered the whole garrison around Him. And they stripped Him and put a scarlet robe on Him. When they had twisted a crown of thorns, they put it on His head, and a reed in His right hand. And they bowed the knee before Him and mocked Him, saying, "Hail, King of the Jews!" Then they spat on Him, and took the reed and struck Him on the head. And when they had mocked Him, they took the robe off Him, put His own clothes on Him, and led Him away to be crucified.

The King on a Cross

Now as they came out, they found a man of Cyrene, Simon by name. Him they compelled to bear His cross. And when they had come to a place called Golgotha, that is to say, Place of a Skull, they gave Him sour wine mingled with gall to drink. But when He had tasted it, He would not drink.

Now Pilate wrote a title and put it on the cross. And the writing was:

JESUS OF NAZARETH, THE KING OF THE JEWS.

Then many of the Jews read this title, for the place where Jesus was crucified was near the city; and it was written in Hebrew, Greek, and Latin.

Therefore the chief priests of the Jews said to Pilate, "Do not write, 'The King of the Jews,' but, 'He said, "I am the King of the Jews."'"

Pilate answered, "What I have written, I have written."

Then the soldiers, when they had crucified Jesus, took His garments and made four parts, to each soldier a part, and also the tunic. Now the tunic was without seam, woven from the top in one piece. They said therefore among themselves, "Let us not tear it, but cast lots for it, whose it shall be," that the Scripture might be fulfilled which says:

"They divided My garments among them, And for My clothing they cast lots."

Therefore the soldiers did these things.

Behold Your Mother

Now there stood by the cross of Jesus His mother, and His mother's sister, Mary the wife of Clopas, and Mary Magdalene. When Jesus therefore saw His mother, and the disciple whom He loved standing by, He said to His mother, "Woman, behold your son!" Then He said to the disciple, "Behold your mother!"And from that hour that disciple took her to his own home.

And those who passed by blasphemed Him, wagging their heads and saying, "You who destroy the temple and build it in three days, save Yourself! If You are the Son of God, come down from the cross."

Likewise the chief priests also, mocking with the scribes and elders, said, "He saved others; Himself He cannot save. If He is the King of Israel, let Him now come down from the cross, and we will believe Him. He trusted in God; let Him deliver Him now if He will have Him; for He said, 'I am the Son of God.'"

Even the robbers who were crucified with Him reviled Him with the same thing.

Jesus Dies on the Cross

Now from the sixth hour until the ninth hour there was darkness over all the land. And about the ninth hour Jesus cried out with a loud voice, saying, "Eli, Eli, lama sabachthani?" that is, "My God, My God, why have You forsaken Me?"

Some of those who stood there, when they heard that, said, "This

Man is calling for Elijah!" Immediately one of them ran and took a sponge, filled it with sour wine and put it on a reed, and offered it to Him to drink.

The rest said, "Let Him alone; let us see if Elijah will come to save Him."

And Jesus cried out again with a loud voice, and yielded up His spirit.

Then, behold, the veil of the temple was torn in two from top to bottom; and the earth quaked, and the rocks were split, and the graves were opened; and many bodies of the saints who had fallen asleep were raised; and coming out of the graves after His resurrection, they went into the holy city and appeared to many.

So when the centurion and those with him, who were guarding Jesus, saw the earthquake and the things that had happened, they feared greatly, saying, "Truly this was the Son of God!"

And many women who followed Jesus from Galilee, ministering to Him, were there looking on from afar, among whom were Mary Magdalene, Mary the mother of James and Joses, and the mother of Zebedee's sons.

Jesus' Side Is Pierced

Therefore, because it was the Preparation Day, that the bodies should not remain on the cross on the Sabbath (for that Sabbath was a high day), the Jews asked Pilate that their legs might be broken, and that they might be taken away. Then the soldiers came and broke the legs of the first and of the other who was crucified with Him. But when they came to Jesus and saw that He was already dead, they did not break His legs. But one of the soldiers pierced His side with a spear, and immediately blood and water came out. And he who has seen has testified, and his testimony is true; and he knows that he is telling the truth, so that you may believe. For these things were done that the Scripture should be fulfilled, "Not one of His bones shall be broken." And again another Scripture says, "They shall look on Him whom they pierced."

Jesus Buried in Joseph's Tomb

Now when evening had come, there came a rich man from Arimathea, named Joseph, who himself had also become a disciple of

Jesus. This man went to Pilate and asked for the body of Jesus. Then Pilate commanded the body to be given to him. When Joseph had taken the body, he wrapped it in a clean linen cloth, and laid it in his new tomb which he had hewn out of the rock; and he rolled a large stone against the door of the tomb, and departed. And Mary Magdalene was there, and the other Mary, sitting opposite the tomb.

Saturday:

Pilate Sets a Guard

On the next day, which followed the Day of Preparation, the chief priests and Pharisees gathered together to Pilate, saying, "Sir, we remember, while He was still alive, how that deceiver said, 'After three days I will rise.' Therefore command that the tomb be made secure until the third day, lest His disciples come by night and steal Him away, and say to the people, 'He has risen from the dead.' So the last deception will be worse than the first."

Pilate said to them, "You have a guard; go your way, make it as secure as you know how." So they went and made the tomb secure, sealing the stone and setting the guard.

Now when the Sabbath was past, Mary Magdalene, Mary the mother of James, and Salome bought spices, that they might come and anoint Him.

Sunday:

He Is Risen

Now after the Sabbath, as the first day of the week began to dawn, Mary Magdalene and the other Mary came to see the tomb. And behold, there was a great earthquake; for an angel of the Lord descended from heaven, and came and rolled back the stone from the door, and sat on it. His countenance was like lightning, and his clothing as white as snow. And the guards shook for fear of him, and became like dead men.

But the angel answered and said to the women, "Do not be afraid, for I know that you seek Jesus who was crucified. He is not here; for He is risen, as He said. Come, see the place where the Lord lay. And go quickly and tell His disciples that He is risen from the dead, and indeed He is going before you into Galilee; there you will see Him. Behold, I

have told you."

So they went out quickly from the tomb with fear and great joy, and ran to bring His disciples word.

The Women Worship the Risen Lord

And as they went to tell His disciples, behold, Jesus met them, saying, "Rejoice!" So they came and held Him by the feet and worshiped Him. Then Jesus said to them, "Do not be afraid. Go and tell My brethren to go to Galilee, and there they will see Me."

The Soldiers Are Bribed

Now while they were going, behold, some of the guard came into the city and reported to the chief priests all the things that had happened. When they had assembled with the elders and consulted together, they gave a large sum of money to the soldiers, saying, "Tell them, 'His disciples came at night and stole Him away while we slept.' And if this comes to the governor's ears, we will appease him and make you secure." So they took the money and did as they were instructed; and this saying is commonly reported among the Jews until this day.

THE NEXT 40 DAYS:

The Road to Emmaus

Now behold, two of them were traveling that same day to a village called Emmaus, which was seven miles from Jerusalem. And they talked together of all these things which had happened. So it was, while they conversed and reasoned, that Jesus Himself drew near and went with them. But their eyes were restrained, so that they did not know Him.

And He said to them, "What kind of conversation is this that you have with one another as you walk and are sad?"

Then the one whose name was Cleopas answered and said to Him, "Are You the only stranger in Jerusalem, and have You not known the things which happened there in these days?"

And He said to them, "What things?"

So they said to Him, "The things concerning Jesus of Nazareth, who was a Prophet mighty in deed and word before God and all the people, and how the chief priests and our rulers delivered Him to be condemned to death, and crucified Him. But we were hoping that it was He who was going to redeem Israel. Indeed, besides all this, today is the third day since these things happened. Yes, and certain women of our company, who arrived at the tomb early, astonished us. When they did not find His body, they came saying that they had also seen a vision of angels who said He was alive. And certain of those who were with us went to the tomb and found it just as the women had said; but Him they did not see."

Then He said to them, "O foolish ones, and slow of heart to believe in all that the prophets have spoken! Ought not the Christ to have suffered these things and to enter into His glory?" And beginning at Moses and all the Prophets, He expounded to them in all the Scriptures the things concerning Himself.

The Disciples' Eyes Opened

Then they drew near to the village where they were going, and He indicated that He would have gone farther. But they constrained Him, saying, "Abide with us, for it is toward evening, and the day is far spent." And He went in to stay with them.

Now it came to pass, as He sat at the table with them, that He took bread, blessed and broke it, and gave it to them. Then their eyes were opened and they knew Him; and He vanished from their sight.

And they said to one another, "Did not our heart burn within us while He talked with us on the road, and while He opened the Scriptures to us?" So they rose up that very hour and returned to

Jerusalem, and found the eleven and those who were with them gathered together, saying, "The Lord is risen indeed, and has appeared to Simon!" And they told about the things that had happened on the road, and how He was known to them in the breaking of bread.

The Apostles Commissioned

Then, the same day at evening, being the first day of the week, when the doors were shut where the disciples were assembled, for fear of the Jews, Jesus came and stood in the midst, and said to them, "Peace be with you." When He had said this, He showed them His hands and His side. Then the disciples were glad when they saw the Lord.

So Jesus said to them again, "Peace to you! As the Father has sent Me, I also send you." And when He had said this, He breathed on them, and said to them, "Receive the Holy Spirit. If you forgive the sins of any, they are forgiven them; if you retain the sins of any, they are retained."

Seeing and Believing

Now Thomas, called the Twin, one of the twelve, was not with them when Jesus came. The other disciples therefore said to him, "We have seen the Lord."

So he said to them, "Unless I see in His hands the print of the nails, and put my finger into the print of the nails, and put my hand into His side, I will not believe."

And after eight days His disciples were again inside, and Thomas with them. Jesus came, the doors being shut, and stood in the midst, and said, "Peace to you!" Then He said to Thomas, "Reach your finger here, and look at My hands; and reach your hand here, and put it into My side. Do not be unbelieving, but believing."

And Thomas answered and said to Him, "My Lord and my God!"

Jesus said to him, "Thomas, because you have seen Me, you have believed. Blessed are those who have not seen and yethave believed."

That You May Believe

And truly Jesus did many other signs in the presence of His disciples, which are not written in this book; but these are written that you may believe that Jesus is the Christ, the Son of God, and that believing you may have life in His name.

Breakfast by the Sea

After these things Jesus showed Himself again to the disciples at the Sea of Tiberias, and in this way He showed Himself: Simon Peter, Thomas called the Twin, Nathanael of Cana in Galilee, the sons of Zebedee, and two others of His disciples were together. Simon Peter said to them, "I am going fishing."

They said to him, "We are going with you also." They went out and immediately got into the boat, and that night they caught nothing. But when the morning had now come, Jesus stood on the shore; yet the disciples did not know that it was Jesus. Then Jesus said to them, "Children, have you any food?"

They answered Him, "No."

And He said to them, "Cast the net on the right side of the boat, and you will find some." So they cast, and now they were not able to draw it in because of the multitude of fish.

Therefore that disciple whom Jesus loved said to Peter, "It is the Lord!" Now when Simon Peter heard that it was the Lord, he put on his outer garment (for he had removed it), and plunged into the sea. But the other disciples came in the little boat (for they were not far from land, but about two hundred cubits), dragging the net with fish. Then, as soon as they had come to land, they saw a fire of coals there, and fish laid on it, and bread. Jesus said to them, "Bring some of the fish which you have just caught."

Simon Peter went up and dragged the net to land, full of large fish, one hundred and fifty-three; and although there were so many, the net was not broken. Jesus said to them, "Come and eat breakfast." Yet none of the disciples dared ask Him, "Who are You?"—knowing that it was the Lord. Jesus then came and took the bread and gave it to them, and likewise the fish.

This is now the third time Jesus showed Himself to His disciples after He was raised from the dead.

Jesus Restores Peter

So when they had eaten breakfast, Jesus said to Simon Peter, "Simon, son of Jonah, do you love Me more than these?"

He said to Him, "Yes, Lord; You know that I love You."

He said to him, "Feed My lambs."

He said to him again a second time, "Simon, son of Jonah, do you love Me?"

He said to Him, "Yes, Lord; You know that I love You."

He said to him, "Tend My sheep."

He said to him the third time, "Simon, son of Jonah, do you love Me?" Peter was grieved because He said to him the third time, "Do you love Me?"

And he said to Him, "Lord, You know all things; You know that I love You."

Jesus said to him, "Feed My sheep. Most assuredly, I say to you, when you were younger, you girded yourself and walked where you wished; but when you are old, you will stretch out your hands, and another will gird you and carry you where you do not wish." This He spoke, signifying by what death he would glorify God. And when He had spoken this, He said to him, "Follow Me."

The Beloved Disciple and His Book

Then Peter, turning around, saw the disciple whom Jesus loved following, who also had leaned on His breast at the supper, and said, "Lord, who is the one who betrays You?" Peter, seeing him, said to Jesus, "But Lord, what about this man?"

Jesus said to him, "If I will that he remain till I come, what is that to you? You follow Me."

Then this saying went out among the brethren that this disciple would not die. Yet Jesus did not say to him that he would not die, but, "If I will that he remain till I come, what is that to you?"

This is the disciple who testifies of these things, and wrote these things; and we know that his testimony is true.

The Great Commission

Then the eleven disciples went away into Galilee, to the mountain which Jesus had appointed for them. When they saw Him, they worshiped Him; but some doubted.

And Jesus came and spoke to them, saying, "All authority has been given to Me in heaven and on earth. Go therefore and make disciples of all the nations, baptizing them in the name of the Father and of the Son and of the Holy Spirit, teaching them to observe all things that I have commanded you; and lo, I am with you always, even to the end of the age." Amen.

The Scriptures Opened

Then He said to them, "These are the words which I spoke to you while I was still with you, that all things must be fulfilled which were written in the Law of Moses and the Prophets and the Psalms concerning Me." And He opened their understanding, that they might comprehend the Scriptures.

Then He said to them, "Thus it is written, and thus it was necessary for the Christ to suffer and to rise from the dead the third day, and that repentance and remission of sins should be preached in His name to all nations, beginning at Jerusalem. And you are witnesses of these things. Behold, I send the Promise of My Father upon you; but tarry in the city of Jerusalem until you are endued with power from on high."

The Ascension

And He led them out as far as Bethany, and He lifted up His hands and blessed them. Now it came to pass, while He blessed them, that He was parted from them and carried up into heaven. And they worshiped Him, and returned to Jerusalem with great joy, and were continually in the temple praising and blessing God. Amen.

— CHAPTER 2 —

KILLING JESUS THROUGHOUT THE CENTURIES

N ow while they were going, behold, some of the guard came into the city and reported to the chief priests all the things that had happened. When they had assembled with the elders and consulted together, they gave a large sum of money to the soldiers, saying, "Tell them, 'His disciples came at night and stole Him away while we slept.' And if this comes to the governor's ears, we will appease him and make you secure." So they took the money and did as they were instructed; and this saying is commonly reported among the Jews until this day (Matt. 28:11-15).

Trying to disprove and thereby kill the biblical Jesus is nothing new. Matthew records that immediately after the news broke in Jerusalem that Jesus' body was missing, Jewish leaders formulated a story to invalidate the resurrection. Could the biblical account be a conspiracy cover-up by Jesus' disciples? Could the account, in Matthew 28:11-15, be a later insertion by church fathers to promote Jesus' resurrection, knowing full well that He did not rise? Or was the early church simply deceived by following an early tradition begun by Jesus' early followers? Such questions have prompted numerous scholars throughout the centuries to continue to search for Jesus' bones, hoping that one day something will turn up. Others continue killing Jesus by refusing to accept all the historical and circumstantial evidence that validates that Jesus was not only killed at the hands of Roman authorities but that he is alive today.

Some argue by the discovery in 1980 of a family tomb in Talpiot, a suburb of Jerusalem, where Jesus' name appears with five other biblical names related to Him in one way or another. This news, however, does not surprise scholars—though it may shock the uniformed public—since for a long time now the media, numerous movements, and a plethora of published manuscripts have sought to redefine the historical and biblical Jesus. Yet as we have seen, this is nothing but a false alarm.

Past Efforts on Killing Jesus

Although many have tried to redefine the biblical Jesus during the first 1,500 years after His life and death, the real "explosion" came after the Reformation.[1] This explosion came in ten new philosophical approaches to the Bible that evolved through time. These ten are inductivism, materialism, rationalism, deism, skepticism, agnosticism, romanticism, idealism, evolution, and existentialism.[2] Today numerous books draw directly from one or more of these philosophies that seek to redefine and thus figuratively kill the biblical Jesus. Going beyond interpreting the historical record at face value, at times this has resulted in authors creating their own radical theories intent on killing Jesus.

Inductivism. Sir Francis Bacon (1561-1626), a lawyer, orator, writer, philosopher, and scientist, became Lord Chancellor in England in 1618 and published his magnum opus *Novum Organum* in 1620.[3] Basically in this work Bacon postulated that experiment and experience are the bases for discovering truth, which became known as the *inductive* method. Obviously this view resulted in separating science from faith, which would later lead to a mythological understanding of Scripture and perhaps influencing the writings of David F. Strauss and Rudolf Bultmann.[4] Under this new system science is at odds with Scripture. The inductive method is not wrong, for how else do we examine facts but to test them? Instead of interpreting science to oppose Scripture, we should understand both as working harmoniously with each other. But under this new system science sits in judgment of Scripture and is the exclusive arbiter of truth, and it accepts Scripture as a valid judge only on spiritual matters.

Materialism. Thomas Hobbes (1588-1679) worked for Francis Bacon for a while and became the promoter of materialism as explained in his work *Leviathan.*[5] He said all reality consists of matter and the visual, and that the spiritual realm is nonexistent. Going one step further than Bacon, Hobbes's ultimately ended in diminishing the Scriptures' relevancy and authority for everyone. Hence Farnell correctly concludes, "Reason now ascends the throne"[6] in a total sense.

Rationalism. Baruch de Spinoza (1632-1677), Jewish born, was expelled from the synagogue for his heretical views.[7] Repulsive to Jews and Christians alike, Spinoza was described at times as a "hideous atheist." In reality he was a "rationalistic pantheist,"[8] which is not technically the same thing. Rationalism interprets all things through reason, not experience, as the primary means to understanding. Natural science is an a priori system by which to measure all truth, and truth is discovered through mathematical equations. This philosophy led to the Enlightenment period. However, unlike many philosophers of that period (e.g., Descartes and Leibniz), Spinoza believed God was in all things (pantheism). Therefore one could not have a loving personal relationship with such a God since He is part of the essence of all creation. Thus Spinoza's system defines "religion as 'the Mind's intellectual love of God.'"[9] Such ideas obviously reveal why he was not popular with Jews and Christians since it contradicts Scripture that teaches God is not like a man nor are His thoughts our thoughts (Num. 23:19; 1 Sam. 15:29; Isa. 55:8-9).

Deism. Herbert of Cherbury (1583-1648), whose ideas were later advanced by Charles Blount (1654-1693), believed that God is separate from creation but that He does not intimately interact with it. Like other philosophical movements, Deists reject any claims to supernatural revelation since God does not reveal Himself in any way other than through creation. Thus natural law, rejecting all forms of miracles, reigns supreme[10] and runs counter to Jewish and Christian thought.

Skepticism. David Hume (1711-1776), though influenced by the three major Enlightenment philosophies of rationalism, deism, and empiricism that preceded him, went beyond them to postulate that all reality exists in the mind and is perceived through the five senses.[11] He influenced many future theologians such as David F. Strauss (1808-1874), F. E. D. Schleiermacher (1768-1834), Ernst Renan (1823-1892) and Adolph Harnack (1851-1930). As Farnell wrote of Hume, "We perceive the data of our senses, but cannot know that there is anything beyond. In Hume's thought, one could not even prove the existence of the human self."[12]

Agnosticism. Influenced by Hume's system Immanuel Kant (1724-1804) went beyond it in trying to synthesize the philosophy of empiricism and rationalism into one system: agnosticism. Nothing, he said, is knowable for sure. Kant distinguished external experience and reality as something existing outside of self, apart from one's internal mechanism that subjectively interprets this reality based on personal bias. Thus the receptor of the mind processes external experiences it perceives according to its own mechanism. That is, "the mind does not perceive these things as they actually are in themselves, for the mind reshapes what it perceives ... In other words, the mind conditions (perhaps better 'colors') everything that it encounters.... One can know only what appears (*phenomenal*), not what really is (*noumenal*). The thing-in-itself is unknowable."[13] Such statements are self-defeating and nonsensical, because if the proposition (nothing is knowable) were true, it predicates something that can be known. But how can it be known when the very statement negates what it purports to know? All religious people who believe God communicates through supernatural revelation reject such a system (including *skepticism*) because it denies the foundation by which a system can be validated and believed, namely, *that God communicates knowable truth based on people's ability to perceive it for what it really is.*

Romanticism. F. E. D. Schleiermacher (1768-1834) is the person most identified with this movement.[14] In response to the intellectual and unemotional philosophy derived from the Enlightenment, Romanticism emphasized feelings, sensualism, fantasy, experience, the individual over the universal, freedom of expression against the order and the controlled. Farnell summarizes the incompatibility between Romanticism, the Bible, and the Jesus of Scripture:

> In summary, for Schleiermacher the Bible may not be propositional authoritative revelation or historically accurate, but it still conveyed religious "experience" relevant to people. He did not speak about the Jesus of history but about the Christ of faith and about the search for the "historical Jesus." In terms of historical-critical interpretation, "what it means to me in my present situation" (namely, eisegesis and application) was more important for Schleiermacher than the original meaning of Scripture (exegesis and interpretation).[15]

Idealism (transcendentalism). G. W. Hegel (1770-1831) was the most influential advocate who promoted *absolute idealism,* which states that mental and spiritual values are more essential to life than matter.[16] Idealism became "the opposite of realism—the view that things exist independently of being perceived—and of naturalism that explains the mind and spiritual values via materialism.... In other words, history, nature, and thought are aspects of the Absolute Spirit coming to self-consciousness."[17] How that happens seems to be mystical. Again, it is impossible to know the historical-biblical Jesus in this system apart from a reconstruction of the available data, but Hegel and its followers eliminated all miracles and advocated that virtue is the ultimate end of religion that enters the mind by means of the Spirit in mystical form.

Evolution. Charles Darwin (1809-1882) popularized this philosophy through two major works, *The Origin of Species* (1859) and *The Descent of Man* (1871).[18] However, he was not the originator of the evolutionary theory since the naturalistic philosophies espoused by him existed long before him.[19] Evolution leaves God out of the picture in assessing reality and asserts that everything that exists (i.e., matter) stems from a natural process that arose by chance and evolves from a simple form of life to a more complex organism. This system has permeated the scientific community. But it has also influenced theological thought by rejecting the Mosaic authorship of the first five books of the Bible and interpreting a gradual development of biblical revelation that stems from the simple to the more complex.[20]

The evolutionary view resulted in rejecting the uniqueness of monotheism (one God), supernatural revelation, and ultimately the biblical Jesus. Hence Wilhelm Bousset (1865-1920) advocated that biblical concepts evolved and were based on ideas stemming from other religions (e.g., Egyptian, Babylonian, mystery religions, and other ancient myths).[21] However, this system contradicts the second law of thermodynamics, which states that all things go from a state of order to disorder. Also evolutionary philosophy ends in a system that believes—without evidence—that all matter appeared out of nothing by chance. The mathematical possibility of this occurring is staggering and is hard to accept. In fact, it takes more faith to believe in that system than in a system that holds that all design must have a Designer.

Existentialism. Søren Kierkegaard (1813-1855) is considered the father of existentialism. Unfortunately, defining existentialism is not easy because others like "Karl Jaspers (1883-1969), Gabriel Marcel (1889-1973) represent the theistic branch. Jean-Paul Sartre (1905-1980), Martin Heidigger (1889-1976, and Albert Camus (1913-1960) represent the atheistic branch."[22] Kierkegaard believed that biblical truths are attained through subjective means, and he disregarded objective means as a path of arriving at religious truth. This, however, does not mean he did not believe in objective truth but that this form of it could not aid one in becoming a person of faith. Thus Kierkegaard wrote, "And so I say to myself: I choose; that historical fact means so much to me that I decide to stake my whole life upon it.... That is called risking; and without risk faith is an impossibility."[23] His paradoxical position describes where his views end in regard to the historicity of the Bible and Christ: "Kierkegaard never denied that Christianity was objectively or historically true, but he felt that the results of historical research are uncertain. Though asserting his personal belief in the historicity of the Bible and Christ, he maintained that objective truth is not essential to Christianity."[24] Perhaps he believed this way since faith was a step beyond historical facts that could not be proven absolutely. However, to believe in something absolutely one does not need to touch or study it in a laboratory. Many people believed George Washington existed and was the first president of the United States, but no one alive saw or touched him in an absolute way. Historical evidence exists that proves this. Part of the problem occurs when many fail to differentiate between the distinctive senses of "history," which is discussed in chapter 3.

One can appreciate Kierkegaard's fervor for having faith and desiring to experience a personal relationship with God and/or Christ. Yet how can one enter into such a relationship or experience Christ apart from the only objective means (the Bible) that conveys that truth? The contradiction is obvious.

Recent Efforts to Kill Jesus

All of these philosophical thoughts have somehow influenced contemporary writers. Today many of these movements and authors directly seek to redefine and thereby kill the biblical Jesus by posing radical theories with meager evidence to support them. These include the (1) *Jesus Seminar* movement; (2) the *National Geographic* television program about the *Gospel of Judas* that supposedly clarifies the relationship between Jesus and Judas, who was wrongly accused of betraying Jesus; (3) Bart Ehrman's *Misquoting Jesus*; (4) James D. Tabor's *The Jesus Dynasty*; and (5) Michael Baigent's *The Jesus Papers*.[25]

The Jesus Seminar began in 1985 with its founder and chairman Robert Funk along with a group of more than seventy liberal New Testament scholars.[26] Its purpose was to determine which words of Jesus in the Gospels were actually His. As a result of a vote from these scholars, using colored beads they decided which were the authentic words of Jesus. Each of the beads had a color that meant something. For example, *red*: "That's Jesus," *pink*: "Sure sounds like Jesus," *gray*: "Well, maybe," and *black*: "There's been some mistake."[27] Ultimately this resulted in publishing a volume *The Five Gospels: The Search for the Authentic Words of Jesus*, which concluded that 82 percent of what Jesus supposedly said was not authentic, 18 percent was somewhat doubtful, and only 2 percent of what the New Testament Gospels record were the words Jesus actually said.[28] Furthermore the Seminar did not regard the New Testament as superior to any other literature of the church or other writings of the day (the Gospel of Thomas is the fifth Gospel as noted in the book title).[29] The Seminar used seven rules called "pillars" in deciding what to accept as authentic. While all seven pillars have numerous logical flaws and have been thoroughly evaluated elsewhere,[30] I would like to answer two of these rules to show the unscholarly biased and flawed system of these scholars.[31]

How can modern scholars existing more than two thousand years after Jesus be better judges in determining Jesus' authentic words than Jesus' contemporaries who wrote the Gospels? Efforts made by contemporary scholarship that seeks to better understand the ancient world are good. But to dismiss early witnesses as easily as the Seminar does is severely problematic. Furthermore, the church fathers, who lived just one to two hundred years after Jesus, testified to the authenticity and authorship of the four Gospels. Unless solid evidence appears to contradict this, one should not dismiss their testimony.

Jesus Seminar scholars reverse the criteria in how to judge the authenticity of a historical document. They assert that *the Gospels are unhistorical until proven otherwise.* That is like saying in the jurisprudence system that a person is guilty until proven innocent. If we used these criteria, we would be left doubting the majority of all historical documents we now possess. Hence on both of these issues Gregory A. Boyd concludes:

> These twentieth-century scholars imagine that they are in a better position to compose the Bible than was the early church of the second and third centuries. If that strikes you as a bit presumptuous, you are not alone. After all, the early church knew all of this literature well, and was in a much better position than we are to know who wrote it and to judge its accuracy.... And despite the presumptuous claims of the Jesus Seminar, most historical scholars argue that the burden of proof should generally lie with the historian who wants to argue that what an ancient document is reporting is not true. A historian, in other words, must generally prove that an ancient account is wrong, not that what an ancient document reports is right.[32]

The discovery of the *Gospel of Judas* was made public on Thursday, April 6, 2006, when the *National Geographic Society* held a press conference at its headquarters in Washington, D.C. This was a little more than a year before *The Lost Tomb of Jesus* was aired on the Discovery Channel on March 4, 2007. In a packed room of more than one hundred news personnel the society announced the discovery of the *Gospel of Judas*. Three days later on Sunday, April 9, 2006, a two-hour documentary on the *National Geographic* channel was televised. Why all the hype? This new document not only asserts that Judas Iscariot was Jesus' best disciple, who was taught by Him in private more than the others,[33] but it also reveals that Jesus urged Judas to betray Him in order to be killed so that Jesus could get out of the flesh (physical body) and into the spirit realm.[34]

While the document is authentic (i.e., it was written around the fourth-century A.D. and is not a contemporary forgery), numerous facts argue against its being a book authorized by the apostles.

First, the church fathers never mentioned such a book.

Second, this Gospel is written in Coptic, whereas Greek is the language of all four canonical Gospels recorded in the first century A.D. This betrays a late date—to which all scholars agree—and one of the reasons why it could not have been approved by the apostles.

Third, the *Gospel of Judas* follows a practice called "pseudonymity" (falsely attributing a name to a document that was actually written by someone else). Obviously this was done in order to gain acceptance by the public.

Fourth, the *Gospel of Judas* sounds like a document with a similar name that Irenaeus, around A.D. 180, condemned.[35] If this is the same document, then this work was already condemned by the late second-century A.D.

While the document can illuminate the church's historical context when Gnosticism flourished, it contributes nothing to understanding more about Jesus or Judas since this document does not date back to the first century A.D. As Ben Witherington III concludes, "To say otherwise is an argument entirely from silence, not from hard evidence."[36]

Misquoting Jesus was written by Bart D. Ehrman in 2005. In it he reiterates much of the material of an earlier work of his, *The Orthodox Corruption of Scripture* (1993).[37] Basically Ehrman believes humans corrupted the text of the Scriptures. He writes, "The Bible began to appear to me as a very human book."[38] He believes that errors in the extant copies of the Scriptures discredit the verbal inspiration and inerrancy of the Bible. Though we only have copies, the function of textual criticism is to compare the 5,700 complete New Testament copies available, plus over 10,000 more copies in Latin, and more than one million quotations from church fathers to arrive at a very precise reading of the original documents.[39]

Ehrman asserts that more than minor differences exist.[40] For example, he cites 1 John 5:7b, which has an alternative reading based on a scribal alteration of the text.[41] However, one can readily arrive at the original reading—when more than one reading appears—by simply doing some comparisons.

Furthermore, contrary to Ehrman, in such places where alternative readings occur *no major doctrines are at stake*. Hence Witherington says, "There is a reason that both Ehrman's mentor in text criticism and mine, Bruce Metzger, has said that there is nothing in these variants that really challenges any Christian belief: they don't. I would like to add that other experts in text criticism, such as Gordon Fee, have been equally emphatic about the flawed nature of Ehrman's analysis of the significance of such textual variants."[42]

In *The Jesus Dynasty*, James D. Tabor seeks to define and "kill" the historical Jesus by postulating that Jesus' true royal dynasty continued through James, his brother, and not Paul (hence the book's title). Tabor claims that Paul, not James, elevated Jesus to divinity.[43] Tabor uses an inconsistent criterion in interpreting passages by choosing those that support his premise, ignoring those that do not, and superimposing his own meaning on others.[44]

Tabor occupies a faculty position at the University of North Carolina at Charlotte and is a trained theologian (with an interest in archaeology) who received his Ph.D. degree from the University of Chicago. Tabor has interesting and helpful archaeological information. His book is well written and easy to read. As Witherington wrote, "Absent from this study are wild theories about Gnostic gospels being our earliest and best sources about the life of Jesus.... Equally refreshing is Tabor's willingness to take serious the historical data not just in the synoptics but also in the Gospel of John."[45] However, I have the same concern as that of Evans who wrote, "I worry about nonexperts who read it and fail to see how tenuous some of the speculation and conclusions are."[46] Interestingly, though Tabor differs from Baigent and Brown on numerous points,[47] all three of them claim that twenty-first-century theories are closer to the truth than the New Testament records written in the first century A.D.

Since Tabor begins with a premise that discounts the supernatural, many of Jesus' miracles are explained away by natural means.[48] For example, he argues that Jesus could not have been born of a virgin since virgins do not bear children.[49] And Jesus could not have risen physically from the dead since dead people do not rise bodily. Tabor simply follows a philosophical bias called "uniformitarianism" (the present is the key to the past).[50]

His method of research to validate a biblical account is extremely flawed. Here are some examples. John the Baptist was also one of two Messiahs.[51] But this position clearly contradicts the Baptist's own admission in John 1:20, "I am not the Christ." Tabor, however, fails to mention this text. This is not surprising since Tabor views numerous accounts in John's Gospel (especially accounts in chapters 1 and 3) as having been altered later by Christians.[52] When presenting evidence why Matthew's name appears in the Talpoit tomb along with Jesus' bones and therefore belonging to Jesus' family, Tabor accepts Luke's account as evidence that Mary's genealogy merged with the line of Levi, thereby showing how a person named Matthew could appear in Jesus' family tomb.[53] This shows how selective and inconsistent are his methods, and how his bias permeates the entire book. He repeatedly accepts one reading of a New Testament text above another without explanation.

While denying the virgin birth Tabor also believes Mary became illegitimately pregnant by a Roman soldier named Pantera, and that she ultimately had sex with not one but three men.[54] Part of Tabor's supposed evidence comes from a second-century A.D. philosopher named Celsus who wrote against Christianity, whose work *Contra Celsum*, is quoted in various places in a rebuttal by Origen, a church father of the third century A.D. He also believes a tombstone inscription bearing the name Pantera discovered in 1859 in Bingerbrück, Germany, may possibly be the father of Jesus who at one time lived in Sidon. Hence he believes Mark 7:24 suggests why Jesus secretly visited that city ("And He entered a house and wanted no one to know it"). He also supports this by noting that some church fathers[55] accepted the point about Pantera. Evans, however, says, "Tabor thinks this supports the historicity of the tradition. Otherwise, why would the church fathers such as Epiphanius take it so seriously? But Epiphanius and later Christian writers are simply trying to fend off slur, and to do so they throw out various proposals, some having more merit than the allegations themselves." In fact Evans correctly concludes that one cannot allege from fourth-century A.D. rebuttals that an earlier tradition for Pantera proposed by Celsus existed other than the time that Celsus himself lived (in the second century A.D.).[56] Tabor has presented no archaeological evidence whatsoever to link Pantera to Jesus. Discovering a Roman tombstone and proposing various outlandish theories does not qualify as credible evidence. These are highly improbable views that go against all the enormous weight of evidence that tilt the scale in the other direction.

Tabor also believes in a *spiritual* rather than a *physical* resurrection,[57] similar to what *The Lost Tomb of Jesus* documentary and *The Jesus Family Tomb* book claim.[58]

Tabor accepts the premise of the *Jesus Seminar* (without mentioning it) that equally recognizes the second-century A.D. Gnostic *Gospel of Thomas* as equal to or perhaps better than the other Gospels.[59] He suggests that there is a "cryptic" clue in Saying 105 that echoes Jesus' illegitimate birth: "One who knows his father and his mother will be called *the son of a whore*."[60] It has been acknowledged by numerous scholars that the *Gospel of Thomas* was written too late (in the second half of the second-century A.D.) to give a clear picture of Jesus, is replete with mystic and condemned Gnostic teachings, and was never accepted as an apostolic Gospel, as the first four hundred years of church tradition clearly shows.[61] To be fair, however, Tabor does not believe all Gnostic accounts are equally valid since he considers the "Infancy Gospel" and other manuscripts that purport to have Jesus' lost years as late and legendary (second to fourth centuries A.D.) and as being entertaining other than informative.[62] Tabor's book has helpful archaeological information, but he fails miserably as a theologian-lawyer who presents a very weak case. Many of his theories are more than speculative and biased; they are unsubstantiated and incredible.

The Jesus Papers appears as Michael Baigent's latest book similar to his conspiracy-fraught tomes of the *Holy Blood, Holy Grail* (1983) and *The Dead Sea Scrolls Deception* (1992). Baigent holds a M.A. degree in mysticism from the University of Kent in England. He claims that Jesus survived the crucifixion and wrote a set of letters in A.D. 45 denying His deity. Baigent says these letters were buried for two thousand years and were finally unearthed in 1960 from a cellar in a house in Jerusalem. Baigent professes to have seen these letters but are lost today.[63] "What evidence does he have?" one may ask.

Baigent alleges that a number of people saw the letters, but he has not produced any evidence of such individuals.

Why should anyone believe Baigent's story?

Baigent admits he does not read Aramaic.[64] However, he wants everyone to believe that he knows for sure what the letters said. The only way he could know the contents of the letters is to have them translated. And if they were translated, how would he know if the translators were lying since only a few people were able to examine the contents of these alleged letters?

It is impossible for any papyrus letter to survive two thousand years in a cellar of a house in Jerusalem, as Evans correctly notes. "I might also mention that Baigent neglects to mention that archaeologists and papyrologists will tell you that no papyrus (plural: papyri) can survive buried in the ground, in Jerusalem, for two thousand years. The only papyrus documents that have survived from antiquity have been found in climates, such as the area surrounding the Dead Sea and the sands of Egypt. No ancient papyri have been found in Jerusalem itself. Jerusalem receives rainfall every year; papyri buried in the ground, beneath houses or wherever decompose quickly. So whatever Baigent saw, they were not ancient papyri found beneath somebody's house in Jerusalem, and they were not letters Jesus wrote."[65]

If the other points are detrimental to Baigent's case, this last point nails the coffin shut on the bizarre assertion that Pilate conspired with Jesus to fake the crucifixion.[66] Why? Because, as Witherington explains, "Baigent's work ... requires that [he] explain away all the evidence we have from Paul (our earlier New Testament writer), from the canonical gospels, from Josephus, and from Roman sources (such as Tacitus and the later Suetonius) that Jesus suffered the extreme penalty and died from crucifixion under and at the hands of Pontius Pilate." Hence, "Not many people are taking seriously Baigent's attempts at revisionist history. It goes against every shred of first-century evidence, Christian or otherwise, that we have about Jesus's [sic] demise."[67] Simply put, the historical and overwhelming evidence shows that Pilate was the primary recipient in killing Jesus.

The Lost Tomb of Jesus documentary and *The Jesus Family Tomb* (*JFT*) book were two recent attempts made to disprove that Jesus rose physically.[68] In 1980, a family tomb was discovered in Talpiot, a suburb of Jerusalem, where Jesus' name appears with five other biblical names related to Him in one way or another. On 26 February 2007, a major press release given by two well-known figures in the film industry claimed to have possibly discovered the lost family tomb of Jesus of Nazareth. Oscar-winning James Cameron (of the Titanic [1997] and director and producer of other blockbusters like The Terminator, True Lies [1984], Aliens [1986], The Abyss [1989], Terminator 2 [1991]) and Emmy-winning Simcha Jacobovici together produced a documentary claiming Jesus' family tomb was found.[69] This aired—not only nationally but also worldwide—on the Discovery Channel on Sunday, March 4, 2007, at primetime. The documentary drew millions of viewers. Also related to the documentary a (now New York Times best seller) book by Simcha Jacobovici and Charles Pellegrino entitled The Jesus Family Tomb: The Discovery, the Investigation, and the Evidence That Could Change History was published by Harper San Francisco on 1 March 2007. Since then a year has passed. They have now renamed the subtitle, revised, and updated the book by adding comments by Jacobovici and answers to objections by James D. Tabor.[70]

This news, however, does not surprise scholars—though it may shock the uniformed public—since this was yesterday's news newly repackaged by savvy men. Since the Jesus family tomb was found in Talpiot, Jerusalem, in 1980 there was clearly no attempted cover-up, as they had implied, since media coverage and publications soon followed the discovery. Clearly the inscription name Mariamne does not refer to Mary Magdalene but to another Mary of the first century. Almost all scholars unanimously disagree with the documentary and book that this ossuary contained the bones of Mary Magdalene. Indeed, there are two better readings of this inscription that were not disclosed by the JFT advocates. Mariamne e Mara could refer to the same person containing two names. Mara is a contraction for Martha and could be the second name.[71] Steven J. Pfaan interpreted this inscription as two names belonging to two separate women. It was common to place the remains of more than one person in an ossuary.[72] By this piece of their puzzle crumbling, the rest of their premise falls apart since all other pieces hinges on this one.

DNA testing disproving motherly kinship between the Jesus son of Joseph ossuary and the Mariamne ossuary does not prove anything since no other DNA testing was done to compare Mariamne with other ossuaries. Even more bizarre is considering that Jesus was married since no evidence exists to validate such a claim. Other possibilities concerning the DNA were not considered regarding the Jesus and Mariamne ossuaries, which hinder the documentary theory. Mariamne could be this Jesus' half-sister, cousin, or a beloved servant who was interred in the family tomb.

The tenth ossuary was never "missing." Since Amos Kloner (one of the most famous and well- know archeologist in Israel) documented the ossuary as plain and non-inscribed, they treated it like other plain ossuaries by placing it outside the courtyard of the Israel Antiquities Authority and together with other plain ossuaries.[73] Furthermore the statistical analysis is only as good as the assumption behind the formulas used to create it. That is, if one piece of the formula fails, it all falls apart. According to the *JFT* proponents, Mariamne has to be Mary Magdalene. Jesus son of Joseph has to be Jesus of Nazareth. Jesus had to be married and fathered a son named Judah. Jose has to be Jesus' brother. Mary had to be His mother. Unfortunately for them, once other information was disclosed it showed the improbability of their hypothesis.

Judaism and the early Christian church also exhibited the common expectation of a future bodily resurrection. Hence the Gospel accounts that mention Jesus' resurrection should not be understood as speaking of a spiritual resurrection, especially when the Gospels record that Jesus ate and was touched by people. Interpreting Jesus' resurrection as spiritual misreads the very point Paul made in 1 Corinthians 15:44. Once *The Jesus Family Tomb* theory becomes exposed to careful scrutiny all Bible students will discover where the real conspiracy lies.

Conclusion

Thus the historical quest to disprove and to kill the biblical Jesus started two thousand years ago continues to thrive today. And although many have tried redefining and killing Jesus anew from the portrait painted in the first-century A.D. New Testament documents, the real upsurge of this attempt came after the Reformation, as seen in the ten philosophical approaches discussed earlier (inductivism, materialism, rationalism, deism, skepticism, agnosticism, romanticism, idealism, evolution, and existentialism).

A number of books today have adopted one or more of these philosophies and seek to redefine and kill the biblical Jesus through bizarre and radical theories void of any scholarly evidence. These are the current ideas and theories that regular folks, pastors, Bible students, professors and many of today's youth (in our schools and universities) are being exposed to without getting a fair and balanced approach to the real facts. Thus, this is the current context and atmosphere in which *Killing Jesus: Is He Alive Today?* book appears and seeks to expose in order to set the record straight.

— CHAPTER 3 —

KILLING THE DOCUMENT THAT
VALIDATES JESUS RISING

I f one can kill the primary evidence that validates the Resurrection,
then all else will collapse. The Bible is that primary piece of evidence
that documents the killing and the rising of Jesus. The death, burial and
resurrection are mentioned specifically in 18 of the 27 New Testament
books and implied in the rest, so there are many verses that relate to
these subjects.[1] Before analyzing the primary source that validates the
killing and rising of Jesus, let us first consider two theories proposed by
theologians.

Most scholars have admitted that early witnesses to Jesus' resurrection believed they really saw Him alive after He had died.[2] But these
scholars differ on how they explain what the witnesses saw. They attempt to explain the Resurrection in one of three ways: the natural
view, the supernatural view, and the agnostic view.[3] The agnostic view
pleads ignorance to what early witnesses saw, while the other two views
are each subdivided into two categories.

For example, the natural view seeks to explain Jesus' resurrection by
either a subjective *internal* means or objective *external* means.

The subjective internal theory says that the witnesses experienced
hallucinations. While many believed they saw Jesus alive, this was just
their imagination.[4] Willi Marxsen held that Peter was influenced to
believe in the risen Jesus by a vision, whose faith then influenced others
to promote the idea that Jesus rose though they themselves did not
personally experience the vision. Marxsen adds that it is impossible to
know "the actual reality" of what Peter saw.[5] To hold this view, however,

one would have to reinterpret the normal meaning of the word "see" when perceiving someone or something objectively, redefine the straightforward testimony of the Gospel accounts of seeing, touching, and eating with the risen Jesus, and reinterpret Paul's terminology in 1 Corinthians 15:1–9 that mentions that a number of people had "seen" the risen Jesus. Hence this view has not been prominent among scholars.

Some who hold to an objective external theory interpret Jesus' resurrection with fantastic explanations. For example, one of the most famous explanations is the "swoon" or "apparent death" view. This view postulates that Jesus merely fainted on the cross, and that after being taken down from the cross and taken to a tomb He somehow survived. Though this view has its advocates, the majority of scholars have rejected this theory since far too many assumptions and exceptions must occur for it to be true, besides having to discard extrabiblical and biblical testimony that says otherwise.[6]

Variations of the naturalistic view exist, but basically this view alleges that Jesus never rose from the dead. Gary R. Habermas concludes, "Each of the naturalistic theories was attacked piece by piece by the liberal scholars in the nineteenth century, as each criticized the other's approaches. In the twentieth century, critical scholarship has largely rejected wholesale the naturalistic approaches to the resurrection."[7]

On the other hand, the supernatural view claims that something actually happened to Jesus after He died. In this view there are also subjective and objective elements as well. The subjective idea of having a personal "vision" was debunked by Theodor Keim, who held that Jesus appeared objectively to the disciples "in the form of heavenly 'telegrams,' revealing his glorified state and convincing them he was alive and well."[8] Although in this view the tomb was not empty, Jesus made supernatural appearances in a noncorporeal way.[9]

Furthermore, some reject the idea that Jesus rose bodily since fallible men wrote the Bible, and since it has a number of errors, who can trust it? This is the allegation made recently by the best-selling author Bart D. Ehrman's *Misquoting Jesus*.[10]

Because many books, monographs, and articles have thoroughly addressed the issue of Jesus' resurrection and whether the Bible is a trustworthy historical document, there is no need to repeat that information exhaustively here.[11] Our scope will be much more limited to address arguments on whether Jesus rose from the dead, and whether He had a spiritual or a physical body.

Before discussing the Resurrection, however, one should first validate the document (the Bible) used to testify of Jesus' resurrection. That is, can the Bible be trusted and thereby give credence to the Resurrection accounts of Jesus of Nazareth?

The Bible as an Accurate Historical Document

A number of scholars agree with the sentiment of Earl Doherty who writes, "We have nothing in the Gospels which casts a clear light on that early evolution or provides us with a guarantee that the surviving texts are a reliable picture of the beginning of the faith."[12] Along with this opinion, people also make an unwarranted assumption: "*difference = contradiction, error, or lack of credibility.*"[13] Another assumption, popularized by Dan Brown's *The Da Vinci Code*, asserts that all of the Bible books were accepted as authoritative on the basis of an unfair vote by the Roman emperor Constantine in the fourth century at the Council of Nicea (A.D. 325).[14]

Before clarifying such allegations, assumptions, and historical blunders, it must be openly stated that showing whether Jesus rose bodily from the grave does not depend on whether one believes in the inerrancy of Scripture. Gary R. Habermas and Michael R. Licona present the "minimal facts" arguments, Too often the objection raised frequently against the Resurrection is, "Well, the Bible has errors, so we can't believe Jesus rose." We can quickly push this point to the side: "I am not arguing at this time for the inspiration of the Bible or even its general trustworthiness. Believer and skeptic alike accept the facts I'm using because they are so strongly supported. These facts must be addressed."... Historians recognize that most writings of antiquity contain factual errors and propaganda. They still can identify kernels of historical truth in those sources. If they eliminated a source completely because of bias or error, they would know next to nothing about the past. Thus, [if one rejects]... the inspiration of the Bible, there was still the collection of historical facts that remained to be answered.[15]

These historical facts, which must be answered by those who reject the inspiration of Scripture, are discussed in this chapter to argue for the veracity of the bodily resurrection of Jesus. Having said this, however, the evidence shows the Bible can be trusted as an accurate historical document that conveys the truth of what happened in Jerusalem over two thousand years ago.

It is a colossal historical blunder to allege that all twenty-seven New Testament (NT) books were deemed authoritative by a mere vote that occurred in the Council of Nicea A.D. 325.

First, the Council of Nicea had nothing to do with forming the canon (or the official recognized list of inspired books) of the NT. Instead this Council convened to settle the long-held belief about the deity of Jesus and His relationship to the Father, since a debate arose between two prominent men of the time. Presbyter Arius of Alexander believed Jesus was created and is not of the same nature as God the Father. Conversely Athanasius believed Jesus is distinct from the Father, but is similar in nature as God.[16] After an almost unanimous vote of 316 to 2, the matter was settled and the long-held belief of the church for two hundred years now officially stood: Jesus is God.[17]

Second, within the first century the Bible claimed for itself to be inspired and people trusted it as God's Word (Matt. 5:17; Luke 10:7; 24:27; Acts 2; 17:11; Gal. 6:16; Eph. 2:20; Col. 4:16; 1 Tim. 5:18; 2 Tim. 3:16–17; Heb. 1:1–2; 2 Pet. 1:19–21; 3:16; Rev. 1:3). Almost all scholars date all NT books within the first century, and some even believe they were all written before A.D. 70.[18]

Followers of the apostles, called church fathers, believed that these books were the inspired Word of God. Men like Ignatius of Antioch (A.D. 35–107) and Polycarp, a disciple of the apostle John (A.D. 65–115), and writings including the Epistle of Barnabas (A.D. 120) and the Epistle of Second Clement (A.D. 140) referred to the NT books as "Scripture." Thus by the middle of the second century most of the books were already considered Scripture by church leaders.[19] By the end of the second century most of the NT books appeared in a list called the Muratorian Fragment (Roman origin), except Hebrews, James, and 1 and 2 Peter. These books were still in question, which proves the rigorous process that took place in the early church before accepting any book as authoritative.[20]

Because fast communication systems (airplanes, telephones, and computers) did not exist in those days, it took a while before all twenty-seven books of the NT were recognized and compiled. By A.D. 367, Athanasius was the first to mention the twenty-seven books of the NT as canonical.[21] Later in two councils all twenty-seven books of our present NT were official recognized. This, however, did not occur simply because someone voted them arbitrarily into a list. F. F. Bruce forcefully says,

> One thing must be emphatically stated. The New Testament books did not become authoritative for the Church because they were formally included in a canonical list; on the contrary, the Church included them in her canon because she already regarded them as divinely inspired, recognizing their innate worth and generally apostolic authority, direct or indirect. The first ecclesiastical councils to classify the canonical books were both held in North Africa—at Hippo Regius in 393 and at Carthage in 397—but what these councils did was not to impose something new upon the Christian communities but to codify what was already the general practice of these communities.[22]

Someone said eloquently, "'The church did not create the Canon: the Canon created the church.' In other words, it is the Word of God from the outside, given key moments in history through His chosen messengers, that calls the people of God into existence. In the fourth century, the church merely published for the sake of clarity what it had always believed."[23] To say otherwise is to make a historical blunder.

Another mistake many scholars and laymen make is assuming that "differences" equal "contradictions." Understanding how to interpret history may be a bit complex and requires careful thought, since the way events are recorded may vary according to a writer's perspective.

Darrell L. Bock illustrates this point by asking the name of the worldwide conflict that occurred at the turn of the twentieth century. "Only a few realize that it was initially called 'The Great War' or the 'War to End All Wars.' Both names expressed the scope of the conflict, which was unprecedented up to that time. The name this conflict is known by today is 'The First World War,' a name it could not have until the Second World War took place. Now whether one refers to this event by its original name, The Great War, or by its alternative, The

First World War, one is looking at the same set of historical events." Thus sometimes an event may be understood and described by its original name or setting that took place or by its subsequent impact after it occurred. Therefore a historian may record an incident from its original perspective or how it was perceived in the aftermath of the event. Both accounts are true but have different perspectives with one description having more details than the other.[24]

Numerous examples of this sort occur in the Bible.[25] That is, similar accounts of the same event may vary according to the perspective a historian wants to emphasize.

Many books have been written discussing problem passages in the Bible and passages that seem to contradict each other.[26] Two examples will suffice to demonstrate the common erroneous assumption that "differences" equal "contradictions."

Matthew 8:6–9 records a centurion asking Jesus to heal his servant. However, in Luke 7:3–8, messengers are the ones asking Him to heal the centurion's servant. Perhaps these are two similar events that describe different occasions in which a centurion had a slave that needed healing. While that may work, for example, in the accounts described with similar details in the Sermon on the Mount and the Sermon on the Plain (Matt. 5:1; Luke 6:17), it seems incredulous here and in a number of occasions.[27] Another way of resolving the issue is to say these accounts contradict each other and are mistaken. Recording such a contradiction, however, makes no sense if people were trying to forge a godly inspired document. It seems they would want to harmonize the text. The better alternative is to say both are emphasizing different details of the same account. Matthew addresses a Jewish audience in whose culture messengers spoke on behalf of a person as if the person/sender was present.[28] "An example in our culture is when the White House press secretary speaks. What is important is not especially who he is but that he speaks for the president. Ancient culture was similar."[29] Thus Matthew summarizes the event as if the centurion is the one speaking to Jesus (normally understood by his Jewish audience), but since Luke addresses a mixed group of Gentiles he gives more details since they would not understand this way of summarizing the event.

Peter's three denials of Jesus seem to clash in the biblical accounts because those accusing him differ (Matt. 26:69–75; Mark 14:66–72;

Luke 22:55–62; John 18:15–18, 25–27). But again, "It may just be that as the denials proceeded, *more than three people* challenged Peter though different accounts note only *some* of those participants."[30]

What may seem contradictory may be resolved by understanding the different perspectives the historians wanted to emphasize.

Another accusation made against the Bible's trustworthiness appears on three levels, as noted by NT textual critic scholar Bart D. Ehrman. (1) Not only do we not have the original documents the apostles wrote, but we also do not posses copies, or copies of the copies of the primary text. All we have are very late copies of the originals.[31] (2) A number of differences also exist in these copies, so much so that "there are more variants among our manuscripts than there are words in the New Testament."[32] (3) "Orthodox" scribes have altered the text so drastically in a number of places that the meaning of the text changes, which results in having a different doctrinal conclusion.[33]

Ehrman's three objections are noted and answered by Daniel B. Wallace.[34] First, Ehrman has no way of knowing how to determine those late third-or fourth-generation copies. We do have "between ten to fifteen copies within a century of the completion of the New Testament."[35] Hence it seems possible that these third- or fourth-generation copies were made from even earlier manuscripts. Ehrman simply gives a false impression.

Second, differences in manuscripts are sometimes compared to what occurs in a "telephone game."[36] Children sit in a wide circle. At one end a child repeats a secret to the one next to him and so on, until the last child repeats the message which by then is terribly distorted. Wallace, however, clarifies the fallacy of this comparison. But the copying of New Testament manuscripts is hardly like this parlor game. Most obviously, the message is passed on in writing, not orally.... Second, rather than one line, multiple lines or streams of transmission are available. These help to function as checks and balances on the wording of the original. A little detective work in comparing, say, three lines of transmission, rather than reliance solely on the last person's account in one line, would help recover the wording of the original story. Third, textual critics don't rely on just the last person in each line but can interrogate several folks who are closer to the original source. Fourth, writers (known as church fathers) are commenting on the text as it is going through its transmissional history. And when there are chronological gaps among the manuscripts, these writers often fill in those gaps by telling us what the text said in that place in their day. Fifth, in the telephone game, once the story is told by one person, that individual has nothing else to do with the story. It is out of his or her hands. But the original New Testament books most likely were copied more than once and have been consulted even after several generations of copies had already been produced.[37]

Furthermore, do we really have more variations in the manuscript copies than we have words in the NT? Ehrman estimated that 400,000 textual deviations exist in the NT. Compared to the 138,162 words in the standard Greek NT this seems unusually high, and it gives the impression that no one could ever arrive at the original text of the Scriptures.[38] Who can believe the Bible's account of the early witnesses of Jesus' resurrection if the copies were corrupted? But the fact is we can. What Ehrman presents as a huge problem is more apparent than real.

Most textual variations have no bearing on the meaning of the Scripture; no major doctrines are in doubt.[39] Most of the differences simply involve a letter that was omitted in a word or added, or a variant spelling of a word, or a synonym. Even when a different word appears in a passage, which supposedly changes its meaning, so many copies exist along with quotations from church fathers that arriving at the original word and meaning of the text is only a matter of doing the necessary investigative work of comparison: internally in the context and externally by looking at the copies available.[40] In fact, the Greek NT manuscripts are unrivaled by any other ancient works as the following chart shows:[41]

"Besides textual evidence from the New Testament Greek manuscripts and from early versions, the textual critic compares numerous scriptural quotations used in commentaries, sermons, and other treaties by early church fathers. Indeed, so extensive are these citations that if all other sources for our knowledge of the text of the New Testament were destroyed, they would be sufficient alone for the reconstruction of practically the entire New Testament."[42] Hence Wallace concludes, "In sum, New Testament textual critics suffer from an embarrassment of riches when their discipline is compared with other Greek and Latin literature. Although it is true that we don't possess the original documents, to say that we don't have the copies of the copies of the original, without further clarification as to what we *do* have, is misleading. Statements like this reveal one of the fundamental flaws in *Misquoting Jesus*: it's not what Ehrman puts into the book that is so troubling but what he leaves out. And what he leaves out is any discussion of the tremendous resources at our disposal for reconstructing the text of the New Testament."[43]

The Physical Resurrection Accepted Historically

Today some scholars say it is incorrect to speak of Jesus' resurrection as "historical." Marxsen believed this, and "a remarkable number of subsequent scholars have followed him in this assertion."[44] Ehrman, in a debate with William L. Craig, argued that one could believe "theologically" that God raised Jesus from the dead but not historically .But this cannot be a historical claim, and not for the reason that he [Craig] imputed to me as being an old, warmed over 18th century view that has been refuted ever since. Historians can only establish what probably happened in the past. The problem with historians is they can't repeat an experiment. Today, if we want proof for something, it's very simple to get proof for many things in the natural sciences; in the experimental sciences we have proof. If I wanted to prove to you that bars of ivory soap float, but bars of iron sink, all I need to do is get 50 tubs of lukewarm water and start chucking in the bars. The Ivory soap will always float, the iron will always sink, and after a while we'll have a level of what you might call predicted probability, that if I do it again, the iron is going to sink again, and the soap is going to float again. We can repeat the experiments doing experimental science. But we can't repeat the experiments in history because once history happens, it's over.[45]

Such a view not only denies the existence of miracles, but also misunderstands how one may refer to "history" in different ways. Noting this kind of error N. T. Wright says, "This proposal appears to be cautious and scientific. It is, however, neither of these things. It involves a rash dismissal of an important question, and a misunderstanding of how science, including scientific historiography, actually works…. This is a classic case of failing to distinguish between the different senses of 'history.'"[46]

Not distinguishing how one may use the word "history" in five different ways has been part of the problem plaguing the "historical Jesus" and the "resurrection of Jesus" debate.[47] Wright succinctly summarizes how the fives senses of the term "history" works, which helps clear the confusion that so often comes with the arguments of those wanting to refute Jesus' physical resurrection.

First, there is history as *event*. If we say something is "historical" in this sense, it happened, whether or not we can know or prove that it happened.

Second, there is history as *significant event*. Not all events are significant; history, it is often assumed, consists of the ones that are. The adjective that tends to go with this is "historic"; "a historic event" is not simply an event that took place, but one whose occurrence carried momentous consequences.

Third, there is history as *provable event*. To say that something is "historical" in this sense is to say not only that it happened but that we can demonstrate that it happened, on the analogy of mathematics or the so-called hard sciences.[48]

Fourth, and quite different from the previous three, there is history as *writing-about-events-in-the-past*. To say that something is "historical" in this sense is to say that it was written about, or perhaps could in principle have been written about. (This might even include "historical" novels).

Fifth and finally, a combination of (3) and (4) is often found precisely in discussions of Jesus: history as *what modern historians can say* about a topic. By "modern" I mean "post-Enlightenment," the period in which people have imagined some kind of analogy, even correlation, between history and the hard sciences. In this sense, "historical" means not only that which can be demonstrated and written, but that which can be demonstrated and written *within the post-Enlightenment worldview*. This is what people have often had in mind when they have rejected "the historical Jesus" (which hereby, of course, comes to mean "the Jesus that fits the Procrustean bed of a reductionist world") in favour of "the Christ of faith."[49]

What then is the sense of the word "history" that we ought to understand when the early witnesses claimed to have seen Jesus or when Paul wrote, "He was buried, and ... He rose again the third day according to the Scriptures" (1 Cor. 15:4)? Were they recording a historical event or writing metaphorically? All the early first-century witnesses spoke of Jesus' resurrection as a historical event that actually occurred according to Wright's first point: "history as *event*." Because we speak of Jesus' resurrection as a historical event, this does not mean it cannot be verified. Many things have happened that cannot be proven scientifically according to point number three but can be verified. For example, "The death of the last pterodactyl is in that sense a *historical* event, even though no human witnessed it or wrote about it at the time, and we are very unlikely ever to discover [scientifically] when it took place." Do we then say this is not a true event when all of the circumstantial evidence points to this being the case? "Similarly, we use the word 'historical' of persons or things, to indicate simply and solely that they existed."[50]

We are now left to answer in the rest of this chapter one question: Did the Hebrews and Christians following the apostles understand the Resurrection to be of a spiritual or physical nature?

Hebrew Scriptures' general thought. For ancient peoples (including those in the Middle East) the *Iliad* written by Homer, was to them what the Old Testament (OT) was for the Jews. Along with Homer much of the other Greek classical works (eight to fifth century B.C.) painted a gloomy picture for the dead who could not return.[51] Even the concept of "resurrection" in the world of Egyptian mummification (or any Canaanite or fertility cults) does not have the same biblical sense.[52] Clarifying this difference in Jon Davies'[53] incorrect application of the term, Wright concludes. "The word denotes, as he sees, a further re-embodiment, a return to a this-worldly life, after a period in which the dead person is *not* alive in this way. Mummification and its other attendant practices, however, imply that the person still is 'alive' in some bodily sense, despite appearances." This does not mean a person comes back to a new bodily form of existence (which appears to be the way the NT uses the word "resurrection") but "'continuing existence in a mummified and hence, in that sense, 'bodily' state after death.'"[54]

Homer's view of life after death took an evolutionary turn in Plato's writings (fifth to fourth century B.C.), which the ancient world considered much like that of the NT.[55] Homer viewed the "'self' being the physical body, lying dead on the ground, while the 'soul' flies away to what is at best a half-life, now the 'self,' the true person, is precisely the soul." But "for Plato, the soul is the non-material aspect of a human being, and is the aspect that really matters. Bodily-life is full of delusion and danger; the soul is to be cultivated in the present both for its own sake and because its future happiness will depend upon such cultivation. The soul, being immortal existed before the body, and will continue to exist after the body is gone. Since for many Greeks 'the immortals' were the gods, there is always the suggestion, at least by implication, that human souls are in some way divine."[56] One can see where the Greco-Roman concept and emperors adopted the idea that they were in some form divine.

Contrary to ancient pagan literature, the general thought in the Hebrew Scriptures was based in attaining a bodily resurrection. Though the OT concept of resurrection is minor, however, later Jewish and Christian interpreters noticed "covert allusions" missed by earlier readers, an ability shared by many including Jesus. Although many scholars agree that for most of the OT the concept of a bodily resurrection meant being "deeply asleep," they also believe later revelation brought this idea to the forefront.[57]

The concept of resurrection appears to have developed in three common stages. "Many Christians have adopted some kind of theory of progressive revelation, according to which the earlier parts of the Old Testament held little or no belief in life after death, some of the more mature parts began to affirm a life beyond the grave, though without being very specific, and then, right at the end of the Old Testament period, some writers began to proclaim the quite different and radically new belief in bodily resurrection." In other words, "This is routinely seen as a kind of crescendo, beginning with near-silence, as it were, of the grave itself, and moving towards the fully orchestrated statement of the theme which will dominate the New Testament."[58]

Though this general understanding is correct, it needs to be modified. Beginning with the Genesis account of the Fall, God would not be triumphant unless the original physical creation was not in someway renewed. Acknowledging this important feature Bock wrote, "The bodily aspect of Jesus' resurrection is key, because in Judaism the belief in resurrection was a belief in a bodily resurrection involving a redemption of the full scope of what God had created (Rom. 8:18–30)."[59] Similarly Witherington states, "This resurrection is linked to actual environmental renewal of the earth itself (see Rom. 8:18–25). The destiny of believers and the destiny of the earth are inexorably linked together."[60] Though not as clear as the third stage that explicitly advocates the concept of physical resurrection, the first stage shows at times the resurrection seed and early plant-life that would later blossom to a mature tree in the New Testament era.[61] However, the Hebrew Scriptures appears not to concentrate on "life after death" or even "with resurrection."[62]

For example, evidence from numerous passages seems to show, perhaps like that of Homer and other Greek classical writers, that the Hebrew Scriptures described death as the final analysis:

> "For out of it you were taken; for dust you are, and to dust you shall return" (Gen. 3:19).

> "For in death there is no remembrance of you; in the grave who will give you thanks" (Ps. 6:5).

> "The dead do not praise the LORD, nor any who go down into silence" (Ps. 115:17).

> "For we will surely die and become like water spilled on the ground, which cannot be gathered up again" (2 Sam. 14:14).

"For the living know that they will die; but the dead know nothing, and they have no more reward, for the memory of them is forgotten. Also their love, their hatred, and their envy have now perished; nevermore will they have a share in anything done under the sun. Go, eat your bread with joy, and drink your wine with a merry heart; For God has already accepted your works. Let your garments always be white, and let your head lack no oil.

Live joyfully with the wife whom you love all the days of your vain life which He has given you under the sun, all your days of vanity; for that is your portion in life, and in the labor which you perform under the sun. Whatever your hand finds to do, do it with your might; for there is no work or device or knowledge or wisdom in the grave where you are going" (Eccl. 9:5–10).

Many more passages exist that describe the temporal nature of human life without any preview of future hope.[63] Unlike Plato's progressive view of death survived by a bodiless soul, "Death itself was sad, and tinged with evil. It was not seen, in the canonical Old Testament, as a happy release, an escape of the soul from the prison-house of the body." Instead, life, the corollary to death, was to be enjoyed to the fullest.[64]

One should not take from these passages (as the predominant thrust of the OT) that Jews did not believe in a future hope of restoration or the continuation of life after death, since it appears in seed form. Even passages describing the temporal nature of life, the hopelessness, and the ineffective state of the dead were merely ways of depicting life as it is viewed from an earthly perspective, or as the writer of Ecclesiastes, would say: life as seen "under the sun."[65]

Rather, ancient Israelites knew of other passages that gave them a living hope beyond the grave (e.g., 2 Sam. 7:12–21;[66] Pss. 72:1–12; 89; Isa. 61:1–11).[67] Too many other passages exist, though some are debatable, to simply dismiss the fact that OT Jews had no hope of the dead returning to life (e.g., Gen. 22:5 [cf. Heb. 11:17–19];[68] Job 19:25–27; 33:15–30; Pss. 16:10–11 [cf. Acts 2:23–31]; 22; 49:1–19; 73; Isa. 26:19; 53:10–12; Ezek. 37:1–14).[69] Yet of all OT passages almost all scholars today agree that Daniel 12:2–3 speaks of a concrete bodily resurrection from the dead.[70] "And many of those who sleep in the dust of the earth shall awake, some to everlasting life, some to shame and everlasting contempt. Those who are wise shall shine like the brightness of the firmament, and those who turn many to righteousness like the stars forever and ever."

Though bodily resurrection was not the predominant belief in the OT it does burst forth, as seen above, in various passages. Certainly this is the case in Daniel 12:2–3.

Resurrection in Jewish sources. However, by the second-Temple period, the time of Jesus, and rabbinic writings this position changed (200 B.C. to A.D. 200). By this period almost all Jews believed in some form of bodily resurrection.[71] Those who believed in the resurrection meant life after death in the sense of a two-stage approach. That is when a person died he existed in a place prepared by God where he waited for a future bodily resurrection, not some ghostly or spiritual disembodiment of eternal existence.[72] Sadducees, a Jewish aristocratic group arising in the second century B.C., however, denied any form of resurrection. Many such passages from the *Wisdom of Jesus ben Sirach* (i.e., Ecclesiasticus) appears to support their view that nothing beyond this life awaited anyone.[73] But similar to those passages of the OT, *Wisdom* (and a few intertestamental texts) emphasizes an earthly perspective of the frailty and fleetingness of life so as to encourage obedience while one lives.[74]

Another view—though a minority position—of a disembodied resurrection of the soul existed in this period, like that in Platonic Greek philosophy, which influenced Judaism of the second century B.C.[75] While such passages (1 Macc. 2:49–70; 4 Macc. 3:18; 6:7; 7:19; 9:22; 10:19; 14:5; 16:25; 17:12; 18) appear to promote the disembodied view of the soul, this interpretation can be questioned. Nothing explicitly states in these texts that the soul will live disembodied. Even one of the most used passages, *Jubilee* 23:27–29, frequently cited to argue for the existence of the disembodied souls, says in the following two verses, "rise up," "bones rest," and "spirits increasing joy," which may describe the two-stage expectation of time between a person's death and resurrection (vv. 30–31). Wright believes this is "the probable interpretation." However, this would then be "the only occurrence in the relevant literature of something that looks like the resurrection language being used to denote something other than new bodily existence." And this would be odd.[76]

Another exception to the predominant teaching of this era appears in Philo's writings. Philo, an Alexandrian Jew, was steeped in Hellenistic philosophy like that of Plato and Aristotle, which taught the immortality of the disembodied soul.[77] But this and the previous positions were not majority views in second–Temple Judaism.

Since first-century Jewish Christians testified of Jesus' resurrection, it is necessary to understand the context in which they made such allegations in order to know how to interpret it.

What became the predominant belief of second-Temple Judaism on the Resurrection comes to the fore unambiguously through the martyrs of the Maccabees. As the Syrian oppressor, Antiochus Epiphanes, wanted Jews to defy their laws, by eating pork and worshiping idols, through the story of a mother and her seven sons who are torture to death, they claim to return victoriously in a new body at the resurrection.

> And when he was at his last breath, he said [the second brother], "You accursed wretch, you dismiss us from this present life, but the King of the universe will raise us up to an everlasting renewal of life, because we have died for his laws" (2 Macc. 7:9).

> After him, the third was the victim of their sport. When it was demanded, he quickly put out his tongue and courageously stretched forth his hands, and said nobly, "I got these from Heaven, and because of his laws I disdain them, and from him I hope to get them back again" (2 Macc. 7:10–11).

> "And when he was near death, he [the fourth brother] said, "One cannot but choose to die at the hands of men and to cherish the hope that God gives of being raised again by him. But for you there will be no resurrection to life!" (2 Macc. 7:14).

> The mother was especially admirable and worthy of honorable memory. Though she saw her seven sons perish within a single day, she bore it with good courage because of her hope in the Lord. She encouraged each of them in the language of their fathers. Filled with a noble spirit, she fired her woman's reasoning with a man's courage, and said to them, "I do not know how you came into being in my womb. It was not I who gave you life and breath, nor I who set in order the elements within each of you. Therefore the Creator of the world, who shaped the beginning of man and devised the origin of all things, will in his mercy give life and breath back to you again, since you now forget yourselves for the sake of his laws" (2 Macc. 7:20–23).

I [the mother spoke privately to her youngest son] beseech you, my child, to look at the heaven and the earth and see everything that is in them, and recognize that God did not make them out of things that existed. Thus also mankind comes into being. Do not fear this butcher, but prove worthy of your brothers. Accept death, so that in God's mercy I may get you back again with your brothers." [This implies the physical reality of returning since God made the physical world from nothing.] (2 Macc. 7:28–29)[78]

A mere reading of the Jewish text of 2 Maccabees 7 makes it impossible to deny belief in a future bodily resurrection.[79] Another political hero of this era, Judas Maccabeus, discovered that the men who died in battle wore under their robes idolatrous tokens of the idol of Jamnia. He urged those alive to pray that God would forgive them (12:40–42), when they rose again.

He also took up a collection, man by man, to the amount of two thousand drachmas of silver, and sent it to Jerusalem to provide for a sin offering. In doing this he acted very well and honorably, taking account of the resurrection. For if he were not expecting that those who had fallen would rise again, it would have been superfluous and foolish to pray for the dead (2 Macc. 12:43–44).[80]

Yet another incident occurred to a Jew called Razi, elder of Jerusalem (2 Macc. 14:37). Before being arrested by the enemy Nicanor and the soldiers, he fell on his own sword (v. 41) while hoping to rise one day by the Lord's power.

But in the heat of the struggle he did not hit exactly, and the crowd was now rushing in through the doors. He bravely ran up on the wall, and manfully threw himself down into the crowd. But as they quickly drew back, a space opened and he fell in the middle of the empty space. Still alive and aflame with anger, he rose, and though his blood gushed forth and his wounds were severe he ran through the crowd; and standing upon a steep rock, with his blood now completely drained from him, he tore out his entrails, took them with both hands and hurled them at the crowd, calling upon the Lord of life and spirit to give them back to him again. This was the manner of his death (vv. 43–46).

Apocalyptic literature of this period, like that of *1 Enoch*, though at times it is not explicitly clear,[81] makes a bold claim for bodily resurrection.

And in those days shall the earth also give back that which has been entrusted to it, And Sheol also shall give back that which it has received, and hell shall give back that which it owes. For in those days the Elect One shall arise, and he shall choose the righteous and holy from among them: For the day has drawn nigh that they should be saved. And the Elect One shall in those days sit on My throne, and his mouth shall pour forth all the secrets of wisdom and counsel: For the Lord of Spirits hath given (them) to him and hath glorified him. And in those days shall the mountains leap like rams, and the hills also shall skip like lambs satisfied with milk, and the faces of [all] the angels in heaven shall be lighted up with joy. And the earth shall rejoice, and the righteous shall dwell upon it, and the elect shall walk thereon (1 Enoch 51:1–5).[82]

Similar to the "Elect One" above, the "Son of Man" together with a righteous remnant will receive a bodily resurrection, which depicts "a judgment scene reminiscent" of Daniel 7:13; 12:2; and Isaiah 52–53.[83]

And the righteous and elect shall be saved on that day, and they shall never thenceforward see the face of the sinners and unrighteous. And the Lord of Spirits will abide over them, and with that Son of Man shall they eat and lie down and rise up for ever and ever. And the righteous and elect shall have risen from the earth, and ceased to be of downcast countenance. And they shall have been clothed with garments of glory (1 Enoch 62:13–15).

First Enoch 91:10 also says, "And the righteous shall arise from their sleep, and wisdom shall arise and be given unto them." Other passages make the same point of the righteous attaining to a future bodily resurrection (*1 Enoch* 96:1–3; 102:4–11; 103:4; 104:1–4; 108:11–15; *Pseudo–Phocylides* 102–105; *Testament of Moses* 10:8–10; *Life of Adam and Eve* 13:3–6; 4; 41:2; 43:2–3; *Sibylline Oracles* 4:179–92; *Testament of Levi* 18:3; *Testament of Judah* 25:4; *Testament of Zebulon* 10:1–3; *Testament of Benjamin* 10:6–9; *4 Ezra* 7:28–44 [Daniel 12:2]; *2 Baruch*

30:1–5; 42:8; 51:5; *Psalms of Solomon* 3:11–16).[84]

In hindsight many Rabbis viewed the Hebrew Scriptures as teaching a bodily resurrection, as seen in the Talmud and the Mishnah.

How, on the basis of the Torah, do we know about the resurrection of the dead? As it is said, "And you shall give thereof the Lord's heave-offering to Aaron the priest" [Num. 18:28]. And will Aaron live forever? And is it not the case that he did not even get to enter the Land of Israel, from the produce of which heave-offering is given? [So there is no point in Aaron's life at which he would receive the priestly rations.] Rather, this teaches that he is destined once more to live, and the Israelites will give him heave-offering. On the basis of this verse, therefore, we see that the resurrection of the dead is a teaching of the Torah....

> R. Simai says, "How on the basis of the Torah do we know about the resurrection of the dead? "As it is said, 'And I also have established my covenant with [the patriarchs] to give them the land of Canaan' [Exo. 6:4]. "'With you' is not stated, but rather, 'with them,' indicating on the basis of the Torah that there is the resurrection of the dead."

> Minim asked Rabban Gamaliel, "How do we know that the Holy One, blessed be he, will resurrect the dead?" He said to them, "It is proved from the Torah, from the Prophets, and from the Writings." But they did not accept his proofs. "From the Torah: for it is written, 'And the Lord said to Moses, Behold, you shall sleep with your fathers and rise up' (Deu. 31:16)." They said to him, "But perhaps the sense of the passage is, 'And the people will rise up' (Deu. 31:16)?" "From the Prophets: as it is written, 'Thy dead men shall live, together with my dead body they shall arise. Awake and sing, you that live in the dust, for your dew is as the dew of herbs, and the earth shall cast out its dead' (Isa. 26:19)."...

> Romans asked R. Joshua b. Hananiah, "How do we know that the Holy One will bring the dead to life and also that he knows what is going to happen in the future?" He said to them, "Both propositions derive from the following verse of Scripture: "As it is said, 'And the Lord said to Moses, Behold

you shall sleep with you fathers and rise up again, and his people shall go awhorring ...' (Deu. 31:16)." "But perhaps the sense is, '[the people] will rise up and go awhoring' He said to them, "Then you have gained half of the matter, that God knows what is going to happen in the future." It has also been stated on Amoraic authority: Said R. Yohanan in the name of R. Simeon b. Yohai, "How do we know that the Holy One, blessed be he, will bring the dead to life and knows what is going to happen in the future? "As it is said, 'Behold, you shall sleep with you fathers, and ... rise again ... (Deu. 31:16)" (bSanh. 90).[85]

All Israelites have a share in the world to come ... And these are the ones who have no portion in the world to come: He who says, the resurrection of the dead is a teaching which does not derive from the Torah, (2) and the Torah does not come from Heaven; and (3) an Epicurean (mSamh. 10:1).

At one time all blessings in the Temple concluded with "forever." When the heretics corrupted [the practice] and said, "There is but one world [but no world to come]," they ordained that they should say, "forever and ever" [thus suggesting the existence of a world to come] (mBer. 9:5).[86]

Jewish leaders also recited daily a common liturgical temple prayer (which perhaps the Sadducees were exempt from repeating). It mentions bodily resurrection as coming from God who gives "life to the dead."[87]

Josephus' (A.D. 37–100) resurrection proclamations have been controversial, but sufficient evidence exists to show that he also followed the common concept of a bodily resurrection.

Do not you know that those who depart out of this life, according to the law of nature, and pay that debt which was received from God, when he that lent it us is pleased to require it back, enjoy eternal fame? That their houses and their posterity are sure, that their souls are pure and obedient, and obtain a most holy place in heaven, from whence, in the revolution of ages, they are again sent into pure bodies (The Jewish War 3.374).

But every good man hath his own conscience bearing witness to himself, and by virtue of our legislator's prophetic spirit, and of the firm security God himself affords such a one, he believes that God hath made this grant to those that observe these laws, even though they be obliged readily to die for them, that they shall come into being again, and at a certain revolution of things receive a better life than they had enjoyed before (Apion 2.218).

Wright correctly says, "Josephus makes the strong claim that belief in the resurrection is supported not only by conscience and the faithfulness of God, but by 'the lawgiver's prophecies.' As we have seen in the rabbis, and shall see in the New Testament, the question of whether the resurrection was prophesied by Moses himself was at the heart of at least some first-century debate on the subject. Josephus is here adopting a clear-cut Pharisaic position, both on the content of the belief and on its biblical basis."[88]

Furthermore the Essenes (Qumran community) described by Josephus appear to have the two-stage approach, in which at death a person's soul survives but later he receives a new body in the Resurrection.[89] Émil Puech's definitive work on the Essenes and their beliefs, especially concerning the Resurrection, is a standard text today.[90] Without having to reduplicate his find, various passages in the Qumran Scrolls bring to bear what the Essenes believed.

For He shall heal the critically wounded, He shall revive the dead, He shall send good news to the afflicted, (Isaiah 61:1) (4Q521 f2ii+4:12)

And the Lord will perform marvelous acts such as have never been, as he said; for he will heal the wounded and will make the dead live, he will bring good news to the poor, he will lead ... and enrich the hungry ... (4Q521 f2ii+1:10–13)

... see all the Lord has made: the earth and all that is in it, the seas and all they contain, and all the reservoirs of waters and torrents ... those who do what is good before the Lord ... like these, accursed. And they shall be for death ... he who gives life to the dead of his people. We shall give thanks and announce to you … of the Lord, who … (4Q521 f7+5ii:1–7)[91] the Reviver raises the dead of His people. (vacat) Then we shall give thanks and relate to you the righteous acts of the Lord which … those destined to die. And He shall open the graves … and open … and … and a valley of death … and a bridge of deeps … the accursed shall languish? … and the heavens shall advance… (4Q521 f7+5ii:6 –14)

Your holy ones. That bodies, covered with worms of the dead, might rise up from the dust to an eternal council; from a perverse spirit to Your understanding (1QHa 19:15)

Then the sword of God shall hasten to the time of judgment and all the children of His truth shall awaken to put an end to the children of wickedness, and all the children of guilt shall be no more. The hero shall draw his bow, and the fortification shall open… as an open country without end. The eternal gates shall open to bring out the weapons of war, and they shall be mighty from one end of the world to the other … But there is no escape for the creatures of guilt, they shall be trampled down to destruction with no remnant. And there is no] hope in the abundance of … , and for all the heroes of war there is no refuge. (vacat) For victory belongs to God Most High… Raise the ensign, O you who lie in the dust, and let the worms of the dead lift a banner for…they cut… in the battles of the arrogant. And He shall cause a raging flood to pass through, which shall not enter the fortified city… for plaster and as a beam for … truth …. (1QHa 14:32–40)[92]

Other texts also indicate this, according to Philip Jenkins. "The evidence of the Dead Sea Scrolls shows that at least some Jews had a highly developed concept of the Messiah in the century before Jesus' career, seeing a figure who healed the sick and raised the dead."[93]

Though the main concerns of the Qumran community lie with maintaining "present purity" and with an expectation of better world to come than the present, various texts nevertheless carry the idea of a bodily resurrection; but this was not a point of debate or dogmatically asserted by them.[94]

Jewish testimony reveals their common belief to be that of a future physical resurrection. Hence Wright said, "The [bodily] resurrection was not simply a doctrine of the Pharisees and their putative successors, the rabbis. All the evidence suggests that, with the few exceptions noted already, it was widely believed by most Jews around the turn of the common era."[96]

Resurrection in Christian sources. Jewish testimony before and during the first-century apostolic era demonstrates that belief in a bodily resurrection was common. But what did the church fathers believe about the Resurrection? Could their view give us a reflection of first-century thought, and do their views reflect similar beliefs of their Jewish predecessors?

Before discussing what the church fathers believed about the resurrection, it is necessary to discount as a predominant view the notion of a fringe group like the "Gnostics," who believed in a symbolic or spiritual Resurrection. First, numerous passages in Gnostic literature explicitly deny bodily resurrection,[97] since according to them the world is evil, and one must return to the prior disembodied state before creation. They believed that a "resurrection" of sorts can occur in this life and that it abides in a person as he gains *gnosis* (knowledge) that will be released on death.[98] Nothing in Gnostic materials agree with Jewish and Christian beliefs about the bodily resurrection, God's goodness, and the orderly creation account.[99] It is clear that nothing in the Gnostic texts reflects what Jewish and first-century sources believed about the future judgment that requires a resurrected body.[100] To suggest that they reflected early Christian thought is wrong and anachronistic since their writings are late (middle second century to the fifth century). Hence it is a mistake to think orthodoxy and Gnosticism were competing beliefs in the first century.[101] Philip Jenkins has correctly said:

> The problem with these reconstructions is the suggestion that both orthodoxy and Gnosticism are equally ancient and valid statements of the earliest Christianity, which they are not. What became the orthodox view has very clear roots in the first century, and indeed in the earliest discernible strands of the Jesus movement; in contrast, all the available sources for the Gnostic view are much later, and that movement emerges as a deliberate reaction to that orthodoxy....

This point [dating late Gnostic works earlier than they are] is illustrated by the debate over the key concept of the Resurrection, which is so fundamental to Pagel's argument. We recall that the orthodox regarded Jesus' resurrection as a specific event that occurred at a given moment in history, while Gnostics viewed it as a continuing symbolic process. There is no doubt that the orthodox position reflected the ideas of the first century, as all the four canonical gospels had before 100 provided their famous accounts of the resurrection and the various appearances to Jesus' followers. But when did the Gnostic interpretation emerge? Most evidence generally cited in support of such a view dates from well into the second century.[102]

Together with Jenkins one can say, "Finding what Gnostics believed about Jesus might be intellectually interesting ... but it brings us no closer to the historical roots of Christianity than does exploring the religious beliefs of nineteenth-century Shakers or Mormons. The Gnostic texts no more than confirm what we already knew about the far fringes of early Christian belief."[103]

The church fathers' beliefs, however, were more in line with Jewish thought but with a slight variance, they taught that a future resurrection is possible because of Jesus' resurrection. Hence we are not surprised that the church fathers, apologists, and later Christians articulated their beliefs in a future Resurrection similar to that of their NT predecessors.

First Clement (first century A.D.) appears to take a two-stage approach of the Resurrection. That is, when Christians die they are temporarily in heaven (see *1 Clem.* 5:4, 7; 6:2; 35:1; 44:5)[104] before receiving a superior resurrection body (*1 Clem.* 24:5 [John 12:24]; 26:1).[105] Clement makes his two-step-postmortem view explicitly in *1 Clement* 50:3 –4:

> Those who by God's grace were perfected in love have a place among the godly, who will be revealed when the Kingdom of Christ visits us. For it is written: "Enter into the innermost rooms for a very little while, until My anger and wrath shall pass away, and I will remember a good day and will raise you from your graves."

He says in another passage, "Let us consider, dear friends, how the Master continually points out to us the coming resurrection of which he made the Lord Jesus Christ the firstfruit when he raised him from the dead" (*1 Clem.* 24:1).

Second Clement (second century A.D.) was a sermon written by an anonymous author, but many scholars continue to refer to it as 2 Clement. The homily stresses the reality of the physical resurrection:

And let none of you say that this flesh is not judged and does not rise again. Understand this: in what state were you saved? In what state did you recover your sight, if it was not while you were in this flesh? We must, therefore, guard the flesh as a temple of God. For just as you were called in the flesh, so you will come in the flesh. If Christ, the Lord who saved us, became flesh (even though he was originally spirit and in that state called us, so also we will receive our reward in this flesh. Therefore let us love one another, that we all may enter into the kingdom of God. (9:1–6).[106]

Ignatius of Antioch (A.D. 35–107) also expounded how believers will likewise be raised from the dead like Jesus.

[Jesus], moreover, really was raised from the dead when his Father raised him up, who—his Father, that is—in the same way will likewise also raise us up in Christ Jesus who believe in him, apart from whom we have no true life. (Letters of Ignatius to the Trallians 9:2)

He reiterates in various letters similar sentiment of how Christians must believe in a physical resurrection (*Letters of Ignatius to the Philadelphia* 8:2; 9:2; *to the Smyrnaeans* 1:2; 12:2).

For he suffered all these things for our sakes, in order that we might be saved; and he truly suffered just as he truly raised himself—not, as certain unbelievers say, that he suffered in appearance only (it is they who exist in appearance only!). Indeed, their fate will be determined by what they think: they will become disembodied and demonic. (Letters to the Smyrnaeans 2:1)

For I know and believe that he was in the flesh even after the resurrection; and when he came to Peter and those with him, he said to them: "Take hold of me; handle me and see that I am not a disembodied demon." And immediately they touched him and believed, being closely united with his flesh and blood. For this reason they too despised death; indeed, they proved to be greater than death. And after his resurrection he ate and drank with them like one who is composed of flesh, although spiritually he was united with the Father. (Letters to the Smyrnaeans 3:1–3)

Polycarp (A.D. 69–155), bishop of Smyrna, similarly to Ignatius believed that Christians will rise from the dead just as Jesus rose (*Letter of Polycarp to the Philippians* 2:1–2; 5:2). Waiting to be martyred, he anticipated like many who died before him, eternal life, which he describes in terms "both of soul and of body, in the incorruptibility of the Holy Spirit" (*The Martyrdom of Polycarp* 14:2; see also 19:2).

The *Didache* (early second century A.D.), which means *teaching*, contained instructions for the Christian community. For the *Didache* the physical resurrection is not a central point of debate. However, while discussing the Eucharist and end time events, the *Didache* makes it clear that it follows the same beliefs as that of other church fathers.

Just as this broken bread was scattered upon the mountains and then was gathered together and become one, so may your church be gathered together from the ends of the earth into your kingdom; for yours is the glory and the power through Jesus Christ forever. (Didache 9:4)

And "then there will appear the signs"[46] of the truth: first the sign of an opening in heaven, then the sign of the sound of a trumpet,[47] and third, the resurrection of the dead—but not of all; rather, as it has been said, "The Lord will come, and all his saints with him." Then the world "will see the Lord coming upon the clouds of heaven."[49] (Didache 16:6–8)

Barnabas (late first century A.D.) demonstrates in his letter the belief in a physical resurrection since he believes Jesus will come in the flesh.

The prophets, receiving grace from him, prophesied about him. But he himself submitted, in order that he might destroy death and demonstrate the reality of the resurrection of the dead, because it was necessary that he be manifested in the flesh. (Letter of Barnabas 5:6)

He reiterates the belief of Jesus rising from the dead and how there will be a "recompense" for those who will be resurrected (*Letter of Barnabas* 15:8–9; 21:1).

The *Shepherd of Hermas* (mid to second century A.D.) is quite ambiguous in espousing the doctrine of the Resurrection. Only one passage mentions the Resurrection. Though a bit unclear, the references to undefiled "flesh" and "spirit" in order to "live to God" seem to indicate resurrection as the future status of Christians (*Shepherd* 60:1–4 [*Parables* or *Similitudes* 5.7.1 –4]).

The *Epistles to Diognetus* (A.D. 150–225),[107] an apologist, comes close to agreeing with the typical Hellenistic dualistic view of the soul versus the body (6:3–5). In the following passage he seems to espouse physical resurrection, but it is difficult to say for sure since it is ambiguous.

> The soul loves the flesh that hates it, and its members, and Christians love those who hate them. The soul is enclosed in the body, but it holds the body together; and though Christians are detained in the world as if in a prison, they in fact hold the world together. The soul, which is immortal, lives in a mortal dwelling; similarly Christians live as strangers amidst perishable things, while waiting for the imperishable in heaven. (Epistles to Diognetus 6:6–8)[108]

Papias (A.D. 60–130), bishop of Hierapolis, clearly demonstrated that he believed in a physical resurrection. Three texts demonstrate this.

> Among other things he says that there will be a period of a thousand years after the resurrection of the dead when the Kingdom of Christ will be set up in material form on this earth. These ideas, I suppose, he got through a misunderstanding of the apostolic accounts, not realizing that the things recorded in figurative language were spoken by them mystically. (Fragments of Papias 3:12)

From this it is clear that in the list of names itself there is one John who is placed among the apostles, and another, John the Elder, whom he lists after Aristion. We have mentioned this fact because of the statement made above, which we have recorded on the authority of a considerable number of people, that the two later epistles of John are not the work of the Apostle but of the Elder. He is the one who is said to have promulgated the Jewish tradition of a millennium, and he is followed by Irenaeus, Apollinarius, and others, who say that after the resurrection the Lord will reign in the flesh with the saints. (Fragments of Papias 7:3)

When he says these things he is hinting, I think, at Papias, who was then bishop of Hierapolis in Asia and flourished in the days of the holy evangelist John. For this Papias, in the fourth book of his Expositions of the Lord, mentioned food among the sources of enjoyment in the Resurrection. Later on Apollinarius believed this doctrine, which some refer to as the millennium.... and Irenaeus of Lyons says the same thing in the fifth book of his Against Heresies and cites in support of his statements the above-mentioned Papias. (Fragments of Papias 16:1)

Caroline Walker Bynum's magisterial work, *The Resurrection of the Body*, concludes, "Early Christianity, rabbinic Judaism, and the Koran[109] all speak of the body that rises as bones or a seed.... By the early third century, polemicists for the resurrection of the flesh assumed a dualist anthropology that saw the human being as a union of soul and body.... A theory of bodily return was, to these thinkers, essential."[110] To believe that people would rise bodily from the dead was the predominant view in this period. The evidence makes this an undisputable point.

Conclusion

Before discussing the Resurrection, we looked at the document (the Bible) that testifies of Jesus' resurrection. The evidence demonstrated that the Bible can be trusted as a historical document, and therefore it gives credence to the resurrection accounts of Jesus of Nazareth.

Furthermore, though the Hebrew Scriptures refer in general more to a temporal fleetingness of life that emphasizes an earthly perspective, the seed and early plant form of the doctrine of a future bodily resurrection appears in various passages. During the second-Temple period and in the translation of the Hebrew Scriptures into Greek, the concept of the Resurrection became "much clearer, so that many passages which might have been at most ambiguous became clear, and some which seemed to have nothing to do with resurrection might suddenly give a hint, or more than a hint, in that direction."[111] Thus almost the majority of Jewish literature recorded from 200 B.C. to A.D. 200 emphasized the belief of a future bodily resurrection. Rabbinic literature (Talmud and Mishnah) also exhibited the common expectation of the dead being raised bodily in the future resurrection. This belief continued to be the dominant conviction of the church fathers who followed their apostolic predecessors.

That people would rise bodily from the dead was the predominant view and background of the period when the witnesses of Jesus' resurrection recorded the NT. A reading of the evidence makes this point undisputable.

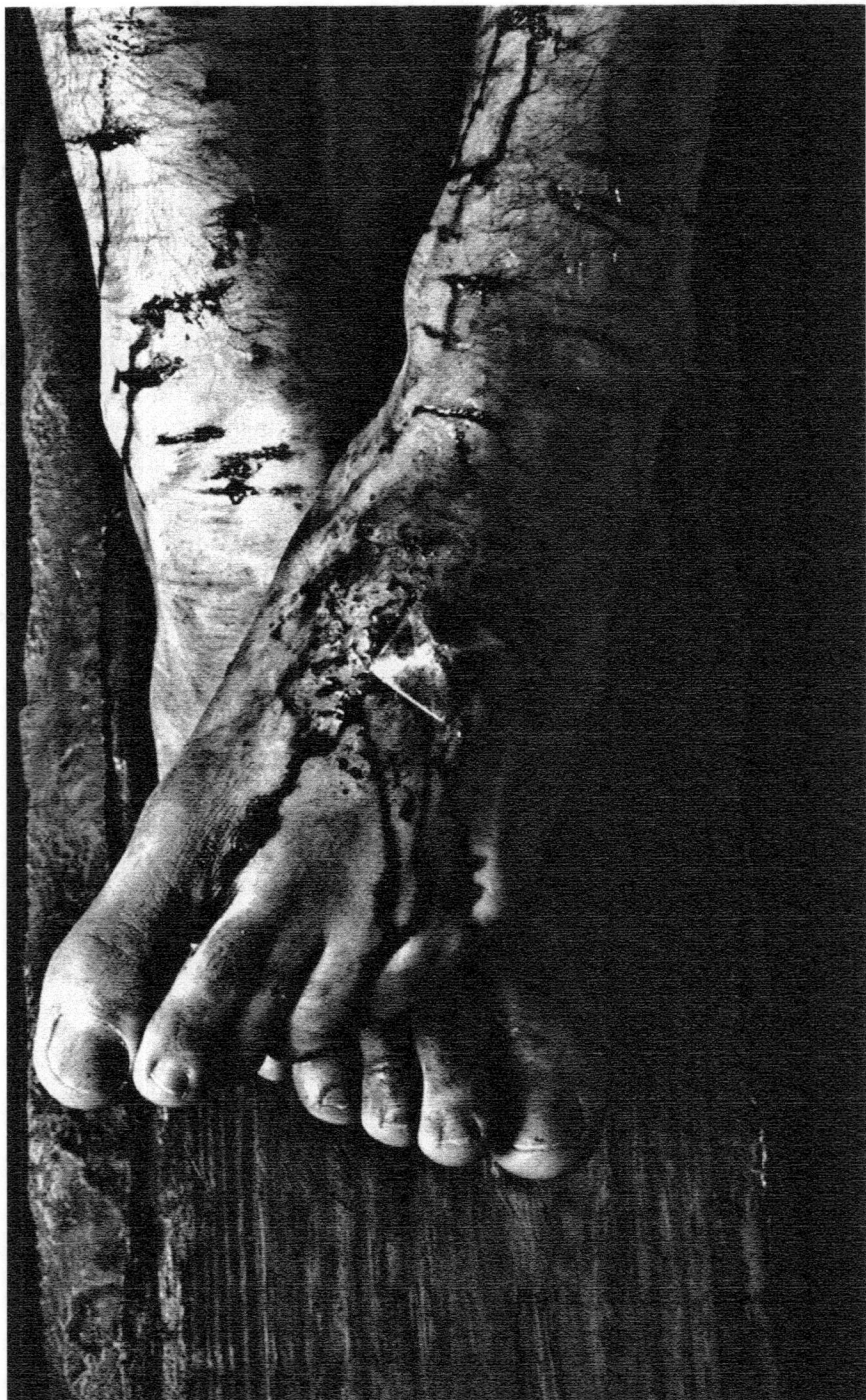

— CHAPTER 4 —

KILLING JESUS BEFORE RISING

If the Gospels afforded us no assistance we would have to imagine how Jesus contrived to give the impression of death, and suggest a way in which his body could have been secured by his friends. It is by no means a novel theory that Jesus was not dead when taken from the cross, and some will have it that he subsequently recovered.... There is no cause to doubt the crucifixion of Jesus, or that he had an assistant to aid him in his bid for survival.[1]

That Jesus really died on the cross needs to be established for various reasons. If Jesus did not die—which is a necessary prelude to rising physically—there can be no forgiveness of sins and eternal life for all who believe in Him (Rom. 6:1–23; 1 Cor. 15:12–23). Furthermore, the OT Law illustrated the necessary shedding of blood in order to forgive sins as seen in its sacrificial Levitical system. If Jesus faked His death, the Christian message is void and worthless, since John testified of Jesus, "Behold! The Lamb of God who takes away the sin of the world!"[2]

One of the best-known books denying that Jesus rose bodily from the grave is *The Passover Plot*, by Hugh J. Schonfield.[3] He argues that Jesus did all He could to fulfill the Old Testament prophecies but that He did not intend to die. Instead He plotted to survive the Crucifixion. Though Schonfield's fictional *Passover Plot* theory was analyzed and found completely wanting,[4] this has not stopped others from making similar allegations.

83

Another conspiracy theory denying Jesus' death on the cross is *The Jesus Conspiracy*, by Elmar R. Gruber. He claims, "A detailed analysis shows that the term used in the Greek original for the thrust of the soldier, *nyssein*, means a light scratch, puncture or stab to the skin, not a thrust with full force, let alone a deep penetration…. Even Origen (185–254), who did actually believe Jesus was dead at the time when the blood and water came out from the wounds, pointed out that corpses do not bleed."[5] Recently best-selling author Michael Baigent claims in *The Jesus Papers*, "Pilate took steps to ensure that Jesus would survive. He spoke with a member of the Sanhedrin and friend of Jesus, the wealthy Joseph of Arimathea."[6]

Could these allegations be true? Was Jesus lightly tortured, thereby making it possible for Him to endure the cross? Did He really die or was He resuscitated instead of resurrected? How does one deal with an empty tomb, or was it not empty, after all?

Jesus Tortured Short of Death

Before Jesus faced the death sentence of crucifixion, Pilate had Him "flogged/scourged" (Matt. 27:26; Mark 15:15; Luke 23:25; John 19:16). Even before being flogged, Jesus underwent six trials and in some of them He was beaten. (see following chart).

Before Jesus ever reached the civil trials He was already punched and slapped in His first religious trial, according to Mark 14:65. "Then some began to spit on Him, and to blindfold Him, and to beat Him, and to say to Him, 'Prophesy!' And the officers struck Him with the palms of their hands."[7]

When Jesus was finally turned over to the Roman guards to be flogged, He was probably already in some physical pain. But what condition was He in after the Roman guards finished?

Before a person received a Roman execution, he was given a preliminary legal flogging, all except women, Roman senators, and soldiers.[8] Though Mel Gibson's movie *The Passion of the Christ* has Hollywood embellishments, one of the things Gibson got correct was perhaps the most gruesome and bloodiest scene, next to the crucifixion, of the flogging of Jesus. Roman guards would inflict just the right amount of pain without killing the victim facing capital punishment. Victims were forcefully stripped of their clothes and tied to a post. Then the guards administered one of the most painful and cruel scourgings ever imaginable. Hebrew Law did not allow more than 40 lashes, but the Romans placed no limitation on them (Deut. 25:3). The scourging instrument was called a flagrum. This was sometimes called the Cat of Nine Tails because it had nine pieces of leather with pieces of sharp bones and metal attached that would "greatly lacerate human flesh" (Figure 15).[9]

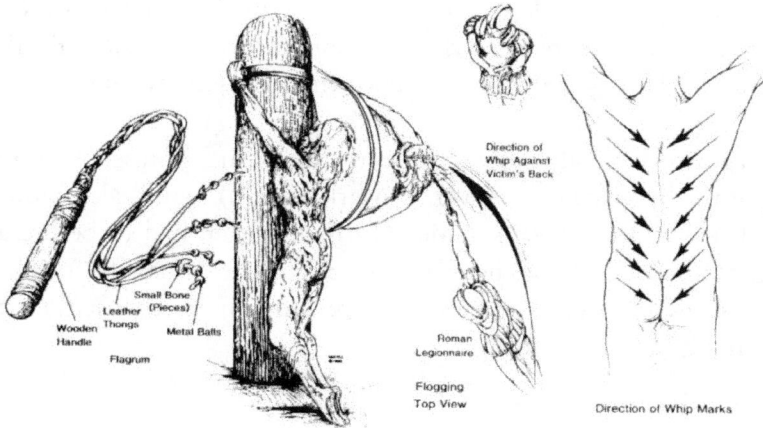

Figure 15. Scourging

The following article describes graphically the medical evidence showing the gruesome torture endured by a crucifixion victim.

As the Roman soldiers repeatedly struck the victim's back with full force, the iron balls would cause deep contusions, and the leather thongs and sheep bones would cut into the skin and Subcutaneous tissues. Then, as the flogging continued, the lacerations would tear into the underlying skeletal muscles and produce quivering ribbons of bleeding flesh. Pain and blood loss generally set the stage for circulatory shock. The extent of blood loss may well have determined how long the victim would survive on the cross.

At the Praetorium, Jesus was severely whipped. (Although the severity of the scourging is not discussed in the four gospel accounts, it is implied in one of the epistles [1 Peter 2:24]. A detailed word study of the ancient Greek text for this verse indicates that the scourging of Jesus was particularly harsh.) It is not known whether the number of lashes was limited to 39, in accordance with Jewish law. The Roman soldiers, amused that this weakened man had claimed to be a king, began to mock him by placing a robe on his shoulders, a crown of thorns on his head, and a wooden staff as a scepter in his right hand. Next, they spat on Jesus and struck him on the head with the wooden staff. Moreover, when the soldiers tore the robe from Jesus' back, they probably reopened the scourging wounds.[10]

John P. Mattingly's observes correctly, "The phrase 'And they bring unto the place of Golgotha' (Mark 15:22a) would also indicate that Christ, unable to walk under His own power, had to be literally brought or borne along the place of execution. Thus, the revolting and horrifying pre-cross sufferings were brought to a close, and the crucifying began" (Figure 16).[11]

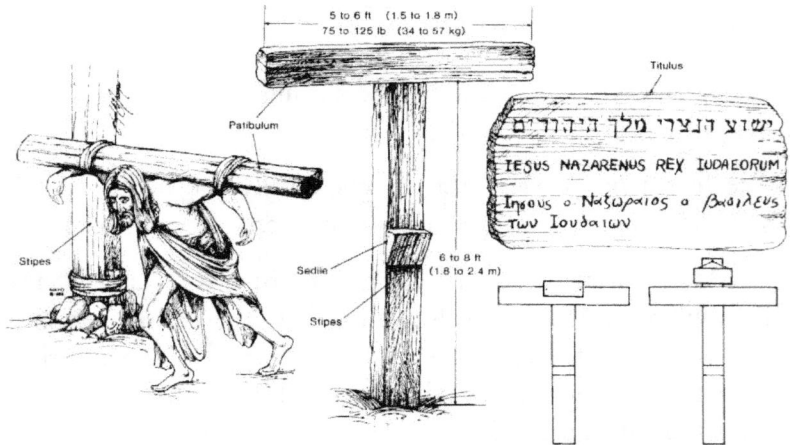

Figure 16. The Cross

In view of these intense suffering how could anyone argue that Jesus survived the crucifixion?

Did He Really Die?

Since skeptics cite the Koran (Surah 4:157) as evidence that Jesus merely pretended to die on the cross, it is necessary to investigate whether He actually died. If He did not die, then He merely resuscitated and was not resurrected. That is not, however, what the biblical and extrabiblical records claim.

Biblical Records. The Scriptures present several facts about Jesus' death. First, as already noted, Jesus was critically injured before He was crucified. After the flogging a crown of thorns was placed on His head, which most certainly intensified the bleeding (Matt. 27:29).

Second, besides being in serious condition before He was put on the cross, Jesus "suffered five major wounds between nine in the mourning and just before sunset (cf. [Mark 15] vv. 25, 33). Four of these were nails used to fix Him on the cross. We know from remains of Palestine crucifixion victims that these nails were five to seven inches long and about three eights inch square."[12] These knife-size nails would certainly result in death (Figure 17).[13]

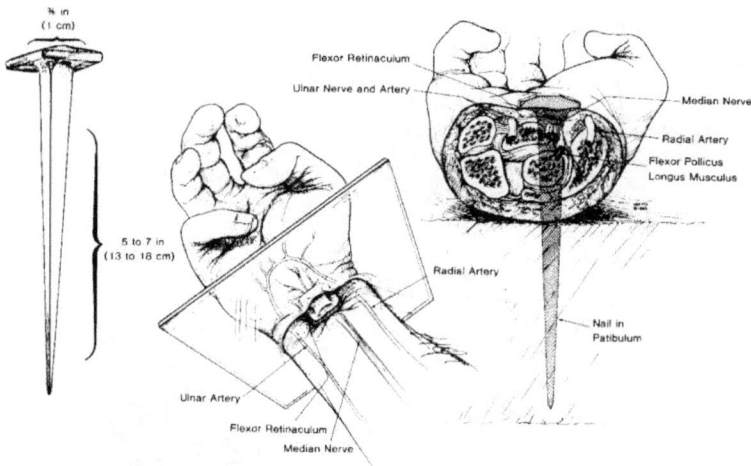

Figure 17. Nails and Crucifixion

Third, Roman soldiers often crucified convicts. Therefore the odds of allowing one to survive crucifixion are zero. In fact they made sure the two criminals crucified with Jesus were dead by breaking their legs. This was necessary since the Sabbath day was approaching and Jewish Law did not permit anyone to remained crucified overnight (Deut. 21:22–23; Mark 15:42). But when the soldiers "came to Jesus came to Jesus and saw that He was already dead, they did not break His legs" (John 19:32–33). Breaking the legs caused a crucifixion victim to suffocate since he could not push himself up to get air (Figure 18).

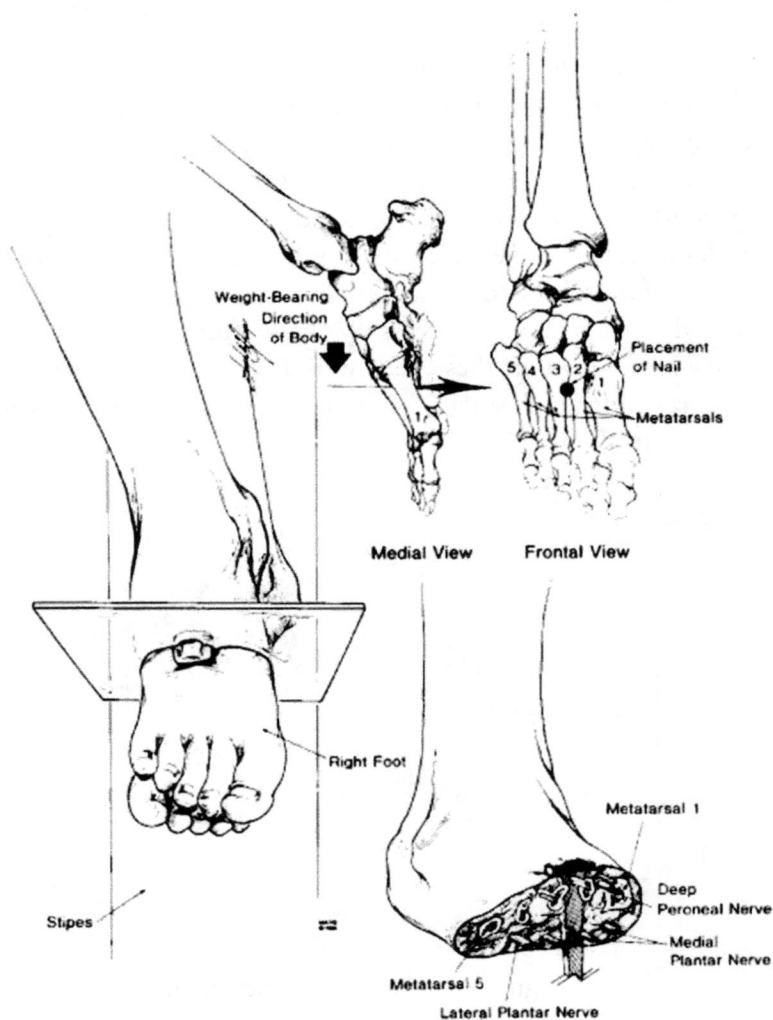

Figure 18. Feet of the Crucified

As Gary R. Habermas describes, "It was typical for a person to hang on the cross for days. However, on occasion when the Romans desired to speed up the process they would employ the *crurifragium*, the act of breaking the legs with a heavy club or mallet. This would prevent the victim from pushing up and exhaling. The cause of death for a crucified victim was simple—he could not breathe." Were the soldiers mistaken in thinking that Jesus was dead? "The soldiers had seen hundreds of men executed by crucifixion. It was routine to know when the victim was dead. He was not pushing up any longer for air."[14]

Furthermore, to insure that Jesus was dead the guards "pierced His side with a spear, and immediately blood and water came out" (John 19:34). The Greek word νύσσω ("pierced") does not refer to a mere "light scratch, puncture or stab to the skin," as Elmar R. Gruber argues.[15] The degree of the "stab" depends on the description given in the context not the word itself.[16] In this case the context clearly attests to Jesus' death. Pilate also verified this according to the biblical record. "Pilate marveled that He was already dead; and summoning the centurion, he asked him if He had been dead for some time" (Mark 15:44). Thus the stabbing was deep enough to penetrate the skin and rupture something since according to John "blood and water came out" (John 19:34; Figure 19).

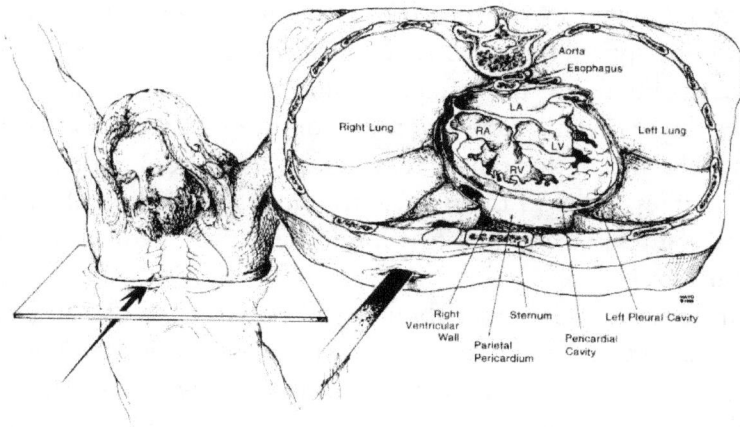

Figure 19. Piercing

Three medical doctors describe what the spear did and the medical results of what probably occurred. "Clearly, the weight of historical and medical evidence indicates that Jesus was dead before the wound to His side was inflicted and supports the traditional view that the spear, thrust between His right ribs, probably perforated not only the right lung but also the pericardium and heart and thereby ensured his death. Accordingly, interpretations based on the assumption that Jesus did not die on the cross appear to be at odds with modern medical knowledge."[17]

Gruber also argues that people do not bleed after death. But this wrongly assumes Jesus was dead for a long time. Jesus was pierced in the "sac" surrounding the heart that contains plenty of blood for a person to bleed even if the heart is not pumping blood.[18]

Fourth, anointing a body with about 75 to 100 pounds of spices, then wrapping it tightly in "strips of linen," and placing it in a cold slab tomb-rock would definitely guarantee asphyxiation or some other form of death if it did not occur on the cross. Imagine the scenario if Jesus had survived the cross? Such is the portrait Habermas paints by explaining liberal scholar David F. Strauss's critique and decisive blow to the swoon theory.

Strauss' [sic] most convincing point concerned Jesus' condition upon reaching his disciples. Very few would doubt that he would be in sad physical shape, limping badly, bleeding, pale and clutching his side. He would obviously be in need of physical assistance and, at any rate, would not appear to be the resurrected and glorified Lord of Life! As Strauss pointed out, the disciples would have gone for a doctor's help rather than proclaim Jesus the risen Son of God! Strauss asserted that even if the swoon theory was conceivable, it still could not account for the disciples' belief in the risen Jesus. Since they did proclaim him to be the resurrected and glorified Lord, the swoon theory is not able to account for the facts.[19]

In fact we know more about Jesus' burial than that of any other historical figure of the past. Wilbur M. Smith wrote, "We know more about the burial of the Lord Jesus than we know of the burial of any single character in all of ancient history. We know infinitely more about His burial than we do the burial of any Old Testament character, or any king of Babylon, Pharaoh of Egypt, any philosopher of Greece, or triumphant Caesar."[20] Yet we do not find anyone questioning whether these individuals died. That is because those who questioned Jesus' death know those who followed these leaders were not claiming they were resurrected. Therein lies the issue, not whether Jesus died but on

whether He was bodily resurrected. Therefore denying Jesus' death is just another way of refuting His physical resurrection.

People just did not survive crucifixion. "Survival of crucifixion was unknown, just as surviving the firing squad, the electric chair, a lethal injection, or the gas chamber is unheard of today. Because the law had decreed the prisoner's death, even if a first attempt failed, procedures would be repeated until the decree was carried out. But death from crucifixion was as certain as any modern method of execution. There was no escape."[21]

Extrabiblical Records. A number of sources outside the Bible also attest to the common Roman practice of crucifixion.[22] The cruel form of punishment of first-century crucifixion is also well documented by scholars.[23] Josephus, Cicero, Tacitus, Lucian of Samosata, Mara Bar-Serapion, the Babylonian Talmud, and even critical scholars testify of Jesus' death.

Josephus wrote, "And when Pilate, at the suggestion of the principal men amongst us, had condemned him to the cross, those that loved him at the first did not forsake him, for he appeared to them alive again the third day, as the divine prophets had foretold these and ten thousand other wonderful things concerning him; and the tribe of Christians, so named from him, are not extinct at this day."[24]

Tacitus describes, "Nero fastened the guilt [of the burning of Rome] and inflicted the most exquisite tortures on a class hated for their abominations, called Christians by the populace. Christus, from whom the name has its origin, suffered the extreme penalty during the reign of Tiberius at the hands of one of our procurators, Pontius Pilatus."[25]

Lucian of Samosata, a Greek satirist, stated, "The Christians, you know, worship a man to this day—the distinguished personage who introduced their novel rites, and was crucified on that account."[26]

Mara Bar-Serapion said, "Or [what advantage came to] the Jews by the murder of their Wise King, seeing that from that very time their kingdom was driven away from them?"[27]

The Babylonian Talmud records, "On the eve of the Passover Yeshu was hanged. For forty days before the execution took place, a herald went forth and cried, 'He is going forth to be stoned because he has practiced sorcery and enticed Israel to apostasy. Any one who can say anything in his favor, let him come forward and plead on his behalf.' But since nothing was brought forward in his favor he was hanged on the eve of the Passover!"[28] The name *Yeshu* is the equivalent Hebrew name for "Joshua," or Greek *Iēsous*, translated in English as "Jesus." The Jews believed that if a person "hung on a tree," the equivalent terminology for crucifixion, he was "accursed of God" (Deut. 21:23).

Critical scholar John Dominic Crossan also believes Jesus died on the cross. "That he [Jesus] was crucified is as sure as anything historical can ever be."[29]

NT critic, Gerd Lüdemann said, "Jesus' death as a consequence of crucifixion is indisputable."[30]

Even liberal scholar, James D. Tabor concludes, "None of these theories appear to have any basis whatsoever in reliable historical sources. I think we need have no doubt that given Jesus' execution by Roman crucifixion he was truly *dead* and that his temporary place of burial was discovered to be empty shortly thereafter."[31]

The Empty Tomb

Many theories are suggested to explain the empty tomb, such as the "swoon theory" which has been mentioned already. The strongest issue that critics of Jesus' physical resurrection have to contend with is that of the empty tomb. Since no one was able to produce the body of Jesus, in order for proponents to disprove the Resurrection, it remains a key argument that points to Jesus' physical resurrection. Hence Smith said, "No man has written, pro or con, on the subject of Christ's resurrection, without finding himself compelled to face this problem of Joseph's empty tomb. That the tomb was empty on Sunday morning is recognized by everyone, no matter how radical a critic he may be."[32]

William L. Craig presents eight reasons why the empty tomb points to Jesus' physical resurrection.[33]

"*The Historical Reliability of the Account of Jesus' Burial Supports the Empty Tomb.*" As Smith mentioned above, we know more about Jesus' burial than the burial of any other historical figure. How does this relate to an empty tomb and a risen Jesus? First, the disciples would not believe in Jesus' resurrection if a body laid in the tomb. Second, even if they were deceived, others living in Jerusalem would not be, since a stroll to the tomb would show that the disciples idea was a hoax. Third, the Roman authorities could easily disprove the Resurrection by exhuming the corpse. "Thus, you see, if the story of Jesus' burial is true, then the story of the empty tomb must be true as well."[34]

"*Paul's Testimony Implies the Fact of the Empty Tomb.*" Paul believed in the empty tomb. The statement, "He was buried" followed by the remark "He was raised" refers to an empty tomb. N. T. Wright also defends this point from critics who accused Paul of not mentioning the empty tomb. "The fact that the empty tomb itself, so prominent in the gospel accounts, does not appear to be specifically mentioned in this passage [1 Cor 15:4], is not significant; the mention here of 'buried then raised' no more needs to be amplified in that way than one would need to amplify the statement 'I walked down the street' with the qualification 'on my feet.' The discovery of the empty tomb in the gospel accounts is of course significant because it was (in all the stories) the first thing that alerted Jesus' followers to the fact that something extraordinary had happened; but when the story was telescoped into a compact formula it was not the principal point. The best hypothesis for why 'that he was buried' came to be part of this brief tradition is simply that the phrase summarized very succinctly that entire moment in the Easter narratives."[35]

Furthermore Paul's witness recorded in 1 Corinthians 15:3–5 was the earliest creed (like the Apostles Creed). Creeds are pithy ways to transmit oral information that is easy to memorize. Numerous scholars believe three years after Paul's salvation (A.D. 33 or 36)[36] or later when he visited Jerusalem and met with James and Peter (Gal. 1:18–19), he received this "creedal" information. Even if he received it later, it could not have surpassed A.D. 51, which is when he first arrived at Corinth.[37] Thus he wrote, "For I delivered to you first of all that which I also received" (1 Cor. 15:3a). Habermas states, "At minimum, we have source material that dates within two decades of the alleged event of Jesus' resurrection and comes from a source that Paul thought was reliable. Dean John Rodgers of Trinity Episcopal School for Ministry comments, 'This is the sort of data that historians of antiquity drool over.'"[38] Therefore Paul's words in 1 Corinthians 15:3–5 testify that he believed and incorporated the message of the empty tomb, and they also show that the earliest creed could not have been "a late legendary development."[39]

"The Empty Tomb Story Is Part of Mark's Source Material and Is Therefore Very Old." If one considers Mark's source (perhaps Peter) to be early, the inclusion of the empty tomb at the end of Mark's Gospel that appear to be grammatically and linguistically linked is telling. If one considers Caiaphas's occupation from A.D. 18 to 37, Mark's source of information comes within only seven years of Jesus' death. Why would anyone circulate a story of a buried man instead of an empty tomb?[40] They would not. Hence this strongly points to the validity of an empty tomb.

"The Phrase 'The First Day of the Week' Is Very Ancient." Contrasting Paul's term "on the third day" (1 Cor. 15:3, NASB) are the women who found the empty tomb "on the first day of the week" (Mark 16:2). Since Paul's "on the third day" creedal statement is accepted to be one of the earliest repeated credos by the church, it seems that if Mark's account was late and legendary, promoters would want to smooth these

statements out. This shows that Mark's creedal statement "on the first day of the week" is perhaps earlier than that of Paul's, thereby removing any doubt of the authenticity of the empty tomb account.[41]

"*The Story Is Simple and Lacks Legendary Development.*" Other than including or excluding various small details because of the Gospel writers different perspectives, the four Gospel accounts on Jesus' burial agree and record a simple and straightforward testimony (Matt. 27:57–28:8; Mark 15:42–16:8; Luke 23:50–24:10; John 19:38–20:8). By contrast, the Gnostic *Gospel of Peter* has embellishments that are obviously legendary; it describes scribes, elders, Pharisees, a number of soldiers, and a huge crowd witnessing "a loud voice in heaven, ... the heavens opened, ... two men come down from there in a great brightness and draw night to the sepulcher. That stone ... started of itself to roll ... both the young men entered in.... And ... three men come out from the sepulcher, and two of them sustaining the other, and the cross following them, and the heads of the two reaching to heaven, but that of him who was led of them by the hand overpassing the heavens. And they heard a voice out of the heavens crying, 'Hast thou preached to them that sleep?' and from the cross there was heard the answer, 'Yea.'"[42] The straightforward and simple explanations of the event in the Gospels argue for the authenticity of the Gospel accounts of the empty tomb.[43]

"*The Tomb Was Discovered Empty by Women.*" Women were the first to witness the empty tomb.[44] Yet in Jewish society women were not considered credible witnesses.

> But let not a single witness be credited; but three, or two at the least, and those such whose testimony is confirmed by their good lives. But let not the testimony of women be admitted, on account of the levity and boldness of their sex, nor let servants be admitted to give testimony on account of the ignobility of their soul; since it is probable that they may not speak truth, either out of hope of gain, or fear of punishment. But if anyone be believed to have borne false witness, let him, when he is convicted, suffer all the very same punishments which he against whom he bore witness was to have suffered (Josephus,

Antiquities 4.219 [4.8.15.219]).[45]

> It is not possible to have a world without either males or females, but happy is the one whose children are males, and woe for him whose children are females (Talmud, bPesahim 65a [5.10.10.1]).[46]

> This is the governing principle: Any evidence that a woman [gives] is not valid, also they are not valid [to offer]. Thus any evidence that a woman [gives] is valid, also they are valid [to offer]. Said Rab Ashi, "This is to say that a person who, by their [that is, Rabbinical] standards, is a robber is valid to offer testimony [normally allowed] of a woman" (Talmud, Rosh Hashanah 22a [1:8]).

As Rosh Hashanah's statement shows, the witness of a woman was viewed as no more reliable than that of a thief. Perhaps this sheds light on why the Jewish disciples did not immediately believe the women's witness of the empty tomb.[47] "And their words seemed to them like idle tales, and they did not believe them" (Luke 24:11). Romans too shared contempt toward women. "Whereas men and women hitherto always sat together, Augustus confined women to the back rows even at gladiatorial shows: the only ones exempt from this rule being the Vestal Virgins, for whom separate accommodation was provided."[48]

Thus, if one were to invent the account of the empty tomb, women would not be the best witnesses to use. Why would someone record the most incredible event in history and risk the chance of embarrassment by using questionable witnesses to verify it? Hence Habermas concludes, "If the Gospel writers had originated the story of the empty tomb, it seems far more likely that they would have depicted men discovering its vacancy and being the first to see the risen Jesus. Why would they not list the male disciples Joseph of Arimathea and Nicodemus and avoid the female issue altogether? If the account of the empty tomb had been invented, it would most likely *not* have listed the women as the primary witnesses, since in that day a woman's testimony was not nearly as credible as a man's. Thus the empty tomb appears to be historically credible in light of the principle of embarrassment."[49]

"The Disciples Could Not Have Preached the Resurrection in Jerusalem Had the Tomb Not Been Empty." As mentioned earlier, if the tomb was not empty a brief stroll to the Jerusalem tomb would have resolved the issue and would have silenced the disciples once for all. But since no one produced a corpse, the preaching of the disciples was clearly based on the fact that Jesus' tomb was empty.

"The Earliest Jewish Propaganda against the Christians Presupposes the Empty Tomb." An early skeptic's attempt to refute the empty tomb appears in Matthew 28:11–15.

Now while they were going, behold, some of the guard came into the city and reported to the chief priests all the things that had happened. When they had assembled with the elders and consulted together, they gave a large sum of money to the soldiers, saying, "Tell them, 'His disciples came at night and stole Him away while we slept.' And if this comes to the governor's ears, we will appease him and make you secure." So they took the money and did as they were instructed; and this saying is commonly reported among the Jews until this day.

By the last phrase, "This saying is commonly reported among the Jews until this day," Matthew recorded an effort in his day to try to refute the physical resurrection of Jesus. In the zealous attempt, however, of those who tried to refute the physical resurrection of Jesus, they did not deny the empty tomb because they admitted, "His disciples came at night and stole Him away." They could not have it both ways: an empty tomb and a nonresurrected Jesus. "The Jewish propaganda did not deny the empty tomb, but instead entangled itself in a hopeless series of absurdities trying to explain it away. In other words, the Jewish propaganda that the disciples stole the body presupposes that the body was missing. Thus, the Jewish propaganda itself shows that the tomb was empty."[50]

Besides, this theory is full of problems. Could the disciples have overpowered Roman guards and stolen the body? Not a chance. Just hours before, they were all scared and abandoned Jesus; and the most fearless, Peter, became fearful and denied Him three times.[51] In addition how could the guards know who took the body since they were sleeping? The best they could do was say, "Someone stole the body?"

Even believing this is problematic. How can anyone sleep through the removal of a rock covering the tomb heavy enough that took a number of men to move? Assuming the thieves were successful, the guards would never claim such a thing because by Roman law they would deserve the death penalty for falling asleep and allowing grave robbers to steal a body on their watch.[52]

Conclusion

Jesus was not lightly tortured. He underwent such a severe mode of torture and execution that it would have been impossible for Him to have survived the cross.

The biblical records verify Jesus' death on the cross, and extrabiblical sources do so as well. Josephus, Cicero, Tacitus, Lucian of Samosata, Mara Bar-Serapion, the Talmud, and even critical scholars, all testify of Jesus' death.

Eight good reasons show that the tomb was empty. It was not empty because Jesus did not die, or because the disciples stole the body. Such theories create more problems than they solve. In fact Craig notes that NT critical scholar and resurrection researcher, Jacob Kremer provides names of twenty-eight scholars (including his) who acknowledge the empty tomb:

> Blank, Blinzler, Bode, von Campenhausen, Delorme, Dhanis, Grundmann, Hengel, Lehmann, Léon-Duffour, Lichtenstein, Manek, Martini, Mussner, Nauck, Rengstorff, Ruckstuhl, Schenke, Schmitt, Shcubert, Schweizer, Seidensticker, Strobel, Stuhlmacker, Trilling, Vögtle, and Wilckens.' [He adds] I can think of at least sixteen more that he failed to mention: Benoit, Brown, Clark, Dunn, Ellis, Gundry, Hooke, Jeremias, Klappert, Ladd, Lane, Marshall, Moule, Perry, Robinson, and Schnackenburg. Perhaps most amazing of all is that even two Jewish scholars, Lapide and Vermes, have declared themselves convinced on the basis of the evidence that Jesus' tomb was empty.[53]

The fact is that Jesus died, and the tomb was empty because He rose physically from the dead. A number of witnesses and various accounts verify this, which is the subject of the next chapter.

— CHAPTER 5 —

KILLING THE CONCEPT OF PHYSICAL RESURRECTION

> While speaking of the positive evidence of the Resurrection of our Lord, it may be further urged that the fact, if true, harmonizes all the other facts of His history.[1]

A miracle is "a surprising and welcome event that is not explicable by natural or scientific laws and is therefore considered to be the work of a divine agency: *the miracle of rising from the grave.*"[2] Some people do not believe in miracles for various reasons. Hence, killing the concept of physical resurrection is a must. However, for those who believe in miracles, accepting the fact that Jesus of Nazareth rose physically rather than spiritually is not shocking.

The Jews believed in disembodied spirits of the dead and spirit-angels according to various passages (e.g., 1 Sam. 28:11–20; 2 Kgs. 19:7; Mark 6:49; Luke 24:39; Heb. 1:7, 14). But this belief is never spoken of as "resurrection." Conversely the concept and Hebrew word היה (*hyh*, "to revive" or "to return life") and the Greek words ἐγείρω (*egeirō*) and ἀνίστημι (*anistēmi*, "rise to life") represent the term "resurrection."[3] This is evident in numerous biblical passages where people were physically raised from the dead back to life (1 Kgs. 17:17–22; 2 Kgs. 4:32–36; 13:20–21; Isa. 26:19; Ezek. 37:3–14; Dan. 12:2–3; Matt. 9:23–25; 27:52–53; Luke 7:11–15; John 11:43–44; Acts 9:36–40; Rev. 11:8, 11).

Some, however, object to calling some of these events (e.g., the raising of Lazarus) "resurrections" because these people (other than

99

Jesus) died again. They prefer to call them "resuscitations." A person who receives CPR (cardiopulmonary resuscitation) after not breathing for a few seconds or minutes may be "revived" or "resuscitated," but this differs from a person who has no vital signs for a long period of time. That person is considered dead and a candidate for resurrection. CPR would not bring this person back from the dead. However, if a person dies for a prolonged period of time and returns to life by a miracle, this may be called a *resurrection*, even though that individual dies again.

All the wicked dead will be raised at the Great White Throne judgment. This is called a "resurrection" even though they will again die after their day in court (Dan. 12:2; Rev. 20:6). Thus the term "resurrection" or "arise" does not imply in itself, apart from qualifiers, *resurrection to everlasting life* (i.e., not to die again), since the word is used of people who return to life to die again. Thus if one is brought back to life by a special miracle, it can be defended biblically as a resurrection. Whether one returns to life and dies again or returns to life never to die again, the person possesses a body, which is a vital element in defining the term "resurrection."

What then is the evidence from the OT and NT passages that preview "the oncoming attraction" of Jesus' physical resurrection? In other words are there passages that show people were raised physically, thereby previewing or hinting that Jesus' physical resurrection was the expected interpretation and nothing new?

Old Testament Resurrection Accounts

Three resurrection accounts testify to the expectancy of a future physical resurrection (1 Kgs. 17:17–22; 2 Kgs. 4:32–36; 13:20–21). Although these individuals died again, these accounts are a preview of the kind of resurrection most Jews anticipated and the way Jesus was expected to rise from the dead, that is, physically instead of spiritually.[4]

Widow's Son. First Kings 17:17–22 records the Bible's first occurrence of a resurrection. Elijah, by God's mandate, met a widowed woman from Zarephath of Sidon who provided nourishment for Elijah in a miraculous way (vv. 17:8–16). While Elijah was there, her son died (vv. 18, 20). Seeing the woman's distraught condition Elijah restored him back to life. "Then the LORD heard the voice of Elijah; and the soul of the child came back to him, and he revived" (v. 22).

Shunammite's Son. Second Kings 4:32–36 also records a resurrection account. A Shunammite woman was distressed when her child died (2 Kgs. 4:25 –32). Elisha, successor of Elijah, restored the child back to life. As Elisha lay on the child, the boy "opened his eyes" (v. 35). "The gradual revival of this boy differs from Elijah's method in 1 Kings 17 where there was instant response to the word (as to Christ in Mark 5:41–42; *cf.* Acts 9:40). This was no mere artificial respiration, and Gehazi was a witness both to the child being dead as well as to his revival which became widely known (8:5)."[5]

Unnamed Man. A similar event occurs in 2 Kings 13:20–21. When a dead man was placed "in the tomb of Elisha," he "touched the bones of Elisha" and immediately "revived and stood on his feet."

All three accounts point to a physical resurrection. Regarding these accounts, N. T. Wright says, "The people concerned would die again. Our main interest in these stories—apart from their participation of stories about Jesus—is their implicit assumptions about death. The life-force (*nephes*, always difficult to translate) departs from the child and returns when Elijah revives him. Elisha's servant tells him that the child has not 'woken up.' This language anticipates some of the key ideas that are used in connection with resurrection itself."[6] That is, though the modes used to revive the children and the dead man in these accounts differs, the stories nevertheless end in the same conclusion: *all were resurrected from the dead.*

The following accounts vary from those of 1 and 2 Kings in that these seem to point to some being permanently resurrected. Various OT passages teach that a group of people in the future will be resurrected physically never to die again, while others will die again.

Decayed Body. Job 19:25–27 seems to reflect a belief that Job expected to see God in the future resurrection. These verses have too many interpretive issues for the scope of this book.[7] Regardless of one's interpretation, however, one important point may be noted.

Verse 26 can be translated in three ways, resulting in completely different meanings:

"And after my skin has been destroyed, yet *in my flesh* I will see God" (NET)

"and after my skin has been thus destroyed, then *from my flesh* I shall see God" (RSV)

"And after my skin, even this body, is destroyed, then *without my flesh* shall I see God" (ASV)[8]

Since the Hebrew preposition מִן (*min*) can be translated "in," "from," or "without," it is difficult to know what Job meant. If one translates the preposition מִן along with the phrase as "*in* or *from* my flesh," Job referred to seeing God once he was restored physically in this life.[9] This translation may also be understood as Job referring to seeing God in his final "new bodily resurrection" after his present deteriorated "skin [i.e., body] is destroyed," which would mean Job reached a level of extraordinary faith.

However, if the correct translation is "*without* my flesh," Job may mean he expected to see God in some kind of a postmortem state, perhaps in his spirit. Perhaps Job refers to "figuratively the eyes of his soul."[10]

Verse 26 reflects a common Hebrew figure of speech called parallelism, where the second line corresponds in some sense with the first line. However, what kind of correspondence these lines have is the question. All possible interpretations fit the category known as "antithetical parallelism," where the second line contrasts the idea of the first line in some sense. But that contrast remains a mystery. Does it contrast the temporal destruction of Job's body to his being restored physically in this life as shown in chapter 42? Does it contrast the total destruction of Job's body to his seeing God when he will receive a new body in the resurrection? (Perhaps Job 33:15–30 refers to the bodily resurrection for which Job longed.) Or perhaps, 19:26 contrasts the total destruction of Job's body to his seeing God after death in his disembodied spirit.[11]

Job seems to have viewed life from a temporal perspective as is typical of wisdom literature and most of the OT (Job 7:7–10; 14:1–14; 16:22). However, since Hebrews 11:17–19 states that Abraham believed in a physical resurrection of some kind (according to Gen.

22:5) perhaps Job's claim is an exception. In fact, many commentators believe that. "Though the passage probably does not itself refer explicitly to resurrection, it was 'built on the same logic' that eventually led to the early Christian viewpoint. Those who still maintain that the passage envisages a post-mortem vindication ... [suggest], in a careful and sensitive argument, that Job makes a 'leap of faith' to a 'life beyond physical decay.'"[12] Whether Job meant he would see God after being restored to health in this life or in his resurrected body, or his disembodied spirit, we cannot be sure. But what is certain is that regardless of Job's present state, he was sure to "see God" who would ultimately vindicate him. This is very comforting for people who now read "explicit passages" referring to the Resurrection, since they, like Job, can have confidence that they will see God who will vindicate them at the resurrection of the dead.

Dust Dwellers Will Live. Isaiah 26:19 mentions a resurrection. But does it refer figuratively to the nation returning from captivity, or literally to the final bodily resurrection of Israelites, or both?

> LORD, in trouble they have visited You. They poured out a prayer when Your chastening was upon them. As a woman with child is in pain and cries out in her pangs, when she draws near the time of her delivery, so have we been in Your sight, O LORD. We have been with child, we have been in pain; we have, as it were, brought forth wind; we have not accomplished any deliverance in the earth, Nor have the inhabitants of the world fallen. **Your dead shall live; together with my dead body they shall arise. Awake and sing, you who dwell in dust; for your dew is like the dew of herbs, and the earth shall cast out the dead.** Come, my people, enter your chambers, and shut your doors behind you; hide yourself, as it were, for a little moment, until the indignation is past. For behold, the LORD comes out of His place to punish the inhabitants of the earth for their iniquity; the earth will also disclose her blood, and will no more cover her slain (Isa. 26:16–20).

Whether one interprets verse 19 (above in bold letters) as referring figuratively to a national "resurrection" from captivity[13] or to a future physical resurrection, one cannot discount the analogy of the pregnant woman giving birth, which pictures actual "deliverance" for those of the earth who have fallen (i.e., died) and who will participate in a bodily resurrection.[14] This is the proper interpretation of verse 19 if one notes the entire context. J. Alec Motyer does just that. "First, the (mere) continuance of the community [figurative resurrection of the nation] as such does not meet the problems that the poem describes. The world has not come to new birth. The continuance of the community does nothing to solve this. Second, relating this passage to its parallel in verses 5–6, it is the inhabitants of the 'lofty city' who *dwell in the dust.* The Lord's people already inhabit the city of salvation.... It is others who need to be drawn in. In this connection *your dead* is more likely to mean 'the dead you are concerned about.'... It is, then, a promise of life for the world: the counterpart of the vision of 25:6–10a. But 25:7–8 looked forward specifically to the abolition of death itself. If we view 26:19 in its context in this way (as in deed we must), then its terms go beyond any figurative significance to the literal sense of a full resurrection."[15] Wright also concludes, as do numerous other scholars, "The original Hebrew refers literally to bodily resurrection, and this is certainly how the verse is taken in the LXX and at Qumran. It is still possible, of course, that here resurrection is, as ... in Ezekiel, a metaphor for national restoration; but the wider passage, in which God's renewal of the whole cosmos is in hand, opens the way for us to propose that the reference to resurrection is intended to denote actual concrete events."[16]

Dry Bones. Ezekiel used the image of resurrection as a metaphor (or metonymy) to illustrate the literal restoration of the nation from captivity (37:11). In chapter 36 God promised to restore Israel and He complied with that promise in the vision given to Ezekiel. Almost all scholars agree with this view.[17] Though this passage does not refer *directly* to a literal bodily resurrection, it does *indirectly* show that Jews must have believed in a future bodily resurrection of the dead. That is, if the OT Jews did not believe in a literal bodily resurrection, as in Isaiah 26:19 and Daniel 12:2–3, then how would they understand the literal return of the nation depicted through the resurrection metaphor? In other words, if there is no corresponding reality of a literal bodily resurrection, there can be no corresponding return of the nation illustrated by the resurrection metaphor. The metaphor is only as effective as the reality it illustrates. If there is no real bodily resurrection, then there is no real return of the nation of Israel.[18]

Dead Rising at the End. Daniel 12:2–3 says, "And many of those who sleep in the dust of the earth shall awake, some to everlasting life, some to shame *and* everlasting contempt. Those who are wise shall shine like the brightness of the firmament, and those who turn many to righteousness like the stars forever and ever."

The word "sleep" is a common metaphor referring to literal death when the body returns to the "dust of the earth."[19] It does not refer to soul sleep.[20] Since the metaphorical word "sleep" means physical death, the metaphorical word "awake" "points to *bodily* resurrection, not simply a renewal of the soul."[21] Two types of resurrections will occur. Those who trusted in God's plan of salvation will be resurrected bodily to receive "everlasting life" and those who did not will be resurrected bodily to receive "everlasting contempt."

Verse 3 portrays "two parallel similes to describe the final state of the resurrected righteous."[22] The resurrected righteous will "shine like the brightness of the firmament," and "like the stars forever and ever." Some writers suggest that this refers to some "astral immortality," or that the righteous in their final state will literally "become stars" at the resurrection. This is incorrect. As Wright correctly suggests, "The two clauses are similes: the passage predicts that the righteous will be *like* stars, not that they will *turn into* stars, nor even that they will be *located among* them."[23]

This is the clearest OT passage on bodily resurrection.[24] Wright said, "There is little doubt that this refers to concrete, bodily resurrection."[25] Similarly John J. Collins observes, "Virtually unanimous agreement [exists] among modern scholars that Daniel is referring to the actual resurrection of individuals from the dead."[26]

New Testament Resurrection Accounts

Six NT resurrection accounts testify to the common physical resurrection Jews witnessed (Matt. 9:23–25; 27:52–53; Luke 7:11–15;

John 11:43–44; Acts 9:36–40; Rev. 11:8, 11). Although these individuals would die again, the accounts show what kind of resurrection most Jews anticipated: a physical resurrection not a spiritual one.

Jairus's Daughter. Matthew 9:23–25 describes Jesus' power over death by resurrecting a girl.[27] The girl's father told Jesus that his daughter had died (v. 18), and he petitioned to Jesus to lay a "hand on her and she will live." A funeral procession was already under way as the flutes sounded and the crowed wailed.[28] This clearly shows, along with terms like "dead," contrast to "live" (v. 18) that the twelve-years-old girl (Luke 8:42) was dead.[29] While the word "sleep" sometimes refers to literal sleep as in Luke 22:46, the term "sleep" (as in the OT) also expressed euphemistically "death."[30] Besides Luke adds that the crowd knew "she was dead" (8:53). "Jesus was not denying that she was actually dead. He was simply comparing her dead condition to sleep. Like sleep, her death was temporary, and she would rise from it."[31]

Widow's Only Son. Luke 7:11–15 also describes a dead man being raised to life by Jesus. While the funeral procession was on its way to bury the dead man, Jesus had compassion on him and "touched the open coffin" and called the dead to "arise" (as He did to Jairus's daughter and Lazarus [Luke 8:54; John 11:43]). Consequently, "So he who was dead sat up and began to speak" (Luke 7:15). Clearly this illustrates another example of a dead person being raised to life physically.

Lazarus of Bathany. John 11:43–44 is perhaps the most telling of all Jesus' miracles. The fact that Lazarus was dead is undisputed. When Jesus asked that "the stone" covering the burial chamber be removed, Martha replied, "Lord, by this time there is a stench, for he has been *dead* four days" (v. 39). Nevertheless to show God's glory in being able to raise the dead to physical life, Jesus "cried with a loud voice, 'Lazarus, come forth!'" And Lazarus "who had died, came out bound hand and foot with graveclothes, and his face was wrapped with a cloth. Jesus said to them, 'Loose him, and let him go'" (vv. 43–44).

Many Saints. Matthew 27:52–53 records one of the most baffling historical event ever witnessed. "The graves were opened; and many bodies of the saints who had fallen asleep were raised; and coming out of the graves after His resurrection, they went into the holy city and appeared to many." Carson suggests, "Matthew does not intend his readers to think that these 'holy people' were resurrected when Jesus died and then waited in their tombs till Easter Sunday before showing themselves.... The 'holy people were raised, came out of the tombs, and were seen by many after Jesus rose from the dead."[32] There must have been a good number of people alive when Matthew recorded this. Thus if this event were not true, many people could have denied it. Many people who witnessed this event may have been included in the "five hundred brethren ... of whom the greater part remain to the present" who witnessed the physical resurrection of Christ and were still alive when Paul wrote 1 Corinthians around A.D. 54-55. "Most likely [these resurrected saints]... were on the earth until the point when Jesus first ascended to His Father following the Resurrection or at least by the time of His final ascension (Acts 1), fifty[33] days later."[34] Therefore it is erroneous to think that Christ's ascended spiritually instead of bodily. "This [ascension] is not the mere ascent of a soul. A bodily ascension fits the Jewish background, especially after a physical resurrection."[35]

Dorcas. Acts 9:36–40 records a bodily resurrection of a gracious lady named "Tabitha, which is translated Dorcas." She "became sick and died" (v. 37). Two men summoned Peter to come (v. 38). When Peter arrived he found many widows crying, but he "put them all out, and knelt down and prayed. And turning to the body he said, 'Tabitha, arise.' And she opened her eyes, and when she saw Peter she sat up" (vv. 39–40). This event is similar to Elisha who resurrected a dead boy (2 Kgs. 4:35) and Christ who resurrected Jairus's daughter (Luke 7:15; 8:54–55). "The parallel is no accident. Peter's ministry shows that Jesus is still at work."[36] The connection reflects the glory of Christ (see John 11:4, 40; cf. vv. 25–27) raising people from the dead bodily.

Two Witnesses. Revelation 11:8, 11 mentions two witnesses of God who will be killed by a satanic messenger (v. 7). After their bodies will be left exposed in the open "three and a half days" for all to see (v. 9), "the breath of life from God entered them, and they stood on their feet" (v. 11). This clearly indicates a bodily resurrection. Robert L. Thomas notes that "the clear allusion is to Ezekiel 37:5, 10, where God sends the breath of life into dead bones, making them live again and stand on their feet (cf. 2 Kings 13:20–21)."[37]

Conclusion

The evidence from the OT and NT passages is overwhelming in giving a "preview of the oncoming attraction" of Jesus' physical resurrection. Numerous passages show that people were raised physically, thereby previewing Jesus' physical resurrection as the expected interpretation.

CHAPTER 6

KILLING THE EVIDENCE THAT HE ROSE PHYSICALLY

The certainty of the apostles was founded on their experience in the factual realm. To them Jesus showed Himself alive "by many infallible proofs" (Acts 1:3). The term Luke uses is "tekmerion," which indicates a demonstrable proof. The disciples came to their Easter faith through inescapable empirical evidence available to them, and available to us through their written testimony. It is important for us, in an age that calls for evidence to sustain the Christian claim, to answer the call with appropriate historical considerations.[1]

The bodily resurrection of Jesus Christ from the dead is the crowning proof of Christianity. Everything else that was said or done by Christ and the apostles is secondary in importance to the resurrection. If the resurrection did not take place then Christianity is a false religion. If it did take place, then Christ is God and the Christian faith is absolute truth.[2]

New Testament (NT) accounts report that Jesus appeared on numerous occasions after His resurrection. He appeared ten times (or eleven counting Paul's witness in Acts 9:1–9) in forty days to different people highlighted in eighteen steps.[3] How one understands the nature of Jesus' resurrection largely depends on how one interprets His postmortem appearances which were witnessed by many people.

Could all these witnesses have been deceived in thinking they saw Jesus? Assuming they saw Him, did He possess the same physical body that came out of the tomb or a totally different body? These and other questions are discussed in this chapter.

Appeared Sunday Morning[4]

Before Jesus rose from the dead Matthew records that angels moved the stone from Jesus' tomb (28:2–4). The other Gospels simply mention the stone was rolled away from the tomb but do not say who did it (Mark 16:4; Luke 24:2; John 20:1), although one assumes "the two men" who "stood by them in shinning garments" were the angels who removed the stone (Luke 24:4; cf. Mark 16:5).

Removing the stone proves Jesus rose physically, not spiritually. Why? Because an incorporeal "body" could have walked through the rock just as spirits pass through doors. The removal of the stone also points to a physical resurrection of the same body that entered the tomb. If Jesus' new physical body had no continuity from the old body that entered the tomb, there would be no need to remove the stone. God could have created a new body while discarding the previous one by leaving it in the grave or simply taking it as He did with the body of Moses (Jude 9). Those who argue for a spiritual resurrection need to address this important detail of the stone's removal, which is mentioned in each of the four Gospels.

While there is continuity in Jesus resurrected body with His old body, there is also discontinuity from that body. This makes Jesus' resurrection body unique from the old one. Both elements of Jesus' resurrection body are clearly evident in the NT.

That same Sunday morning the women (Mary Magdalene, Mary the mother of James, and Salome) "bought spices, that they might come and anoint" Jesus, but found no body (Mark 16:1). Two points may be noted here. First, why use women to verify the empty tomb if they were not considered credible witnesses in Jewish society?[5] If one were making this up, another scenario would make a better argument to further the lie. Second, if Jesus rose "spiritually," why highlight the point that the tomb was empty (Luke 24:3)? If He had been raised spiritually, the tomb could just as well have contained Jesus' dead body for a long time. A number of critical scholars acknowledge the empty tomb, but what of the resurrection body? An empty tomb does not fit a spiritual body hypothesis, unless one assumes a scenario like that of Moses. Jesus' resurrection appearances in the Gospels debunk this view.

John chose to highlight how Mary Magdalene left, perhaps before seeing the angels as the other two women did (Mark 16:5–7), to tell Peter and John. They ran to the tomb and verified (at about 6:30 a.m.)[6] Mary Magdalene's testimony, found the tomb empty with "the linen cloths lying" in the grave and the "handkerchief that had been around His head ... folded together in a place by itself." Once John arrived he "saw and believed." Then the Greek explanatory conjunction "for" (*gar*) begins verse 9 as a clarification of how they had not yet understood that Scripture prophesied that Jesus "must rise again from the dead" (John 20:1–9). J. Carl Laney notes how both of these disciples did not understand that a number of Old Testament (OT) prophecies verified this (cf. Ps. 2:7; 16:10; Isa. 52:10; 53:10–12).[7] However, other prophecies they failed to apprehend may also include Jesus' prediction of His death and resurrection (John 12:27–32; Mark 8:31; 9:31; 10:33–34).[8] Chapters 11 and 12 discussed how people in the OT expected and prophesied that the Messiah would rise physically.

Jesus' *first appearance* occurred when Mary Magdalene encountered Him on her return to the tomb at about 7:00 a.m.[9] Mary went ahead of the other women, found the tomb empty, and ran to tell the disciples before the other women got there. Later she returned before any of the other first group of women saw Jesus. Unlike John, who believed He had risen just by seeing the empty tomb, Mary sat outside the tomb crying. Suddenly Jesus appeared to her and she tried clinging to Him. Jesus, however, did not allow her to do so. Again this demonstrates the physical nature of Jesus' resurrection. One can tell the difference between a physical and a spiritual disembodied being. Thus how could Mary want to "cling" to a spirit (John 20:11–18; Mark 16:9–11)?[10]

Jesus' *second appearance* occurred when another group of women returned to the sepulcher and saw and "held Him by the feet and worshiped Him" (Matt. 28:9). How could these women hold the "feet" of a spirit?

Furthermore we described in chapter 4 the problems with the story of the Jewish leaders and guards and concluded that such a story is impossible to believe (Matt. 28:11–15). The soldiers could not have

been asleep to see who took the body, and if they admitted that the
disciples took the body they would receive the death penalty under
Roman law for falling asleep on guard duty or allowing a prisoner to
escape (Acts 12:19; 16:25–27). An empty tomb here argues for a raised
body.[11]

Appeared Sunday Afternoon

Jesus' *third appearance* (about 4:00 p.m.) was to Peter. On Sunday
afternoon Peter saw Jesus but that is all of the information given. If they
talked or did something else together is unknown. All the Bible says is,
"The Lord is risen indeed, and has appeared to Simon!" (Luke 24:34;
cf. 1 Cor 15:5). Since all the other accounts highlight the physical
nature of Jesus' resurrection, we have no reason to think the phrase
"the Lord has risen" refers to a spiritual resurrection. Usually the Greek
term *egeirō* ("raise") refers to physical resurrection (e.g., Matt. 27:52;
John 11:12; 1 Cor. 15:15, 29, 32, 35, 52).[12] Hence Peter witnessed a
physically risen Jesus.

Jesus' *fourth appearance* on resurrection Sunday afternoon occurred
on the road to Emmaus to Cleopas and an unnamed companion (Mark
16:12–13; Luke 24:13–32). As both men were on their way to Emmaus,
a city "seven miles from Jerusalem, … Jesus Himself drew near and
went with them" but they did not recognize Him because "their eyes
were restrained" (Luke 24:13, 15–16). While walking with them, Jesus
elicited an explanation regarding their sad state of affairs regarding the
Jerusalem headlines of the day: the death, burial, and resurrection of
Jesus of Nazareth (24:17–24). If Jesus' bones had been in the grave
or removed, someone would have known. But that is not the case.
News travels quickly in a small place, and both of these disciples of
Jesus were informed of the events, yet they doubted. Even this account
rings authentic, for it shows the human incredulity of people who were
present when those things took place, and heard firsthand witnesses
but doubted. Without recognizing Jesus yet, He sought to remove their
doubts by showing how all that transpired to Jesus of Nazareth was
taught, predicted, and accomplished according to the OT.

> Then He said to them, "O foolish ones, and slow of heart
> to believe in all that the prophets have spoken! Ought not the
> Christ to have suffered these things and to enter into His glory?"

And beginning at Moses and all the Prophets, He expounded to them in all the Scriptures the things concerning Himself (Luke 24:25–27).

Jesus' admonition, "O foolish ones, and slow of heart to believe," only makes sense if both disciples should have known and believed what the Hebrews Scriptures ("Moses and all the Prophets)" taught, but they did not. Hence one cannot claim—according to Jesus' very words—that His suffering, death, and resurrection were not known. Responsible ignorance cannot replace revealed truth according to Jesus. While numerous passages come to mind of what Jesus may have mentioned in this walk-along Bible study, those passages discussed in chapters 10–13 may well have been discussed (Gen. 12:3; 15:6; 22:5 [cf. Heb. 11:17–19]; 2 Sam. 7:12–16; Pss. 16:8–11; 22; 89; Isa. 53:1–12).

Since both men did not seem startled when talking to this unknown person (Jesus) as they would be to a spirit, their conversation was to a man with a corporeal body. This is further confirmed when Jesus stayed with them that "evening" and revealed Himself to them and they finally understood the Scriptures. But once this occurred "He vanished from their sight" (Luke 24:29–32). Obviously Jesus' disappearance does not detract from the reality of His possessing a body. Philip, the apostle, was guided by God's Spirit to instruct an Ethiopian eunuch about Jesus being the one prophesied in Isaiah 53, and then he disappeared similar to the way Jesus disappeared.[13] "Now when they came up out of the water, the Spirit of the Lord caught Philip away, so that the eunuch saw him no more; and he went on his way rejoicing" (Acts 8:39). Yet Philip had not died, and he continued ministering, as seen later in Acts 8:40 and 21:8. If this occurred to a person not yet resurrected, how much more so it could have occurred to Jesus, who regained His glorified state when He was resurrected (John 17:5; Rom. 1:4)?[14] Though Jesus had a body, it was now a glorified body after the resurrection with newfound powers not limited to matter, time, and space.

Appeared Sunday Evening

Jesus' *fifth appearance* occurred on resurrection Sunday evening when both of the Emmaus disciples returned to Jerusalem and were gathered with the ten apostles. Thomas was absent (John 20:24). As the Emmaus disciples recounted their story, "Jesus Himself stood in the midst of them, and said to them, 'Peace to you.' But they were terrified and frightened, and supposed they had seen a spirit" (Luke 24:33–37; John 20:19–20).

Here is one of the strongest argument against believing Jesus rose spiritually instead of physically. If ever there was a time to clarify someone's mistaken interpretation about the nature of Jesus' resurrection, it was now when the disciples believed that when they saw Jesus they encountered a spiritually resurrected being. Notice Jesus' clarification:

> And He said to them, "Why are you troubled? And why do doubts arise in your hearts? Behold My hands and My feet, that it is I Myself. Handle Me and see, for a spirit does not have flesh and bones as you see I have." When He had said this, He showed them His hands and His feet. But while they still did not believe for joy, and marveled, He said to them, "Have you any food here?" So they gave Him a piece of a broiled fish and some honeycomb. And He took it and ate in their presence (Luke 24:38–43; cf. John 20:19–25).

Jesus pointed to His hands and feet to show them the crucifixion marks, which argues for interpreting His resurrection body as possessing a certain continuity with that of His former state but without diminishing any of the dissimilarity of His newly glorified state. Jesus summoned then to "handle" (i.e., to touch) Him and see that it was physically He since "a spirit does not have flesh and bones as you see I have" (Luke 24:39). Darrell L. Bock explains this as follows:

> Luke 24:39 is the only text that describes the resurrected body as having flesh and bones. This is not a phantom or a vision.... It is the raised Jesus whose body has been brought back to life. It has characteristics of the physical body, though it carries those characteristics in a way that the old body could not (e.g., this new body will not perish and it can appear and vanish) and in ways that make his initial appearance startling, not the appearance of merely another disciple.[15]

Even after the disciples touched Jesus, "they still did not believe for joy, and marveled" (v. 41). This can mean either that they remained in disbelief, or that what they were witnessing was so incredible to them that they are amazed. "In other words, this does not express doubt but overwhelming and paralyzing realization (the servant's response to Peter in Acts 12:14 shows a similar paralysis of natural action resulting from joy)."[16] This shows how Luke used the term "marvel." "Luke uses θαυμάζω (thaumazō, to marvel) to express reaction to miraculous events or to teaching (cf. Luke 1:63; 2:18; 4:22; 7:9; 8:25; 9:43; 11:14; 20:26). The combination of joy and amazement suggests the second option."[17]

But in case any suspicion remained whether a ghost was talking, "Jesus removed all doubt and freed them from any sense of terror at his presence by asking for something to eat.... A meal shows that it is Jesus and not a phantom, and it also indicates table fellowship and oneness."[18] Spirits do not eat meals. This passage along with the following one should dispel any notion that Jesus did not rise physically.

Appeared the Following Sunday

Jesus' *sixth appearance* occurred a week later on the following Sunday when all eleven apostles were present. Since Thomas had not believed the report of the ten disciples, he said, "Unless I see in His hands the print of the nails, and put my finger into the print of the nails, and put my hand into His side, I will not believe" (John 20:25). Then, "after eight days His disciples were again inside, and Thomas with them. Jesus came, the doors being shut, and stood in the midst, and said, 'Peace to you!'" (v. 26). Now comes the telling part. To prove to Thomas, similarly as to the ten disciples, that He was not a ghost, Jesus told him, "Reach your finger here, and look at My hands; and reach your hand here, and put it into My side. Do not be unbelieving, but believing." To which Thomas replied, "My Lord and my God!" (vv. 27–28). No one reading this account can dispute that Jesus' revelation to Thomas dispels any notion that He possesses a corporeal body similar to the body that entered the tomb, since the crucifixion marks were visible, but yet it was still unique since He could appear and disappear. As C. K. Barrett notes, "John was evidently of the opinion that the resurrection body, though it could pass through closed doors, could also be handled; it was physically 'real.'"[19] This is the same body that was buried and rose. Thus one cannot believe in the resurrection of Jesus and still hold the notion that an ossuary contained the bones of Jesus of Nazareth.

Appeared Thirty-two Days Following

Jesus' *seventh appearance* occurred thirty-two days later when He appeared to seven disciples by the Sea of Tiberias as they were fishing (John 21:1–14). Verse 4 records, "Jesus stood on the shore; yet the disciples did not know that it was Jesus." Baiting them for a response that would allow Him to perform one last miracle and reveal Himself, He asked them, "'Children, have you any food?' They answered Him, 'No'" (v. 5). He replied, "'Cast the net on the right side of the boat, and you will find some.'" So they cast, and now they were not able to draw it in because of the multitude of fish." Once they were all on the shore with Jesus after having recognized Him, Jesus served as host. Having prepared breakfast He "took the bread and gave it to them, and likewise the fish." That Jesus appears bodily here is obvious. A spirit would not prepare and eat a breakfast. His preparing breakfast serves as a transition to the following incident in which He commissioned Peter to the work of the ministry.[20]

Jesus' *eighth appearance* happened within those thirty-two days when He commissioned the eleven disciples in a mountain in Galilee (Matt. 28:16–20; Mark 16:15–18). However, perhaps "a large crowd accompanied them, and many scholars believe this would be the occasion for the five hundred witnesses Paul references (1 Cor. 15:6)."[21] In Matthew 28:17 there seems to be a change in subject indicated by the Greek grammatically construction *hoi de* ("but some") from the previous clause "they worshiped." Hence the "some" who "doubted" (which refers more to *hesitate* than to *unbelief*)[22] were perhaps the five hundred witnesses that "were less sure how to react,"[23] which was the typical response of those who first encountered the resurrected Jesus. Regardless, everyone saw Jesus, not some ghostly apparition.

In Jesus' *ninth appearance* He appeared to His half-brother James (1 Cor. 5:7). Surely James saw something compelling that made him become a believer in Jesus, whom he had denied up to the Resurrection (John 7:5). N. T. Wright notes how "James is not mentioned as a follower of Jesus at any point of the gospel narratives."[24] Perhaps Jesus' physical resurrection convinced James to believe in Him as the Messiah.

In Jesus *tenth appearance* at Jerusalem, He instructed His disciples to wait for the coming of the Holy Spirit ten days later (Luke 24:44–49; Acts 1:3–8). In Luke 24 Jesus seems to have repeated the Great Commission He gave earlier in Matthew 28:19–20.

While on the Mount of Olives, Jesus ascended in a cloud. In fact Jesus' physical return is only as good as His physical departure according to Scripture. "Now when He had spoken these things, while they watched, He was taken up, and a cloud received Him out of their sight. And while they looked steadfastly toward heaven as He went up, behold, two men stood by them in white apparel, who also said, 'Men of Galilee, why do you stand gazing up into heaven? This same Jesus, who was taken up from you into heaven, will so come in like manner as you saw Him go into heaven'" (Acts 1:9–11). Since the Messiah, Jesus, will return physically according to numerous OT passages, certainly He departed physically. If He did not depart physically, how could He return physically so that "His feet will stand on the Mount of Olives" (Zech. 14:4)?

Apparent or Actual Physical Resurrection: 1 Corinthians 15:44

Regarding the resurrection bodies of believers Paul wrote, "It is sown a natural body, it is raised a spiritual body. There is a natural body, and there is a spiritual body" (1 Cor. 15:44).[25] Interestingly this passage actually says the opposite of what most people claim. Many wrongly interpret the words "spiritual body" to mean an "immaterial" body (i.e., composed of "spirit") or a body composed of a semi-spiritual "light substance."[26]

The Gospel accounts of Jesus' resurrection show that He possesses a body with continuity and discontinuity of His former state. Now Paul made the same point in 1 Corinthians 15:1–50. "Jesus' own appearances, in which he eats and is seen and touched by others, reveal the first-century Christians who held to Christianity held to a resurrection hope. The model was Jesus, the firstborn from the dead (Col. 1:15–20). In fact, this clear teaching of the Gospels necessitates a *physical* resurrection."[27]

Paul argued contextually from what people witnessed in the Gospels about Jesus' bodily resurrection. They were now witnesses taking the stand to bolster Paul's argument from 15:1–8. Paul obviously witnessed the resurrected Jesus on the road to Damascus (Acts 9:1–9). Whether he had other encounters with Jesus cannot be known for sure (e.g., 2 Cor. 12:2). Furthermore Paul contrasted how resurrection overcomes death, which can only mean in Judaism *physical resurrection*, or else Adam's curse on the whole creation that brought physical death to mankind has really not been overturned (1 Cor. 15:12–23; Gen. 3:1–22).[28]

In 1 Corinthians 15:35, Paul rhetorically asked, "How are the dead raised up? And with what body do they come?" He explains it by a metaphor through the seed sprouting (vv. 36–38) and by numerous contrasting analogies that the resurrection body contains continuity but discontinuity from one's former earthly existence. He says,

> All flesh is not the same flesh, but there is one kind of flesh of men, another flesh of animals, another of fish, and another of birds. There are also celestial bodies and terrestrial bodies; but the glory of the celestial is one, and the glory of the terrestrial is another. There is one glory of the sun, another glory of the moon, and another glory of the stars; for one star differs from another star in glory (vv. 39–41).

Paul could not mean the resurrection body is "immaterial," because that would argue against the point he made that all matter (flesh) is not of the same "kind" of substance. The contrasts in the analogies are not denoting two different substances of human existence ("immaterial-spirit" vs. "material-flesh") but two different "kinds" of material substance ("material-spirit-controlled" vs. "material-fleshly-controlled").[29] All these analogous comparisons have different "kinds" of matter; hence the same is true of the resurrection body. It will not be of the same kind of material substance that we now possess but will nevertheless be of some bodily material substance.

Three parallel negative terms also indicate modes of existence, not substance: "corruption" (decay), "dishonor" (disgrace), and "weakness" (vv. 42–43).[30] Hence Wright observes,

> In the concluding section of the chapter, Paul will stress the distinction between a body which is corruptible, i.e., which can and will decay, die and ultimately disintegrate altogether, and a body of which none of this is true (verses 50b, 52b, 53,

54). This contrast of corruption/incorruption, it seems, is not just one in a list of differences between the present body and the future one, but remains implicit underneath the rest of the argument, not least between the present humanity in its *choikos* ('earthly') state, ready to return to dust, and the new type of humanity which will be provided in the new creation. The fundamental leap of imagination that Paul is asking the puzzled Corinthians to make is to a body which cannot and will not decay or die: something permanent, established, not transient or temporary.[31]

In fact Paul's use of the adjectives "natural" (*psychikos*) and "spiritual" (*pneumatikos*) in the Corinthian letter do not refer to objects or persons composed of immaterial or material substance.[32] Instead he employed the terms to emphasize what kinds of powers are controlling a person.[33] Either a person is controlled by a *fleshly, carnally,* or *humanly* force, or he is controlled by the *Spirit* (1 Cor. 2:13, 15; 3:1; 14:37).[34] Believers in Corinth were failing to live according to the Spirit. And so in 1 Corinthians 15:44 Paul epitomized the ultimate victory over the *fleshly* (πσψξηικοσ) nature that controls unbelievers (2:14) but that can also drive believers to act in similar ways (3:1).[35] Hence in 1 Corinthians 15:44 Paul seemed to follow his early use of *pneumatikos*.[36] In addition, it seems that if Paul wanted to indicate that the resurrection body was an "immaterial-spiritual" entity, he would have used the adjective *pneumatinos*, whose ending *nos* emphasizes the body's spiritual nature.[37]

All "exegetical, theological, and lexicographical evidence" goes against saying the words "spiritual body" refers to an "immaterial body."[38] Instead, as seen by the overwhelming majority of commentators, "Paul is speaking in v. 44 of a *mode and pattern of intersubjective life directed by the Holy Spirit.*"[39] F. F. Bruce points to the fact that verse 45 refers to the life-giving Spirit.[40] C. K. Barrett says the "spiritual body" is "the new body animated by the Spirit of God."[41] Two points of contrasts, belonging to two different realms, controlled by two different drives are what Paul conveyed in v 44.[42]

The "natural body" refers to the complete person composed of matter and spirit that belongs to this fallen Adamic realm where two controlling powers (the "flesh" and the "Spirit" in Gal. 5–6) are fighting to gain control of a believer. Conversely, the "spiritual body" refers to the complete person composed of a uniquely powerful material-sinless body and a renewed spirit (cf. Rom. 6:6)[43] that is Christlike and belongs to His redeemed realm.[44] Thus the resurrection body will be perfectly suited to obey God in everything through a body controlled by the Spirit.[45] That is the goal of the "spiritual body."

A link then exists between Jesus' resurrected body and the kind of body that believers will possess. That is, "This provides a constructive connection between the salvific and ethical character of the body directed by the Holy Spirit and character of Christ's own raised body in later traditions of the canonical Gospels as 'more' but not 'less' than an earthly physical body. In these resurrection traditions Jesus Christ was not always immediately 'recognized (John 20:14, 15; 21:12; Luke 24:13–20) but his personal identity was recognized in terms of sociophysical gestures and characteristics (Luke 24:31; John 20:16, 20, 27–28; action, voice, hands, side)."[46] Similar to Christ, believers will have a body unique that will function marvelously under the new realm but will also be able to be recognized as the person he or she was before.[47]

Conclusion

All the witnesses in the NT clearly believed and give evidence that they saw Jesus. Also they touched, ate, and conversed with Him after He rose bodily from the dead. Believers were able to examine Jesus with their five senses. Hence no doubt should remain in concluding that Jesus possessed a physical body. His resurrected body was similar in some sense to the one in which He was buried, but also it was uniquely different since now time and spatial barriers do not limit it.

Similarly Paul argued in 1 Corinthians 15:1–58 that believers will possess a uniquely physical body called a "spiritual body," because it will be perfectly suited to obey God through the power of the Spirit.

After examining the evidence of all the accounts of Jesus' resurrection and Paul's explanation of the resurrection, the NT clearly validates that Jesus rose physically.

— Chapter 7 —

KILLING PROPHECIES OF OT AND NT RESURRECTION

Peter Stoner in *Science Speaks* [shows] that coincidence is ruled out by the science of probability. Stoner says that by using the modern science of probability in reference to eight prophecies... "We find that the chance that any man might have lived down to the present time and fulfilled all eight prophecies is 1 in 10^{17}." That would be 100,000,000,000,000,000.[1]

Josh McDowell notes that an estimated 300 Old Testament (OT) references were fulfilled in some sense or other in the person of Jesus of Nazareth.[2] To get an idea of just how impossible it is to suggest that this is mere coincidence, McDowell acknowledges Stoner's equation of probabilities of just eight of these prophecies coming true in Jesus. "Stoner illustrates it by supposing that 'we take 10^{17} silver dollars and lay them on the face of Texas. They will cover all of the state two feet deep. Now mark one of these silver dollars and stir the whole mass thoroughly, all over the state. Blindfold a man and tell him that he can travel as far as he wishes, but must pick up one silver dollar and say that this is the right one. What chance would he have of getting the right one? Just the same chance the prophets would have had of writing ... eight prophecies and having them all come true in any one man, from their day to the present time, providing they wrote them in their own wisdom."[3] If the number increased just a bit, such as forty-eight prophecies being fulfilled in Jesus, the number according to Stoner jumps to ten followed by one hundred and fifty seven zeros.[4] The number is staggering.

We noted in the previous chapter that people being raised from the dead was nothing new, and their resurrections preview the fact that

Jesus rising physically was nothing strange or unexpected. However, are there any OT passages that specifically predict the resurrection of Jesus of Nazareth that were fulfilled in the New Testament (NT)? Yes! At least two such prophecies clearly predicted the resurrection of Jesus of Nazareth.

Psalms 16:8–11 and Acts 2:25–32

A complete analysis of this passage is beyond the scope of this book. However, enough details exist that many scholars interpret it as David prophesying of the resurrection of the Messiah, which Peter confirms in Acts 2:25–32.

OT Passage: Psalm 16:8–11

I have set the LORD always before me; because He is at my right hand I shall not be moved. Therefore my heart is glad, and my glory rejoices; my flesh also will rest in hope. For You will not leave my soul in Sheol, nor will You allow Your Holy One to see corruption. You will show me the path of life; in Your presence is fullness of joy; at Your right hand are pleasures forevermore.

NT Passage: Acts 2:25–32

For David says concerning Him:
"I foresaw the LORD always before my face,
For He is at my right hand, that I may not be shaken.
Therefore my heart rejoiced, and my tongue was glad;
Moreover my flesh also will rest in hope.
For You will not leave my soul in Hades,
Nor will You allow Your Holy One to see corruption.
You have made known to me the ways of life;
You will make me full of joy in Your presence.'

"Men and brethren, let me speak freely to you of the patriarch David, that he is both dead and buried, and his tomb is with us to this day. Therefore, being a prophet, and knowing that God had sworn with an oath to him that of the fruit of his body, according to the flesh, He would raise up the Christ to sit on his throne, he, foreseeing this, spoke concerning the resurrection of the Christ, that

His soul was not left in Hades, nor did His flesh see corruption. This Jesus God has raised up, of which we are all witnesses.

Numerous views seek to explain how Psalm 16:8–11 was used by Peter in Acts 2:25–32.[5] However, Gregory V. Trull has argued convincingly that although Psalm 16 refers primarily to David's confidence in Yahweh, because of the covenant relationship (2 Sam. 7:12–16; Acts 2:30), in Psalm 16:10b "David employed the term חָסִיד [Holy One] to refer to a later recipient of the dynastic covenant, the Messiah. The description of a resurrection before does not depict David's experience. So one may conclude that he spoke of another. This other One was linked to David through the enduring promise of the dynastic covenant. So they were related, yet distinct. David spoke of the resurrection of חָסִיד, Messiah, the ultimate recipient of David's promise."[6] David spoke of himself in general terms of a resurrection in 10a, "You will not leave my soul in Sheol." Then he referred to the physical resurrection of the Messiah in 10b, "nor will You allow Your Holy One to see corruption."[7] Several facts argue indisputably that David's prophecy of the Messiah's physical resurrection was fulfilled in Jesus according to Peter's sermon in Acts 2:25–32.

1. "In the psalm David shifted from a first-person pronoun in verse 10a ('my soul') to the third [sic, second] person חָסִיד [Holy one] in verse 10b. The word חָסִיד extends beyond David to his seed, the Messiah, and the resurrection also extends beyond David to the unique experience of Christ."[8]

2. The LXX translation διαφθοράν ("corruption") of the Hebrew word שַׁחַת ("pit") is not wrong since it is consistently rendered "corruption" elsewhere in the Hebrew Scriptures by the translators of the LXX. Hence David was not referring to imminent physical deliverance from death but to a deliverance from bodily corruption/ decay from the dead by the Messiah rising bodily from the grave.[9]

3. Chapter ten and eleven of this book, as well as Trull's dissertation chapter three, shows that David could have believed in a bodily resurrection,[10] which concept is the predominant thought in Judaism at the time Peter cited Psalm 16:10 in Acts 2:27.[11]

4. Peter said David spoke of "Him" (i.e., Jesus Christ) as a "prophet,"
   and thus he knew God would not leave Jesus' body in the grave.
   Thus Peter consciously spoke prophetically that God would raise the
   Messiah according to his straightforward and literal use of language
   in Acts 2:25–32.[12] If one does not discount the miraculous nature of
   prophecy, one can see how David could have spoken prophetically
   of Jesus' bodily resurrection in the OT (cf. 1 Pet. 1:10-11; 2 Pet.
   1:19–21).

5. David's tomb was moved to Jerusalem where all could witness it,
   according to Peter's words in Acts 2:29.[13] Hence David could not
   have referred literally, as Peter also confirmed, to escaping bodily
   decomposition in the grave. Hence David and Peter refer to Jesus
   Christ as the one who was raised bodily from the grave.

6. Paul's sermon in Acts 13 also reflects similar ideas as that of Peter's
   use of Psalm 16.[14]

Thus we conclude that David prophesied—with limited
knowledge—in Psalm 16:8–11 that the future Messiah would be bodily
resurrected, which ultimately guaranteed his covenant relationship of
an eternal dynastic ruler and his eternal life before God who was at
his "right hand" ([מִימִינִי], i.e., "God's proximity to him ... to protect
him," which terms form the brackets in vv. 8, 11).[15] Furthermore Peter
affirmed that David spoke in Psalm 16:8–11 of Messiah's physical
resurrection.

Peter's commentary on Psalm 16:8–11 reveals important insights
into the understanding of this key Old Testament passage. Verse 10b is
a prophecy by David of Messiah's resurrection. As a prophet David had
foresight of the Messiah's resurrection, and as a recipient of the Davidic
Covenant he had insight into its ultimate fulfillment in Messiah's
rule. The phrase Peter used to introduce the quotation, "David spoke
concerning Him," shows that Psalm 16:10b focused on the Messiah
rather than himself. The distancing of David from the referent of the
psalm becomes even clearer through Peter's words about David's tomb.
The decay of David's body attested to Peter's point that David spoke
not of himself but of the Messiah. Clearly then in Acts 2:25–32 Peter
quoted Psalm 16:8 –11, specifically the single line in verse 10b, as a
direct prophecy from David concerning the Messiah's resurrection.[16]

This proves in NT times believing that Jesus rose bodily was nothing new.[17] In fact it was prophesied and fulfilled in Jesus of Nazareth

Isaiah 53:10–12

Yet it pleased the LORD to bruise Him; He has put Him to grief. When You make His soul an offering for sin, He shall see His seed, He shall prolong His days, And the pleasure of the LORD shall prosper in His hand.

He shall see the labor of His soul, and be satisfied. By His knowledge My righteous Servant shall justify many, for He shall bear their iniquities.

Therefore I will divide Him a portion with the great, and He shall divide the spoil with the strong, because He poured out His soul unto death, and He was numbered with the transgressors, and He bore the sin of many, and made intercession for the transgressors.

Few would debate that a clear reference to resurrection appears in this passage. Hence John N. Oswalt concludes, "The point is to say in the most vivid language that the Servant's life will not be futile after all…. But whether Isaiah intends to speak of resurrection or not, this much is clear, as Westermann points out: it is only on the other side of the Servant's death that the deliverance and ours may be realized."[18] As N. T. Wright wrote, "There is no explicit mention of resurrection itself, and only an oblique statement of what will happen to the servant after his death (53.11). But it is clear that the servant (a) dies and is buried (53.7–9), and (b) emerges in triumph, however densely expressed (53.10–12)"[19]

Though one may argue that words in Romans 4:25; 1 Corinthians 15:3; and Galatians 1:4 may refer to Jesus' substitutionary atonement indicated by Paul's use of the formula "according to the Scriptures,"[20] how can this not include the victory of the resurrection that follows the suffering Servant mentioned by Isaiah 53:10–12?[21] Paul certainly included the resurrection following Jesus' atonement for sin in Romans 4:25, and this is very similar to that of Isaiah 53:10–12.[22] The clauses,

"He shall see His seed, He shall prolong His days" and "He shall divide the spoil with the strong" (vv. 10, 12) reflect the Servant's physical resurrection.

Various scholars have noticed an implicit picture of physical resurrection in Isaiah 53:10–12. Merrill C. Tenney said, "The prophet, speaking of the Servant, presents contrasting pictures of suffering and triumph. The two cannot be simultaneous; one must follow the other. In the given sequence the triumph follows the suffering, thereby implying resurrection."[23] John A. Martin views the clause "He shall see His seed" as a reference to Jesus' physical resurrection.[24] G. W. Grogan says that after the Servant's suffering "comes vindication ... [by] the opening of a new life beyond that death."[25] Luke 22:37 quotes part of the last section in Isaiah 53:12 as being fulfilled in Jesus, which quotation in part may be suggestive of the entire Isaiah 53 passage. This prophecy fits perfectly with what was recorded in the Gospels and the letters of the NT about Jesus' death and bodily resurrection. Moreover, Norman L. Geisler and Ronald M. Brooks write, "Also, the Old Testament teaches the Resurrection by logical inference. There is clear teaching that the Messiah was to die (cf. Ps. 22; Isa. 53) and equally evident teaching that He is to have an enduring political reign from Jerusalem (Isa. 9:6; Dan. 2:44; Zech. 13:1). There is no way to reconcile these two teachings unless the Messiah who dies is raised from the dead to reign forever. Jesus died before He could begin to reign. Only by His resurrection could prophecies of the messianic kingdom be fulfilled."[26]

The OT indirectly testifies of a Servant's death and resurrection that cannot fit anyone else other than Jesus Christ. That Isaiah's passage points to a physical resurrection is indicated by verses 10–12 and is also verified by the fact that Israel in the OT period believed God can and would resurrect the righteous bodily from the grave.[27]

Conclusion

Clearly two OT passages specifically predict the resurrection of Jesus of Nazareth that were verified as fulfilled in the NT. There are other passages that implicitly or explicitly[28] refer to the Jewish expectation of physical resurrection, but I have taken a conservative approach in showing only two in order to show that the OT did predict the physical resurrection of Jesus of Nazareth, which are fulfilled in the NT.

— Chapter 8 —

Killing the Resurrection That Transforms Lives

That "something" was so dramatic it completely changed eleven men's lives, so that all but one died a martyr's death. That something was an empty tomb! An empty tomb that a 15-minute walk from the center of Jerusalem would have confirmed or disproved. Even after two thousand years since that time, mankind hasn't forgotten the empty tomb nor the resurrection appearances of Jesus Christ.[1]

We are living in an age where many things are believable without thinking critically or investigating the validity of a truth claim. Hence many cults dupe people into giving up their time, talents, and treasures for a lie in the name of religion. Conversely and equally true, in our scientific and postmodern era few things are believable unless they can be verified in a laboratory. In such an age Josh McDowell's words resonate more than ever in regards to Jesus' resurrection. "If you wish to rationalize away the events surrounding Christ and His resurrection, you must deal with certain imponderables."[2]

These "imponderables" are the enormous evidence not easily dismissed that argues for Jesus' resurrection, which in turn guarantees the future of all who believe in Him alone. This chapter covers these "imponderables" regarding Jesus' resurrection that no amount of pedigrees, rationalization, or coincidence can explain away.

The Resurrection Does Not Contradict Science
James B. Conant, a former president of Harvard University, defines science as follows. "Science is an interconnected series of concepts and

conceptual schemes that have developed as a result of experimentation and observation, and are fruitful of further experimentation and observations."[3] In a scientific-explosion age many people refuse to believe anything not tested numerous times in a controlled environment that results in a fixed and stable outcome. McDowell affirms a similar sentiment today. "Many people advocate that nothing can be accepted as true unless it can be proven scientifically. When speaking on the historical aspects of the resurrection in a university classroom, I am constantly confronted with the question, 'Can you prove it scientifically?' I immediately reply, 'No.' The modern scientific method does not apply when researching the factuality of the events surrounding the *death, burial and resurrection of Jesus Christ. Science is unable to investigate it.*"[4]

Correctly defined, science then also disqualifies macroevolution (as a valid explanation of the origins of all species) since no one has ever scientifically showed one kind of species changing into another (e.g., a fish changing into a bird). Origins and destinies are always outside the realm of science since they cannot be reproduced in a laboratory.

However, there is a difference between scientific proof and historical proof. Since most people have not seen a dead person rise, they conclude dead people do not rise. But such a conclusion limits reality and truth to the mind of what an individual can perceive. This results in setting people as the ultimate arbiter of what can and cannot happen based on experiments done today. Logically this does not follow. If we have not seen, touched, or experienced something, that does not mean it did not occur in the past (since we were not there to witness it) or that it will not occur in the future (since we are waiting to validate it). At worst, one should be an agnostic (saying "I am not sure" or "I do not know") about the resurrection of Jesus. At best, one can arrive at a certain conclusion about the resurrection of Jesus of Nazareth by studying the circumstantial evidence just as we study other historical events, and examine the impact the event has had historically.

People accept our legal system's way of arriving at the truth regarding criminals and whether they will be incarcerated or freed, or executed or allowed to live. And yet people refuse to apply the same criteria to ascertain whether Jesus was or was not raised from the dead. McDowell's lucid explanation strikes at the heart of the matter in how to distinguish scientific and circumstantial legal evidence necessary to arrive at an informed conviction of the truth.

Testing the truth of a hypothesis by the use of controlled experiments is one of the key techniques of the modern scientific method. For example, somebody says, "Ivory soap doesn't float." So I take the person to the kitchen, put eight inches of water in the sink at 82.7°, and drop in the soap. Pluck. Observations are made, data are drawn, and a hypothesis is empirically verified: Ivory soap floats.

Now if the scientific method was the only method of proving something, you couldn't prove that you went to your first hour class this morning or that you had lunch today. There's no way you can repeat those events in a controlled situation.

Now here's what is called the legal-historical proof, which is based on showing that something is fact beyond a reasonable doubt. In other words, a verdict is reached on the basis of the weight of the evidence. That is, there's no reasonable basis for doubting the decision. It depends upon three types of testimony: oral testimony, written testimony, and exhibits (such as a gun, bullet, notebook). Using the legal method of determining what happened, you could pretty well prove beyond a reasonable doubt that you were in class this morning: your friends saw you, you have your notes, the professor remembers you.

The scientific method can be used only to prove repeatable things; it isn't adequate for proving or disproving many questions about a person or event in history. The scientific method isn't appropriate for answering such questions as "Did George Washington live?" "Was Martin Luther King a civil rights leader?" "Who was Jesus of Nazareth"? "Was Robert Kennedy attorney general of the U.S.A.?" "Was Jesus Christ raised from the dead?" These are out of the realm of scientific proof, and we need to put them in the realm of legal proof.[5]

N. T. Wright points out the ultimate reason people reject the bodily resurrection of Jesus. "Not that science has disproved Easter, but that Easter challenges the social and political pretensions of modernism, both right wing and left wing" to respond ethically to "submit to the kingdom of God."[6] Whether consciously aware of it or not, ulterior motive can drive people to think irrationally or to be dishonest about the evidence confronting them. Anyone investigating the resurrection of Jesus can be convinced without a doubt whether the claims of Scripture are true or false.[7] The credibility of the evidence will cause one either to reject this truth that lies outside the scientific realm or accept it.

Logical Testimony of the Resurrection

Scripture records the words of Jesus' enemies taking steps to prevent His resurrection. "On the next day, which followed the Day of Preparation, the chief priests and Pharisees gathered together to Pilate, saying, 'Sir, we remember, while He was still alive, how that deceiver said, "After three days I will rise." Therefore command that the tomb be made secure until the third day, lest His disciples come by night and steal Him away, and say to the people, "He has risen from the dead." So the last deception will be worse than the first.' Pilate said to them, 'You have a guard; go your way, make it as secure as you know how.' So they went and made the tomb secure, sealing the stone and setting the guard" (Matt. 27:62–66).

Resurrection Enemies Validate It. "In fact, you might say that both the Jews and the Romans outwitted themselves when they took so many precautions to make sure Jesus was dead and remained in the grave. These 'security precautions'—taken with the trial, crucifixion, burial, entombment, sealing and the guarding of Christ's tomb—make it very difficult for critics to defend their position that Christ did not rise from the dead!"[8] Jewish leaders could have produced a body but did not. "Instead, they continually resisted the apostle's teaching, but never attempted to refute it."[9] Why? Because there was no physical body to present, they had no excuse, and they could not accuse the disciples of stealing Jesus' body since they took all the necessary measurements to stop the Resurrection from happening. Hence the enemies of the Resurrection argue strongly in favor of the validity of the event.

Rome, the Seal, and the Stone Validate It. Rome's silence also argues for the validity of the event. If Jesus did not rise and the disciples made up the story, there should be at least one historical Roman document denying the event since His resurrection was widely heralded across the empire. Even in Jerusalem we hear of nothing from Rome, other than Pilate's amazement at Jesus' speedy death (Mark 15:44). John R. Stott also concludes that the silence of the enemies of Christ is "as eloquent a proof of the resurrection as the apostles' witnesses."[10]

What about the seal placed on the tomb? A. T. Robertson explains that the sealing was done "probably by a cord stretched across the stone and sealed at each end as in Dan. 6:17. The sealing was done in the presence of a Roman guard who was left in charge to protect this stamp of Roman authority and power."[11] In fact, "The consequences of breaking the seal were severe. The FBI and CIA of the Roman Empire were called into action to find the man or men responsible. When they were apprehended, it meant automatic execution by crucifixion upside down. Your guts ran into your throat."[12] Would the frightened disciples who abandoned Jesus hours before (Mark 14:50) and who knew the penalty behind breaking a Roman-burial seal do this? The Romans "did their best to prevent theft and the resurrection ... but they overreached themselves and provided additional witness to the fact of the empty tomb and the resurrection of Jesus."[13] How could anyone overpower the guards and break the Roman seal?

The stone was another problem. What impressed Sunday-morning witnesses was that the stone was rolled away. Their shock came not only because of the missing corpse but also because of their concern over who moved the stone. All four Gospels mention the stone (Matt. 28:2; Mark 16:3–4; Luke 24:2; John 20:1) because it was a significant barrier to the physical resurrection of Jesus. The stone probably weighed anywhere from 200 pounds to two tons, which would mean several people would be needed to move it. Furthermore the stone may have been in an inclined position, which would have made it all the more difficult to move.[14] Nevertheless the fact that all four Gospels state that it was moved and no record exists to dispute it argues strongly for Jesus' physical resurrection.

Who Moved the Body: Man, Satan, or God? By logical deduction we can answer this question. What man would challenge Rome and dare tamper with a Roman seal? Enemies of Jesus would not want to steal the body. They wanted to disqualify Him as a prophet since they remembered His resurrection predictions (Matt. 12:38–40; 27:62–67; John 2:18–22). Jewish leaders took all precautions to prevent the tomb from being broken into. Therefore they would not steal the body.

Satan wanted Jesus to remain dead for various reasons. First, Jesus is Satan's enemy and who probably knew of the ancient prophecy of his defeat by the Messiah, who he now knows is Jesus (Gen. 3:15; Rom. 16:20). Second, Jesus' resurrection would mean His sacrifice was accepted as a valid payment to redeem mankind (Rom. 3:21–4:25; 1 Cor 15:12–26). Third, Jesus' resurrection would give hope and increase the number of His followers. Would Satan want all of this? Keeping Jesus dead and entombed would be a decisive victory for the prince of darkness; therefore he would not steal the body or deceive anyone about Jesus' resurrection.

God is the one responsible for raising Jesus from the dead. To be more precise, the entire Trinity raised Jesus from the dead. Peter and Paul said God the Father raised Jesus from the dead (Acts 2:24; 3:15; 4:10; 10:40; 13:23, 30, 37). Paul also noted that God the Holy Spirit raised Jesus from the dead (Rom. 8:11). And Jesus claimed to raise Himself from the dead. "No one takes it from Me, but I lay it down of Myself. I have power to lay it down, and I have power to take it again. This command I have received from My Father" (John 10:18). All three members of the Trinity were involved in the physical resurrection of Jesus Christ.

Transformation as Evidence of the Resurrection

The Disciples. At Jesus' trials the disciples abandoned Jesus (Mark 14:50). However, something miraculously happened to them. Peter denied Jesus three times (vv. 65–72). But fifty days later he defied the Jewish leaders when asked not to preach the Resurrection and salvation in Jesus' name (Acts 2–4; 10:1–4). How could one account for this extraordinary change apart from the physical resurrection of Jesus? Many of Jesus' followers witnessed boldly for Jesus. In fact most of them were martyred because of their witnessing for Jesus.

1. Stephen was the first martyr of the church. His death came around A.D. 35. The Jews stoned him to death (Acts 7:59).

2. James, the son of Zebedee and the brother of the Apostle John, was

the first of the twelve apostles to be martyred. He was executed by king Herod Agrippa I of Judea in A.D. 44 (Acts 12:1–2).

3. Matthew is said to have traveled to Ethiopia and associated with Candace (see Acts 8:27). "Some writings say he was pinned to the ground and beheaded with a halberd in the city of Nadabah (or Naddayar), Ethiopia, in circa A.D. 60."

4. James, the less, was Jesus' half brother who wrote the NT letter. Before the Resurrection and throughout Jesus' ministry, it is very probable he did not believe in Jesus as the Messiah (see John 7:5). Yet, he became a believer and also the leader of the Jerusalem church (Acts 12:17; 15:13–29; 21:18–24). He died about A.D. 66. Josephus records that Ananus ordered James to be put to death by stoning. However, "Hegesippus, an early Christian writer, quoted by the third-century Christian historian Eusebius, says James was cast down from the Temple tower. This version of his death further states that he was not killed by the fall, and so his head was smashed in with a fuller's club, which may have been a club used to beat clothing, or a hammer used by blacksmiths."

5. Matthias took the place of Judas Iscariot (Acts 1:15–26). Later he was stoned and beheaded in Jerusalem. (His year of death is unknown.)

6. Andrew, Peter's brother, according to tradition preached the gospel in Asiatic nations. While in Edessa he was killed by crucifixion on an X-shaped cross that later became known as "St. Andrew's Cross." (His year of death is unknown.)

7. Mark, who wrote the Gospel, according to tradition was "dragged to pieces by the people of Alexandria when he spoke out against a solemn ceremony for their idol Serapis." (His year of death is unknown.)

8. When Peter, the brother of Andrew, left Rome, Jesus, according to Hegesippus, appeared to him and told him to return because he was to glorify Jesus through a similar death (cf. John 21:19). Nero around A.D. 64 then captured Peter. He asked to be crucified upside down since he did not consider himself worthy to die as

Jesus did.

9. Paul was arrested for the second time around A.D. 64 (about the same time Peter was arrested). When fire broke out in Rome, many believed Nero started it, but he blamed the Christians. Paul was beheaded around A.D. 66.

10. Jude, brother of James and half brother of Jesus, who wrote the little letter in the New Testament (NT), was crucified at Edessa (like Andrew) around A.D. 72.

11. Bartholomew, according to tradition, preached in various countries, and "then translated the Gospel of Matthew into the language of Easy-Indian and taught it in that country. His pagan enemies cruelly beat and crucified him." (His year of death is unknown.)

12. Thomas spread the gospel in "Persia, Parthia, and India. In Calamina, India, he was tortured by angry pagans, run through with spears, and thrown into the flames of an oven." (His year of death is unknown.)

13. Luke was probably a Gentile who was Paul's companion on many missionary journeys. He wrote the Gospel of Luke and the Book of Acts. Though no one knows for sure how or when he died, an "early source says that he went to Greece to evangelize, and was there martyred by being hung from an olive tree in Athens in A.D. 93."

14. John the apostle, and brother of James, gets credit for the establishing the seven churches in Revelation: Ephesus, Smyrna, Pergamum, Thyatira, Sardis, Philadelphia, and Laodicea. From Ephesus John was arrested and sent to Rome where he was thrown into a caldron of boiling hot oil. Still alive afterward, Emperor Domitian then banished him to the Island of Patmos, where he penned the Book of Revelation. After leaving Patmos, John returned to Ephesus, where he died a non-martyr's death, becoming the only one of these fourteen who did not die violently.[15]

The fact that they were willing to die for what they believed validates that what they saw and believed was true. Logically this in itself does not prove that what they believed was correct or right. Other people with different beliefs have died for what they believed to be true. That does not make their beliefs credible or true.

Agreed, but this misses the point: The disciples' willingness to suffer and die for their beliefs *indicates that they certainly regarded those beliefs as true.* The case is strong that they did not willfully lie about the appearances of the risen Jesus. Liars make poor martyrs.

No one questions the sincerity of the Muslim terrorist who blows himself up in a public place or the Buddhist monk who burns himself alive as a political protest. Extreme acts do not validate the truth of their beliefs, but willingness to die indicates that they regarded their beliefs as true. Moreover, there is an important difference between the apostle martyrs and those who die for their beliefs today. Modern martyrs act solely out of their trust in beliefs that others have taught them. The apostles died for holding to their own testimony that they had *personally* seen the risen Jesus. Contemporary martyrs die for what they *believe* to be true. The disciples of Jesus died for what they *knew* to be either true or false.[16]

It would be senseless for the disciples to die for a lie since they were the actual witnesses of their claims, not what someone else told them. Hence their testimony and martyrdom argues strongly for the validity of the bodily resurrection of Jesus.

Saul the Christian Persecutor to Paul the Christian Propagator

What can be said of Saul of Tarsus, later called Paul, who persecuted the Christians and then became a propagator of the Christian message? In the Book of Acts (7:58; 8:1–3; 9:1–19; 22:1–16; 26:9–23) Luke recorded how Paul not only consented to the stoning of Stephen but also persecuted the church in order to extinguish its members and promoters. He was a Pharisee and a strict observer of the Law of Moses (Acts 22:9–11; Gal. 1:22–23); but when on the road to Damascus to persecute Christians everything changed for him in one instant when he saw the risen Jesus. After that point until his martyrdom, he began preaching, "Jesus is the Christ" (Acts 9:1–22).

In Philippians 3:1–10 Paul gives a pithy biographical testimony of his conversion that is related to Jesus' resurrection. Paul became the apostle to the Gentiles and he also led many Jews to faith in Christ

(Rom. 1:16; 11:13). He also wrote no less than thirteen letters that form part of the NT.[17]

What could have made a man change so drastically from a foe to a friend, from a persecutor to a promoter, and from Saul the murderer for the Sanhedrin to Paul the messenger of the Savior? One simple answer: Paul met the risen Jesus! "Certainly a skeptic may comment that Paul's conversion is no big deal, since many people have converted from one set of beliefs to another. However, the cause of Paul's conversion makes his different. People usually convert to a particular religion because they have heard the message of that religion from a secondary source and believed the message. Paul's conversion was based on what he perceived to be a personal appearance of the risen Jesus. Today we might believe that Jesus rose from the dead based on secondary evidence, trusting Paul and the disciples who saw the risen Jesus. But for Paul, his experience came from primary evidence: the risen Jesus appeared directly to him. He did not merely believe based on the testimony of someone else."[18]

Psychologically people do not change in a blink of an eye, unless something radical happens to them. One cannot explain the historical account of what happened to Paul psychologically apart from his seeing the risen Christ. What selfish motive would he have in going from a highly educated, wealthy, and respected member of the Sanhedrin to join a persecuted group, become a blue-collar worker, receive beatings, remain on the run throughout his life, and become almost certain to end as a martyr? People lie for their best interests not to bring problems and calamity on themselves. Paul did not lie; he told the truth, and that often leads to persecution, especially when one preaches Jesus Christ (Mark 4:17; Acts 11:19; 13:50; Gal. 5:11; 6:12; 2 Tim. 3:12).

Paul's conversion may perhaps be the most compelling evidence that validates the Christian faith and Jesus' resurrection. Elias Andrews said, "Many have found in the radical transformation of this 'Pharisee of the Pharisees' the most convincing evidence of the truth and power of the religion to which he was converted, as well as the ultimate worth and place of the Person of Christ." In fact Archibald MacBride, former professor at Aberdeen University, wrote, "Besides his [Paul's] achievements ... the achievements of Alexander and Napoleon pale into insignificance."[19] Paul's radical change and lifelong commitment to promote Christianity in spite of persecution also argues strongly for the bodily resurrection of Jesus.

The Church and Changed Lives

How could the Christian church continue to thrive today as it has throughout the centuries without having solid evidence and believing the primary apostolic testimony of the resurrection of Jesus? Norval Geldenhuys said it best. "It is historically and psychologically impossible that the followers of Jesus, who at His crucifixion were so completely despondent and perplexed, would within a few weeks thereafter enter the world (as they did) with such unheard-of joy, power and devotion, if it had not been for the fact that He had risen from the dead, had appeared to them, and had proved that His claims to be the Son of God were genuine."[20]

The early church of the first and second centuries knew most of the men who witnessed the resurrection of Jesus (e.g., Polycarp was a disciple of the Apostle John), which in turn influenced them to become martyrs in order to promote the message of the gospel that propelled the church to exponential growth. Someone has correctly said, "The seed of the church was built on the blood of the martyrs."[21] Such was the building blocks of the church. In just a couple of centuries six million martyrs forged the edifice of the building that Jesus, the prophets, and the apostles founded (Eph. 2:20).

One cannot account for the changed lives of Jesus' disciples unless they experienced something radical. My own testimony is a case in point.

I cannot attest to ever seeing the resurrection of Jesus, but I can attest to experiencing His resurrection power that changed my life forever. Unfortunately before I became a Christian in my early twenties, I grew up in the "*locumi* religion" (also known in the Cuban community as "Santeria"). This is a mixture of Roman Catholicism with African voodoo. Supernatural occurrences were easy for me to believe. As a teenager I saw numerous supernatural occurrences that defy scientific laws (e.g., the law of gravity). Once a high priest of the religion came to my house and did numerous religious rites, supposedly to rid the place of bad spirits. I do not know if the spirits left, but once seeing various pieces of irons go up a flight of stairs and land in front of my mother and me, a chicken faint and rise at the sound of the man's voice, and seeing a coconut float in the air, I wanted to leave. This might sound comical, but it is true. I witnessed it with my own eyes. Yes, I could have been fooled, but what about the other three people in the room with me who saw the same thing? Furthermore this was just one day's occurrence. There were many more bizarre things I witnessed in that religion. I believed in the supernatural and that God existed. This religion, however, did nothing to change and make me a better person.

In my late teens and early twenties I became worse. My track record read like a bad grocery list: burglary (arrested five times), grand theft, petty theft, theft (three times), loitering, possession of burglary tools, trespass (three times), defrauding innkeeper (two times), evading transit fare, cocaine possession (two times), forced strong-arm robbery (three times), dealing in stolen property (two times), petit larceny (three times), obstruction of police officer (three times), resisting arrest (two times), battery on a police officer, alcohol violation and four drug rehabilitation programs. All of this occurred between 1986 and 91.

I could not make sense of life. But then when I met Jesus Christ the direction of my life changed. He became the ultimate key that unlocked the enormous amount of questions in my soul that nothing and no one could open. True, some people change apart from a relationship with Jesus Christ. But they do not change *radically* without Him. Furthermore, as I looked into many other religions, philosophies, and scientific ideas, nothing made sense other than what Jesus' resurrection represented for everyone who simply believes in Him receives eternal life.

Now that I had purpose in life through my relationship with Christ, my "grocery list" began to change—and radically. I earned a B.A. with high honors from Trinity International University, where I later served as an adjunct faculty member for three years. I earned a Th.M. with honors and a Ph.D. from Dallas Theological Seminary. I was on the National Dean's List twice and also given twice the Outstanding Young Man of America award for professional achievement, superior ability, and exceptional community service. At Dallas Seminary I was also awarded the J. Dwight Pentecost Ph.D. scholarship for excellence in Bible Exposition. I have also been pastoring for the past ten years.

All these things—wonderful as they are—are rubbish compared to the surpassing knowledge of Jesus Christ, who changed me. I share them to show the contrast of what I was before and what God has made of me. The radical change began when I simply *believed in Christ's promise that I could receive eternal life* (John 1:12; 3:16; 5:24; 6:40, 47; 11:25-27). Jesus did a miracle of radical proportions in changing my life, and He can do it with anyone, because He died for our sins and rose again on the third day according to the Scriptures (Isa. 53:1–12; Rom. 4:24–25; 1 Cor. 15:3–4).[22]

Conclusion

Once we understand how to distinguish scientific and circumstantial legal evidence, we can then arrive at an informed conviction about the resurrection of Jesus.

Having looked at some of these evidences, the following points are clear. Enemies of the Resurrection actually helped solidify the testimony that validates its authenticity. For example, the empty tomb, the broken seal, the removal of the large stone, and the silence of Rome in not producing a body can only be logically and historically explained by the physical resurrection of Jesus.

That is not all. The disciples' transformed lives validate Jesus' resurrection. From running scared to proclaiming boldly the Resurrection that resulted in most of them being martyred argues for the authenticity of their having seen the risen Jesus.

Furthermore, how does one account for the change in Saul, the most antagonist person of the Christian faith to becoming an advocate of it? Only the risen Jesus appearing to Paul can explain this change.

In fact, because Jesus had met many believers and had directly spoken to the apostles after His resurrection, early church followers were willing to face martyrdom. Exponentially the church grew because of this, which continues to thrive today.

I have witnessed various supernatural things. Those things are as real as the words on these pages. More real than that, however, is the impact Jesus Christ had in my life in changing me from a "train wreck" to a "trusted worker" for Him, who willingly gave Himself for me and rose from the dead—so that all who by faith alone in Him believe His promise of eternal life can be sure they possess it (John 1:12; 3:16; 5:24; 6:40, 47; 11:25–27; Rom. 3:21–4:25; Eph. 2:8–9).

— CHAPTER 9 —

KILLING JESUS: ANSWERS TO OBJECTIONS

Although a book alone could be written on the topic that answers objections to the Physical Resurrection, the authors and promoters of one book that we will answer in this chapter are those objections raised by *The Jesus Family Tomb*. The subtitle of the book has been reworded, and comments by Simcha Jacobovici and answers to objections by James D. Tabor have been added.[1] Jacobovici's portion simply recounts unknown events that occurred on February 26, 2007, and the aftermath, once the documentary and book were released. Tabor, however, answers a number of objections that scholars have made against the film and the book. Below are his answers to objections and our responses to his answers, as well as the final word to-date on the Talpiot tomb's statistical calculation.

Our First Response

Tabor said, "In terms of Christian faith… the Resurrection of Jesus does not have to be understood as a literal 'flesh and bones' event, with Jesus ascending to heaven as a physical being."[2]

First, Tabor misses the point that if Jesus only rose spiritually it does not overturn the spiritual and physical curse that fell on humanity and the earth at creation.[3] Furthermore, second-Temple Judaism, the apostolic fathers, and Christians understood the Resurrection as a physical event. Tabor presents no evidence to the contrary other than suggesting the common argument from 1 Corinthians 15:44. However he adds a new twist that Jesus' physical body can be viewed as similar to that of angels who on occasions assumed what appeared to be a human body. That is, angels were seen eating with Abraham in Genesis 18 but yet they possessed a spiritual nature. While that is true, Tabor fails to note that the materializing of angels is not the same as a person being born, dying, and rising from the dead (something angels do not experience).

We have already shown this in this book that the terminology "rising" and "resurrection" was always understood as the entire person physically rising not solely the immaterial part of man. Thus it will be with Abraham, Isaac, and Jacob, since they were made physical literal promises of a land (Gen. 15:18–21; Heb. 11:8–10) to be enjoyed in some physical sense. Furthermore, according to Hebrews 11:17–19, Abraham believed in a physical resurrection (Gen. 22:5) as he viewed the receiving of Isaac as if he was dead.

To say that the materializing of angels is the same as Jesus' resurrection body is to compare apples with oranges, since angels do not die and by their very nature are spiritual not physical beings. Conversely, Jesus took on a human nature. Thus what governs Jesus is not what governs angels. Moreover, similarities do not prove identity. That is, because Jesus can materialize and dematerialize at will does not prove He rose spiritually. All that this proves is that His resurrection body is now not limited to time, matter, and space, as was His former body. But it is a body nonetheless with special powers at its disposal. Much like angels can venture into the material world while maintaining their original ties to the spiritual world, Jesus and all resurrected Christians can venture into the spiritual world while maintaining their original ties to the material world. All that Tabor proves by mentioning that angels can materialize and eat is that they can materialize. That, however, fails to prove that Jesus rose spiritually. To say Jesus rose spiritually because angels are spiritual beings that can materialize is a non sequitur and faulty logic.

Our Second Response

Tabor answers the objection that Jesus' family was poor and could not afford a family tomb by proposing the following hypothesis. "Although they arose from peasant origins, it is not at all clear that Jesus and his family were destitute or poor in later life." He adds that

Jesus' "family had artisan skills" and had supported their families and mother. Furthermore He had loyal followers who financially supported Him (Luke 8:1–3). Besides, Joseph of Arimathea could have donated a tomb.[4] However, no evidence of such a donation exists, which most likely would not go unnoticed if such were the case.[5] Why does Tabor not address the Holy Sepulcher burial place of Jesus instead of positing such a highly improbable hypothesis? He also assumes his conclusion that Jesus rose spiritually in order to formulate his view that His women supporters mentioned in Luke 8:1–3 could have donated a family tomb. Why would such a donation exist if Jesus rose physically from the dead? The answer is obvious. One has to assume no physical resurrection for such a "tomb donation hypothesis" to work. This is simply a case of assuming one's conclusion.

Along with James and Jude, probably all of Jesus' family became believers after His resurrection. Thus, if they were not rich before becoming believers, it seems the chances of becoming wealthy after becoming believers is less since they would most likely be involved in the ministry (e.g., Acts 15 and the letters of James and Jude). Since Christians were harshly treated in Jerusalem, once a Jew made an open profession of Christ, making a living became harder, not easier. Perhaps that is what gave rise to the letter to the Hebrews. Jewish-Christians were under peer pressure to return to Judaism and many where abandoning Christianity. In addition the evidence suggests that poor saints were in the Jerusalem church and needed financial help, a need Paul helped meet (2 Cor. 8–9; Rom. 15:25–27).

Our Third Response

Tabor correctly claims, "The reading 'Yeshua, son Yehosef,' or 'Jesus, son of Joseph,' has been confirmed by several of the world's leading epigraphers, including Dr. Frank Cross of Harvard University."[6] However, what he does not admit is that many scholars have acknowledged the reading *Yeshua* but with doubts.[7]

He further tries to deemphasize the scrappy handwriting of the name *Yeshua* on this inscription by stating that this is typical of inscriptions since even the inscription of "Joseph, son of Caiaphas, the wealthy and influential high priest who resided over the trial of Jesus, is quite difficult to read."[8] Not only is the opposite true, but most ossuaries documented in Rahmani's catalogue are clearly readable unlike the *Yeshua* inscription. This is why, unlike most others, it has a question mark next to its name.

Tabor also claims "more formal and theological designations such as 'Jesus of Nazareth' and 'Jesus the Christ' became popular decades later."[9] Yet the evidence in Rahmani's catalogue shows otherwise. Furthermore all experts (Joe Zias, Jodi Magness, and L. Y. Rahmani) have said, regardless of the period, "In Jerusalem's tombs, the deceased's place of origin was noted when someone from outside Jerusalem and its environs was interred in a local tomb."[10] Tabor, however, does not provide a shred of evidence for his claim.

Our Fourth Response

Tabor does not believe that the names found in the Talpiot tomb are all that common. "The Rahmani collection does not include all inscribed ossuaries found in the Jerusalem area for the period, but the name frequencies and distributions appear to be fairly representative of our large body of data."[11] He refers to the 231 inscribed ossuaries in Rahmani's catalogue. Not only have all onomastic experts said these names are common, thus contradicting Tabor, but also 231 inscribed ossuaries are a fairly small number according to the estimated 80 thousand Jerusalem residents of the time. If we include the four million residents of the region, this makes the number 231 almost insignificant. Pointing to the limited amount of documented ossuaries in Rahmani's catalogue hinders instead of helps Tabor's point.

Our Fifth Response

Tabor objects to the view that "Mariamne and Mara" could refer to two women, Mariam and Martha, but he does not cite any evidence in support that the names refer to one individual. Tabor simply restates that *Mara* meant in Aramaic "lord" or "mistress," and that this "could very well fit a woman such as Mary Magdalene."[12] Asserting a statement does not make it true. Where is the evidence other than what the book already states? Tabor's answer does not add anything new.

Our Sixth Response

Tabor originally denied that Jesus was married and called it a "gripping fiction" that is "short on evidence."[13] He has now changed his mind saying, "Jesus was married."[14]

The only so-called "strong evidence" he claims is Paul's lack of reference to Jesus' singleness when recommending celibacy, which would have clinched Paul's argument.[15] However, Tabor fails to recognize three points. First, Paul calls celibacy a "gift from God" (1 Cor. 7:7), which allows one to devote more time and effort to the Lord's work (vv. 32–35). Is not that the whole purpose for Jesus' coming to earth (see John 18:37)?[16]

Second, Paul did not need to refer to Jesus when speaking of celibacy because Jesus had spoken of this already in Matthew 19:10–12. That is why Paul wrote that the revelation from 1 Corinthians 7:12 and following is being added by him ("But to the rest I, not the Lord"), since Jesus did not speak about mixed marriages among believers and non-believers. Paul did not need to mention Jesus' singleness because it was common knowledge that Jesus promoted that the ultimate state of existence to do the Lord's work necessitated remaining single (Matt. 19:12). Would Jesus promote celibacy as the highest form of existence to serve the Lord and do less Himself? Hence Paul also promoted celibacy.

Third, Tabor says 1 Corinthians 9:5 does not mention the names of Jesus' brothers wives, or children, which suggests that they were not celibate. Thus "silence does not equal celibacy."[17] True, but this is not silence. In fact this works against Tabor's point, for if Paul wanted to strengthen his point, mentioning Jesus' marriage would have clinched the argument. Instead Paul mentioned the marriage of apostles, Jesus' brothers and Peter's, but not Jesus' marriage. Tabor then actually reverses the logic and point of the passage.

Final Statistical Note

Everyone knows the majority of scholars rejected the statistical analysis from Prof. Andrey Feuerverger, because of the enormous unsubstantiated assumptions (given to him by Jacobovici) needed for his calculations to work. The most recent statistical analysis done by Randall Ingermanson gives a more reasonable number of a 2% probability that the Talpiot tomb belongs to Jesus and His family.[18]

Ingermason arrives at a 2% probability by first noting that there were an estimated 128 men at that time in Jerusalem that were named

"Jesus son of Joseph." This leaves 1 in 128 (1%) that the Jesus of Talpiot is Jesus of Nazareth.

Being conservative, Ingermason qualified some of the previous assumptions made by Feuerverger, some of them worked for and some worked against the Talpiot hypothesis. Thus he concluded the name Maria was far too common to help the Talpiot hypothesis. The name "Yoseh" is a customary contraction of "Yehosef," one of the most common names of that period. Besides the "New Testament data asserts that Jesus was buried in a tomb very close to the execution site (a couple of miles from Talpiot [John 19:41])." A number of other observations made by Ingermason were anticipated in this book.[19] Though most scholars at the January 2008 symposium gave no chance of this being the tomb of Jesus of Nazareth, the best Talpiot hopefuls can say is what Ingermason concluded. "My best estimate is that the probability of authenticity is less than 2%. Based on my best understanding of what the scholars say, the probability may well be much lower than 2%. But I don't believe it is higher than 2%."[20]

Conclusions

Jacobovici and Tabor add nothing new that makes their case more believable. Other points made by Tabor have already been anticipated in this book and answered. Most of the information, especially pages 228–34, of the revised book are rehashing previous arguments, but without any supporting materials. The revised and updated volume adds nothing compelling to their arguments, other than make various logical fallacies and restate former ideas with various twists. Furthermore, the recent statistics done of 2% probability of the Talpiot tomb being that of Jesus of Nazareth puts the final nail on the Talpiot statistical coffin.

ENDNOTES

Chapter One
All passages in this chronology of the last week of Christ came from http://www.biblegateway.com/ . We thank them for allowing us to print this valuable timeline.

Chapter Two
[1] F. David Farnell succinctly notes this very thing through the anti-supernatural philosophical bias that has always existed: "Philosophical opposition to the supernatural is not new. Paul encountered such in Athens (Acts 17:16-34), for his biblical world-view included the resurrection of the material body, but that of his philosophical listeners had no room for the supernatural. Philosophy's clash with Christianity in the New Testament appears in Colossians, 1 John, 2 Peter, Jude, and Revelation 2–3. It emerged early in the post-Apostolic church and continued through the Middle Ages. It was not until the Reformation corrected hermeneutical abuses of philosophy that a resolution of the problem surfaced. But just after a hundred years after the Reformers, philosophy reasserted itself to haunt the church" ("Philosophical and Theological Bent of Historical Criticism," in *The Jesus Crisis: The Inroads of Historical Criticism into Evangelical Scholarship*, ed. Robert L. Thomas and F. David Farnell [Grand Rapids: Kregel Publications, 1998], 85). See also Norman L. Geisler, "Inductivism, Materialism, and the Rationalism: Bacon, Hobbes, and Spinoza," in *Biblical Errancy: An Analysis of Its Philosophical Roots*, ed. Norman L. Geisler (Grand Rapids: Zondervan Publishing House, 1981), 11-19. By noting the helpfulness of Farnell's essay in this section it does not mean I completely endorse all the chapters in the *Jesus Crisis*.

[2] These are not exhaustive but are the ten major philosophical systems foundational to Thomas Hobbes, "Leviathan," in *Great Books of the Western World*, ed. Robert M. Hutchins et al., vol. 23 (Chicago: William Benton, 1952). Usually historical criticism is opposed to an orthodox view of the Bible. These views are thoroughly explained by Farnell, "Philosophical and Theological Bent," 85-131.

[3] See Francis Bacon, "Novum Organum," in *Great Books of the Western World*, 30:133-34.

[4] Farnell, "Philosophical and Theological Bent," 121.

[5] Hobbes, "Leviathan," 41-49.

[6] Farnell, "Philosophical and Theological Bent," 89.

[7] Benedict de Spinoza, "Biographical Note, Benedict de Spinoza," in *Great Books of the Western World*, 31:354.

[8] Colin Brown, *Christianity and Western Thought* (Downers Grove, IL:

InterVarsity Press, 1990), 185-86. These terms are noted by Farnell, "Philosophical and Theological Bent," 89.

[9] Farnell, "Philosophical and Theological Bent," 89.

[10] Ibid., 94. Men like Matthew Tindal (1655-1733), John Toland (1670-1722), Anthony Collins (1676-1729), and others also followed this system of thought.

[11] Ernest C. Mossner, *The Life of David Hume*, 2nd ed. (Oxford: Clarendon Press, 1980), 612. David Hume states, "The idea of substance as well as that of a mode, is nothing but a collection of simple ideas, that are united by the imagination, and have a particular name assigned them, by which we are able to recall, either to ourselves or others, that collection," (*A Treatise of Human Nature*, ed. Ernest C. Mossner [New York: Penguin, 1969], 63).

[12] Farnell, "Philosophical and Theological Bent," 97, 99. John Locke (1632-1704), George Berkeley (1685-1753), and others also followed the same system.

[13] Ibid., 100; cf. Immanuel Kant, *Critique of Pure Reason*, ed. Vasilis Politis (New York: Everyman, 1993), 30-68; Colin Brown, *Philosophy and the Christian Faith* (Downers Grove, IL: InterVarsity Press, 1968), 96.

[14] Other promoters of this view include Jean Jacques Rousseau (1712-1778), Johann Wolfgang Goethe (1749-1832), Friedrich Schiller (1759-1805) and Friedrich Hölderlin (1770-1843).

[15] Farnell, "Philosophical and Theological Bent," 103, 106.

[16] Proponents of this philosophy also include Johann Gottlieb Fichte (1762-1814) and Friedrich W. J. von Schelling (1775-1854).

[17] Farnell, "Philosophical and Theological Bent," 107.

[18] Charles Darwin, *The Origin of Species by Means of Natural Selection; or, the Preservation of Favored Races in the Struggle for Life* (n.p.: n.p., 1859; reprint, New York: J. A. Hill, 1904); Charles Darwin, *The Descent of Man and Selection in Relation to Sex* (London: J. Murray, 1871).

[19] Farnell correctly acknowledges the origins of Darwinian thought. "To a large extent, the hypothesis of evolution resulted from a presupposition exclusion of God and religion from science and stemmed from the philosophies prevalent immediately before and during the Enlightenment (for example deism, agnosticism, uniformitarianism—'the present is the key to the past and'—and atheism" ("Philosophical and Theological Bent," 110), For a more detail discussion see John C. Hutchinson, "Darwin's Evolutionary Theory and 19th-Century Natural Theology," *Bibliotheca Sacra* 152 (July-September 1995): 334-54.

[20] This is known as the Documentary Hypothesis theory (also known as the JEDP theory) in which scholars seek to determine how the Scriptures were formulated by determining how different terms and phrases are employed and who wrote them. Evolutionary theology, however, ultimately led to the well-known form-critical analysis of the New Testament popularized by

Karl L. Schmidt (1891-1956), Martin Dibelius (1883-1947), and Rudolph Bultmann (1884-1976). Form-critical analysis espouses that the Christian community gradually developed the four Gospel accounts from the simplest form—including oral accounts—to a more complex written account.

[21] See Wilhelm Bousset, *Kyrios Christos,* trans. John E. Steely (Nashville: Abingdon Press, 1970). Conceptual parallels appear in a number of pagan religions with that of Christianity. However, many of these parallels are not identical; neither is Christianity dependent on their religious neighbors for their theology. In fact in many cases (e.g., the mystery religions) it can be shown that the opposite is true. For a thorough and excellent treatment showing similarities and distinctions between pagan and Christian religion and thereby demonstrating Christianity's uniqueness see Gregory A. Boyd, *Jesus Under Siege* (Wheaton, IL: Victor Books, 1995), 43-62, and J. Ed Komoszewski, M. James Sawyer, and Daniel B. Wallace, *Reinventing Jesus: How Contemporary Skeptics Miss the Real Jesus and Mislead Popular Culture* (Grand Rapids: Kregel Publications, 2006), 219-62.

[22] For a thorough discussion of these views see Frederick Copleston, *Contemporary Philosophy, Studies of Logical Positivism and Existentialism* (New York: Barnes and Noble, 1972), 148-200, cited in Farnell, "Philosophical and Theological Bent," 113-14.

[23] Søren Kierkegaard, *The Journals of Søren Kierkegaard,* trans. and ed. Alexander Dru (New York: Harper & Brothers, 1959), 185.

[24] Farnell, "Philosophical and Theological Bent," 115. For more on these issues see Kierkegaard, *Journals of Søren Kierkegaard,* 109; Paul R. Sponheim, *Kierkegaard on Christ and Christian Coherence* (New York: Harper & Row, 1968), 173-264.

[25] Bart D. Ehrman, *Misquoting Jesus: The Story Behind Who Changed the Bible and Why* (San Francisco: HarperSanFrancisco, 2005); James D. Tabor, *The Jesus Dynasty: The Hidden History of Jesus, His Royal Family and the Birth of Christianity* (New York: Simon & Schuster, 2006); Michael Baigent, *The Jesus Papers: Exposing the Greatest Cover-up in History* (San Francisco: HarperSanFrancisco, 2006). Although not as recent as these other contemporary works intent on redefining the historical and biblical Jesus, there are numerous others including Earl Doherty, *Challenging the Verdict* (Ottawa: Age of Reason, 2001); John D. Crossan, *Jesus: A Revolutionary Biography* (San Francisco: Harper SanFrancisco, 1994); Bart D. Ehrman, *The Orthodox Corruption of Scripture: The Effect of Early Christological Controversies on the Text of the New Testament* (Oxford: Oxford University Press, 1993); Burton L. Mack, *The Lost Gospel: The Book of Q and Christian Origins* (San Francisco: Harper SanFrancisco, 1993); M. Baigent and R. Leigh, *The Dead Sea Scrolls Deception* (New York: Summit, 1992); John D. Crossan, *The Historical Jesus: The Life of a Mediterranean Jewish Peasant* (San Francisco: HarperSanFrancisco, 1991); H. Koester, *Ancient Christian Gospels*

(Philadelphia: Trinity Press, 1990); Burton L. Mack, *A Myth of Innocence* (Philadelphia: Fortress Press, 1988); Marcus J. Borg, *Jesus: A New Vision* (San Francisco: Harper & Row, 1987); M. Baigent, R. Leigh, and Henry Lincoln, *Holy Blood, Holy Grail* (New York: Dell, 1983); Ron Cameron, *The Other Gospels: Non-Canonical Texts* (Philadelphia: Westminster Press, 1982); H. Koester, *Introduction to the New Testament II: History and Literature of Early Christianity* (Philadelphia: Fortress Press, 1982); J. M. Robinson and H. Koster, *Trajectories through Early Christianity* (Philadelphia: Fortress Press, 1971).

26 See note 31 for a better idea of how many scholars are involved. The *Jesus Seminar* gives the misguided impression that the majority of scholars agree with them. Actually it is just the opposite.

27 Robert W. Funk, Roy W. Hoover, and the Jesus Seminar, *The Five Gospels: The Search for the Authentic Words of Jesus*, ed. R. Funk and J. V. Hills (New York: MacMillian Publishing, 1993), 37.

28 Boyd, *Jesus Under Siege*, 88.

29 See Ibid., 24; Funk, Hoover, and Seminar, *The Five Gospels*, 1-36, acknowledge this same conclusion.

30 Komoszewski, Sawyer, and Wallace, *Reinventing Jesus*, 39-50; Craig A. Evans, *Fabricating Jesus: How Modern Scholars Distort the Gospels* (Downers Grove: InterVarsity Press, 2006), 46-51; Craig L. Blomberg, "Where Do We Start Studying Jesus?" in *Jesus Under Fire: Modern Scholarship Reinvents the Historical Jesus*, ed. Michael J. Wilkins and J. P. Moreland (Grand Rapids: Zondervan Publishing House, 1995), 19-22.

31 Clearly the *Jesus Seminar* gives the impression by the constant use of the word "scholar" that anyone disagreeing with their conclusion is unscholarly. But the opposite is true. "As a matter of fact, a great many scholars, from a wide variety of persuasions, disagree with elements of this highly controversial list of 'pillars.'" Furthermore the *Seminar* also gives the impression that they represent the majority of scholars but they do not. "Indeed, the conclusions of the Jesus Seminar participants are usually representative only of the left-most fringe of the New Testament scholarship" (Boyd, *Jesus Under Siege*, 89-91). Hence, "Sometimes, for example, the phrase 'some two hundred scholars' has occurred. To someone unacquainted with the immensity and complexity of higher education in America, two hundred scholars may seem an impressively large number. In fact, however, it is a very small number when placed against the number of New Testament scholars alone who are involved in the work of SBL (at least half of the 6, 900 members of the organization), let alone the thousands more with substantial scholarly training in the New Testament who for personal or ideological reasons do not take part in the society's activities. And even the number *two hundred* is somewhat misleading, since it includes all of those who were part of the Seminar's proceedings in any fashion—by receiving its mailings, for

example, or reading its reports" (Luke Timothy Johnson, *The Real Jesus: The Misguided Quest for the Historical Jesus and the Truth of the Traditional Gospels* [San Francisco, CA: HarperSanFrancisco, 1996], 2). See also pages 1-27 for another thorough analysis of the *Jesus Seminar* movement and its founders.

[32] Boyd, *Jesus Under Siege*, 24-25, 91 (italics his).

[33] Evans, *Fabricating Jesus*, 242, acknowledges this as well.

[34] See Ben Witherington III, *What Have They Done with Jesus? Beyond Strange Theories and Bad History—Why We Can Trust the Bible* (San Francisco: HarperSanFrancisco, 2006), 7, also sees this dichotomy of flesh and spirit played out. Evans explains the details involving the discovery: "At the best investigators can determine, a leather-bound codex (or ancient book), whose pages consist of papyrus, was discovered in the late 1970s perhaps in 1978, in Egypt, perhaps in a cave. For the next five years the codex, written in the Coptic language [Egyptian language written in Greek letters], was passed around the Egyptian antiquities market. In 1983 Stephen Emmel, a Coptic scholar, ... concluded that the codex was genuine (that is, not a forgery) and that it probably dated to the fourth century. Subsequent scientific test confirmed Emmel's educated guest" (*Fabricating Jesus*, 240). The *Gospel of Judas* actually appears in pages 33-58 in the book (Codex Tchacos) that contains three other tractates.

[35] Irenaeus wrote, "They [the Gnostics] declare that Judas the traitor was thoroughly acquainted with these things [i.e., that Cain and others derived their being from above and did not suffer injury], that he alone, knowing the truth as no others did, accomplished the mystery of the betrayal; by him all things, both earthly and heavenly, were thus thrown into confusion. They produce a fictitious history of this kind, which they style the *Gospel of Judas*" (*Against Heresies* 1.31.1).

[36] Witherington, *What Have They Done with Jesus?* 8.

[37] Komoszewski, Sawyer, and Wallace also note, "These criticisms were made of his earlier major work, *Orthodox Corruption of Scripture*, from which *Misquoting Jesus* has drawn extensively. Yet, the conclusions that he put forth there are still stated here without recognition of some of the severe criticisms of his work the first go-around" (*Reinventing Jesus*, 112). For a complete bibliography of both of Ehrman's books see note 25. See also chapter 3 where Bart D. Ehrman's *Misquoting Jesus* is examined.

[38] Ehrman, *Misquoting Jesus*, 11.

[39] This topic will be discussed in chapter 3. For answers to a similar argument see Komoszewski, Sawyer, and Wallace, *Reinventing Jesus*, 65-73, 275.

[40] Ehrman, *Misquoting Jesus*, 208.

[41] See Komoszewski, Sawyer, and Wallace, *Reinventing Jesus*, 113-14.

[42] Witherington, *What Have They Done with Jesus?* 7. Since Ehrman studied in two locations—which teach the approach explained here—Evans is baffled by Ehrman's position and concludes: "I must admit that I am puzzled by

all this. If not at Moody Bible Institute, then surely at Wheaton College, Ehrman must have become acquainted with a great number of textual variants in the biblical manuscripts. No student can earn a degree in Bible and not know this. Yet Bible students are not defecting in droves. I am also puzzled by Ehrman's line of reasoning. For the sake of argument, let's suppose that the scribal errors in the Bible manuscripts really do disprove verbal inspiration and inerrancy, so that the Bible really should be viewed as a *human book* and not as *God's words*. Would we lose everything as a result? No. Moderate and liberal Christians have held essentially this view for a century or more. The real issue centers on what God accomplished in Jesus of Nazareth" (Evans, *Fabricating Jesus*, 27-28). For more on Ehrman's position see ibid., 28-33, and Komoszewski, Sawyer, and Wallace, *Reinventing Jesus*, 110-17. See also chapter 3 that discusses Ehrman's position further.

[43] Tabor, *Jesus Dynasty*, 273-74.

[44] Others have also noticed Tabor's dubious approach (Witherington, *What Have They Done with Jesus?* 299-300; Evans, *Fabricating Jesus*, 217-20).

[45] Witherington, *What Have They Done with Jesus?* 293.

[46] Evans, *Fabricating Jesus*, 217.

[47] Contrary to Baigent and Brown, Tabor admits that Jesus could not have faked His death but was actually killed by the Romans. He believes this event has biblical and historical support. Citing Mark 16:6; Matthew 28:1-7; and Luke 24:2-5, he concludes, "None of these theories appear to have any basis whatsoever in reliable historical sources. I think we need have no doubt that given Jesus' execution by Roman crucifixion he was truly *dead* and that his temporary place of burial was discovered to be empty shortly thereafter" (Tabor, *Jesus Dynasty*, 229-30, italics his). Of course, Tabor's citing the biblical account of the Resurrection does not mean he interprets it as Jesus rising physically. Instead he believes Jesus' body was moved to the city Tsfat outside of Galilee (ibid., 233-38). He also believes Jesus rose spiritually. See Appendix.

[48] Witherington also makes the same observation (*What Have They Done with Jesus?* 293-295).

[49] Tabor, *Jesus Dynasty*, 59.

[50] See note 19.

[51] Tabor, *Jesus Dynasty*, 137, 243.

[52] Ibid., 43, 135, 140.

[53] Ibid., 56-57.

[54] Ibid., 64-72, 76-77.

[55] Irenaeus, *Against Heresies* 78.7.5; Epiphanius (A.D. 315-403).

[56] Evans, *Fabricating Jesus*, 218.

[57] Tabor, *Jesus Dynasty*, 230-37.

[58] Ibid., 232. Interestingly, Tabor seems to admit this. "In Judaism to claim that someone has been 'raised from the dead' is not the same as to claim

that one has died and exists as a spirit or soul in the heavenly world. What the gospels claim about Jesus is that the tomb was empty, and that his dead body was revived.... He was not a phantom or a ghost, though he does seem to 'materialize' abruptly, and at times is first unrecognized, then suddenly recognized by those who saw him. But Paul seems to be willing to use the term 'resurrection' to refer to something akin to an apparition or vision" (ibid.). But interestingly Tabor actually believes Jesus rose spiritually. See Appendix. See also chapter 4 where overwhelming evidence shows that the Hebrew concept—by in large—of resurrection was bodily not spiritually.

59 He says about the *Gospel of Thomas*: "It is clearly the most precious lost Christian document discovered in the last two thousand years" (ibid., 63).

60 Ibid. (italics his).

61 Ben Witherington III, *The Gospel Code: Novel Claims about Jesus, Mary Magdalene and Da Vinci* (Downers Grove, IL: InterVarsity Press, 2004), 96-109.

62 Tabor, *Jesus Dynasty*, 86. Yet he contradicts himself since he accepts the above quotation from the *Gospel of Thomas* as a valid historical reference that he thinks illuminates Jesus' illegitimate birth. He also accepts late traditions in other places as well (ibid., 64-72, 233-38). A similar observation was made by Witherington, *What Have They Done with Jesus?* 230.

63 Baigent, *Jesus Papers*, 269-70.

64 Ibid., 269, 271.

65 Evans, *Fabricating Jesus*, 216.

66 Baigent, *Jesus Papers*, 126-32.

67 Witherington, *What Have They Done with Jesus?* 7

68 Simcha Jacobovici and Charles Pelegrino, *The Jesus Family Tomb: The Evidence Behind the Discovery No One Wanted to Find* (San Francisco: HarperOne, 2007), 213-34. For a thorough response to these and outlandish and wild conspiracy theories see René A. López, *The Jesus Family Tomb Examined: Did He Rise Physically?* (Springfield, MO: 21stCentury Press, 2008).

69 See chapter nine for answers to Jacobovici and Tabor's rebuttal of the majority of evangelical consensus regarding their responses and allegation of having discovered the family tomb of Jesus of Nazareth.

70 Amos Kloner, "A Tomb with Inscribed Ossuaries in East Talpiyot, Jerusalem," *Atiquot* 29 (1996): 17; Levy Yitzhak Rahmani, *A Catalogue of Jewish Ossuaries in the Collections of the State of Israel*, eds. Ayala Sussmann and Peter Schertz (Jerusalem: Israel Antiquities Authority, 1994), 222-23.

71 Stephen J. Pfann, "Interview by Darrell L. Bock of Stephen J. Pfann to Help Identify Inscriptions" [online] (accessed April 4, 2007) available from http://media.bible.org/mp3/bock/profpfann030807.mp3.

Chapter Three

1 http://www.jesuswalk.com/resurrection/4_resurrection-significance.htm

2 Gary R. Habermas, "Mapping the Recent Trend toward the Bodily Resurrection Appearances of Jesus in Light of Other Prominent Critical Positions," in *The Resurrection of Jesus: John Dominic Crossan and N. T. Wright in Dialogue*, ed. Robert B. Steward (Minneapolis: Fortress Press, 2006), 79–81.

3 These categories and explanations that follow are derived from ibid., 82–92.

4 German liberals promoted this view beginning the second half of the nineteenth century and into the twentieth century. See Gerd Lüdemann, *The Resurrection of Jesus: History, Experience, Theology*, trans. John Bowden (Minneapolis: Fortress Press, 1994); Gerd Lúdemann and Alf Ozen, *What Really Happened to Jesus: A Historical Approach to the Resurrection*, trans. John Bowden (Louisville, KY: Westminster John Knox Press, 1995).

5 Willi Marxsen, *The Resurrection of Jesus of Nazareth*, trans. Margaret Kohl (Philadelphia: Fortress Press, 1970), 88, 94, 96–97. He says the disciples "were all like Thomas and so an appearance was necessary. But this answer will hardly be thought satisfactory. Alternatively one might say that appearances really happened, so why should they not be reported? This may be admitted. But it is essential to add that an appearance was not necessary in order that the ten should believe; for they believed before. And this means that their faith too was dependent on the appearance to Peter. We can therefore now answer the question put earlier. Since the appearance to Peter led others to faith, the functional aspect was bound up with first appearance from the very beginning.... So although the functional aspect is not expressly named in the formula ('Jesus appeared to Peter'), the function is none the less implicit and is to be read into it" (ibid., 90).

6 See chapter 4 for an analysis of this view.

7 Habermas, "Recent Trend toward the Bodily Resurrection Appearances of Jesus," 86. For or an impressive list of scholars who reject the naturalistic view see below in this chapter.

8 This is the explanation succinctly given by Habermas (ibid., 87 n. 43).

9 Hans Grass, *Ostergeschehen und Osterberichte*, 2nd ed. (Göttingen: Vandenhoeck and Ruprecht, 1962), 93, 118–19, 242, 279. This appears in Habermas, "Recent Trend toward the Bodily Resurrection Appearances of Jesus," 87 n. 44.

10 Bart D. Ehrman, *Misquoting Jesus: The Story Behind Who Changed the Bible and Why* (San Francisco: HarperSanFrancisco, 2005). In this book Ehrman asserts that the Bible cannot be trusted because it has numerous errors. In a debate between William Lane Craig and Bart D. Ehrman at College of the Holy Cross, Worcester, Massachusetts, on March 28, 2006, Craig said, "Sadly, Dr. Ehrman came to radically different conclusions as a result of his studies. In his most recent book he poignantly describes how he came to lose his teenage faith. I'm not sure, based on Dr. Ehrman's writings, whether he still believes in Jesus' resurrection or not. He never denies it. But he

does deny that there can be historical evidence for Jesus' resurrection. He maintains that there *cannot* be historical evidence for Jesus' resurrection. Now this is a very bold claim, and so naturally I was interested to see what argument he would offer for its justification. I was stunned to discover that the philosophical argument he gives for this claim is an old argument against the identification of miracles which I had studied during my doctoral research and which is regarded by most philosophers today as demonstrably fallacious" (p. 3, italic his). Later in the debate Ehrman admitted, "I'm a historian dedicated to finding the historical truth. After years of studying, I finally came to the conclusion that everything I had previously thought about the historical evidence of the resurrection was absolutely wrong" (p. 9). Ehrman does not deny the resurrection nor does he affirm it. He is agnostic about it since he believes the concept of the Resurrection as a miracle cannot be verified in history. Whether that is true will be discussed later in this chapter. He says, "What about the resurrection of Jesus? I'm not saying it didn't happen; but if it did happen, it would be a miracle. The resurrection claims are claims that not only that Jesus' body came back alive; it came back alive never to die again. That's a violation of what naturally happens, every day, time after time, millions of times a year. What are the chances of that happening? Well, it'd be a miracle. In other words, it'd be so highly improbable that we can't account for it by natural means. A theologian may claim that it's true, and to argue with the theologian we'd have to argue on theological grounds because there are no historical grounds to argue on. Historians can only establish what probably happened in the past, and by definition a miracle is the least probable occurrence. And so, by the very nature of the canons of historical research, we can't claim historically that a miracle probably happened. By definition, it probably didn't. And history can only establish what probably did. I wish we could establish miracles, but we can't. It's no one's fault. It's simply that the canons of historical research do not allow for the possibility of establishing as probable the least probable of all occurrences. For that reason, Bill's four pieces of evidence are completely irrelevant. There *cannot* be historical probability for an event that defies probability, even if the event did happen. The resurrection has to be taken on faith, not on the basis of proof" (p. 12 italics his). For a complete analysis of the debate see William Lane Craig and Bart D. Ehrman, *Is There Historical Evidence for the Resurrection of Jesus? A Debate between William Lane Craig and Bart D. Ehrman* (online transcript: http://www.holycross. edu/departments/ crec/website/resurrection-debate-transcript.pdf, March 28, 2006, accessed November 5, 2007), 3, 9, 12.

[11] We need not duplicate here the enormous number of tomes written on Jesus' resurrection. For a good bibliography (though not exhaustive) of primary and secondary references of works on the Resurrection see Gary R. Habermas and Michael R. Licona, *The Case for the Resurrection of Jesus*

(Grand Rapids: Kregel Publications, 2004); N. T. Wright, *The Resurrection of God*, Christian Origins and the Question of God, vol. 3 (London: SPCK, 2003).

[12] Earl Doherty, *Challenging the Verdict* (Ottawa, ON: Age of Reason, 2001), 39. Some of those scholars are Bart D. Ehrman, *The Orthodox Corruption of Scripture: The Effect of Early Christological Controversies on the Text of the New Testament* (Oxford: Oxford University Press, 1993); *idem, Lost Christianities: The Battles for Scripture and the Faiths We Never Knew* (New York: Oxford University Press, 2003); *idem, Misquoting Jesus*; Robert W. Funk, Roy W. Hoover, and the Jesus Seminar, *The Five Gospels: The Search for the Authentic Words of Jesus*, ed. R. Funk and J. V. Hills (New York: MacMillian Publishing, 1993).

[13] Darrell L. Bock, *Can I Trust the Bible?* (Norcross, GA: Ravi Zacharias International Ministries, 2001), 18.

[14] Dan Brown, *The Da Vinci Code: A Novel* (New York: Doubleday, 2003), 233–35.

[15] Habermas and Licona, *Case for the Resurrection of Jesus*, 44–45.

[16] The Council of Nicea of A.D. 325 recorded the following: "We believe in one God, the Father All-sovereign, maker of heaven and earth, and all things visible and invisible; And in one Lord Jesus Christ, and the only-begotten Son of God, Begotten of the Father before all ages, Light of Light, true God of true God, begotten not made, of one substance with the Father, through whom all things were made; who for us men and for our salvation came down from the heavens, and was made flesh of the Holy Spirit and the Virgin Mary, and became man, and was crucified for us under Pontius Pilate, and suffered and was buried, and rose again on the third day according to the Scriptures, and ascended into the heavens, and sits on the right hand of the Father, and comes again with glory to judge living and dead, of whose kingdom there shall be no end: And in the Holy Spirit, the Lord and the Life-giver, that proceeds from the Father, who with the Father and Son is worshipped together and glorified together, who spoke through the prophets: In one holy catholic and apostolic church: We acknowledge one baptism unto remission of sins. We look for resurrection of the dead and the life of the age to come."

[17] James L. Garlow and Peter Jones respond to the ridiculous allegation of Brown in, *The Da Vinci Code*, 233, in which he claimed this was a close vote of 316 to 2 (*Cracking Da Vinci's Code* [Colorado Springs, CO: Victor, 2004], 95). Correctly, Darrell L. Bock points out that what occurred at Nicea was not a vote to make Jesus God. "This council and the creed represented what a sizable number of Christian communities had believed for more than two hundred years.... The vote at Nicea, rather than establishing the church's beliefs, affirmed and officially recognized what was already the church's dominant view" (*Breaking the Da Vinci Code: Answers to Questions Everyone's Asking* [Nashville: Thomas Nelson, 2004], 102.

[18] Out of a number of scholars that date all New Testament books within the first century John A. T. Robinson seems to make the best argument (*Redating the New Testament* [Philadelphia: The Westminster Press, 1976]). A. Harnack, C. E. Raven, and a number of contemporary scholars today also believe all NT books were written before A.D. 70.

[19] F. F. Bruce, *The New Testament Documents: Are They Reliable?* 6th ed. (Grand Rapids: Wm. B. Eerdmans Publishing, 1981), 25. Garlow and Jones also observe this in *Cracking Da Vinci's Code*, 139.

[20] This fact goes against a current popular opinion that believes competing Christianities and other religious "Gnostic" books existed and were also considered inspired.

[21] Bruce, *New Testament Documents*, 25.

[22] Ibid., 27.

[23] Garlow and Jones, *Cracking Da Vinci's Code*, 141. For an easy to read explanation of how the books of the Bible were formed, authoritatively accepted, and historically reliable see Josh D. McDowell, *The New Evidence that Demands a Verdict* (Nashville: Thomas Nelson, 1999), 17–68; Norman L. Geisler and William E. Nix, *A General Introduction to the Bible: Revised and Expanded* (Chicago: Moody Press, 1986).

[24] Bock, *Can I Trust the Bible?* 18–19.

[25] A number of these examples are explained by Bock (ibid., 19–28).

[26] Formidable volumes addressing these issues are Robert Anderson, *Misunderstood Texts of the New Testament* (Grand Rapids: Kregel Publications, 1991); Gleason L. Archer, *Encyclopedia of Bible Difficulties* (Grand Rapids: Zondervan Publishing House, 1982); F. F. Bruce, *The Hard Sayings of Jesus*, The Jesus Library, ed. Michael Green (Downers Grove, IL: InterVarsity Press, 1983); J. Carl Laney, *Answers to Tough Questions From Every Book of the Bible: A Survey of Problem Passages* (Grand Rapids: Kregel Publications, 1997).

[27] For example see Jesus' baptism (Matt. 3:17; Mark 1:11; John 1:30–34), temptation (Matt. 4:1–11; Luke 4:1–13), and other places described in the books mentioned in note 26.

[28] The following volumes point out how messengers can speak on behalf of others and can be addressed as if they are the person who sent them. J. C. L. Gibson, *Canaanite Myths and Legends*, ed. G. R. Driver (Edinburgh: T. & T. Clark 1978), 42; Samuel A. Meier, *The Messenger in the Ancient Semitic World*, Harvard Semitic Monographs, ed. Frank Moore Cross, vol. 45 (Atlanta, GA: Scholars Press, 1988), 184.

[29] Bock, *Can I Trust the Bible?* 19.

[30] Ibid., 21 (italics his).

[31] Ehrman, *Misquoting Jesus*, 10.

[32] Ibid., 90.

[33] Ibid., 208.

34 Darrell L. Bock and Daniel B. Wallace, *Dethroning Jesus: Exposing Popular Culture's Quest to Unseat the Biblical Christ* (Nashville: Thomas Nelson, 2007), 38–76. Other scholars have also exposed a number of Ehrman's errors. See Craig A. Evans, *Fabricating Jesus: How Modern Scholars Distort the Gospels* (Downers Grove, IL: InterVarsity Press, 2006), 25–31; Ben Witherington III, *What Have They Done with Jesus? Beyond Strange Theories and Bad History—Why We Can Trust the Bible* (San Francisco: HarperSanFrancisco, 2006), 7.

35 Bock and Wallace, *Dethroning Jesus*, 43–44.

36 Ibid., 44.

37 Ibid., 44–45. Wallace, interestingly, documents how Tertullian, an early church father, reprimanded someone for doubting the original manuscripts of Scripture and pointed the skeptic to visit the churches where the "very thrones," or place, where the apostles read the text in "their own *authentic writings*." Debatable as it is, this could refer to either the original text or copies of it (ibid., 45, [italics his]).

38 This type of thinking is all too prevalent in postmodernism. Interestingly Wallace said, "To be skeptical about the text of the New Testament is essential to a postmodern agenda, in which all things are possible but nothing is probable. The only certainty of postmodernism is uncertainty itself. Concomitant with this is an intellectual pride—pride that one 'knows' enough to be skeptical about all positions" (J. Ed Komoszewski, M. James Sawyer, and Daniel B. Wallace, *Reinventing Jesus: How Contemporary Skeptics Miss the Real Jesus and Mislead Popular Culture* [Grand Rapids: Kregel Publications, 2006], 66).

39 Ben Witherington writes, "There is a reason that both Ehrman's mentor in text criticism and mine, Bruce Metzger, has said that there is nothing in these variants that really challenges any Christian belief: they don't. I would like to add that other experts in text criticism, such as Gordon Fee, have been equally emphatic about the flawed nature of Ehrman's analysis of the significance of such textual variants" (*What Have They Done With Jesus?* 7).

40 Wallace explains this in a succinct way in *Dethroning Jesus*, 52–71. For a more detail discussion in how the science of textual criticism (i.e., the investigation involved at how to arrive at the original text) works see Eldon Jay Epp and Gordon D. Fee, *Studies in the Theory and Method of New Testament Textual Criticism*, Studies and Documents, ed. Irvin Alan Sparks, vol. 45 (Grand Rapids: Wm. B. Eerdmans Publishing, 1993); Bruce M. Metzger and Bart D. Ehrman, *The Text of the New Testament: Its Transmission, Corruption, and Restoration*, 4th ed. (New York and Oxford: Oxford University Press, 2005).

41 With some modifications this chart is based on the following two sources: Komoszewski, Sawyer, and Wallace, *Reinventing Jesus*, 71; and Josh McDowell, *Evidence That Demands a Verdict: Historical Evidences for the Christian Faith*, vol. 1 (San Bernardino, CA: Here's Life Publishers, 1972),

42–43.

[42] Metzger and Ehrman, *Text of the New Testament*, 126.

[43] Komoszewski, Sawyer, and Wallace, *Reinventing Jesus*, 50–51 (italics his).

[44] Wright, *Resurrection of God*, 15. See the discussions in Christopher F. Evans, *Resurrection and the New Testament* 2nd ed., Studies in Biblical theology, no. 12. (London: SCM Press, 1970); Marxsen, *Resurrection of Jesus of Nazareth*; C. F. D. Moule and Willi Marxen, *The Significance of the Message of the Resurrection for the Faith in Jesus Christ*, trans. Dorothea M. Barton and R. A. Wilson, 2nd ed., Studies in Biblical theology, no. 8 (Naperville, IL: A. R. Allenson, 1968).

[45] Craig and Ehrman, *Historical Evidence for the Resurrection of Jesus* (accessed), 12.

[46] As Wright correctly explains, this view says "both too little and too much." "Too little: in standard positivism fashion it appears to suggest that we can only regard as 'historical' that to which we have direct access (in the sense of 'first-hand witness accounts' or near equivalent). But, as all real historians know, that is not in fact how history works. Positivism is, if anything, even less appropriate in historiography than in other areas. Again and again the historian has to conclude, even if only to avoid total silence, that certain events took place to which we have no direct access but which are the necessary postulates of that to which we do have access. Scientists, not least physicists, make this sort of move all the time; indeed, this is precisely how scientific advances happen. Ruling out as historical that to which we do not have direct access is actually a way of not doing history at all. "As a result, this view also says too much. On its own epistemology, it ought not even to claim access to the disciples' faith. Even the texts themselves do not give us direct access to this faith in the way that Marxsen and others seem to regard as necessary. All we have in this case are texts; and though Marxsen did not address this question, the same relentless suspicion, applied in regular postmodern fashion, might lead some to question whether we even have those. If, in other words, you want to be a no-hold-barred historical positivist, only accepting as historical that to which you have (in this sense) direct access, you have a long and stony road ahead of you. Few if any actual practicing historians travel by this route" (*Resurrection of God*, 15–16).

[47] Ibid., 12–13.

[48] To say that history must be a provable event "is somewhat more controversial." For example, "To say 'x may have happened, but we can't prove it, so it isn't really *historical*' may not be self-contradictory, but is clearly operating with a more restricted sense of 'history' than some of the others" (ibid., 13).

[49] Except for the arrowhead pointers everything else comes from Wright (ibid., 12–13 [italics his]). The historical Jesus argument attempted at locating the person of Jesus in light of first-century culture and strips away all supernatural

attributes. Conversely, the Christ of faith does little to anything in locating the Jesus of history but only attributes the theological and supernatural elements attributed to Him. The correct view is to hold to both a historical first-century understanding of Jesus' culture and an unbiased acceptance of supernatural elements attributed to Him that were recorded and witnessed by many of that day. Not keeping these distinct resulted in the confusion that appears in John D. Crossan, *The Historical Jesus: The Life of a Mediterranean Jewish Peasant* (San Francisco: Harper SanFrancisco, 1991), xxvii.

[50] Wright, *Resurrection of God*, 12. For further discussion how theologians have used these five views of history see pages 14–31.

[51] Ibid., 32–47. For example, in *Iliad* 24.549–51, the last sentence literally translates this concept emphatically: "you will not resurrect him [*oude min ansteseis*] before you suffer as further evil." See also *Iliad* 24.756; Aeschylus *Eumenides* 647ff.; Sophocles *Electra* 137–39; Aeschylus *Agamemnon* 565–69, 1019–24, 1360ff.; Euripides *Helena* 1285–87; Aristotle *De Anima* 1.406b.3–5; Aristophanes *Ecclesiazusae* 1073–74; Herodotus 3.62.3ff. (ibid., 32–33 n. 1– 4, see also n. 5–9).

[52] Edwin M. Yamauchi's research suggests that the Christian concept of resurrection is absent in the fertility cults of Tammuz, Adonis, Attis, Osiris, and Baal. "Furthermore, P. Lambrechts has shown recently that the belief in the resurrection of Adonis and in the resurrection of Attis was a late development. In the case of Adonis, the beautiful youth beloved of Aphrodite, who was slain by a boar, Lambrechts points out that there is no trace of a resurrection in the pictorial representations of Adonis or in the early texts — Sappho, Aristophanes, Plutarch, Pausanias, Theocritus" ("Tammuz and the Bible," *Journal of Biblical Literature* 84 [September 1965]: 290). Therefore the typical accusation that Christians derive the resurrection concept from these cults is false.

[53] For his view see Jon Davies, *Death, Burial, and Rebirth in the Religions of Antiquity* (New York: Routledge, 1999), 28–39.

[54] Wright, *Resurrection of God*, 47 (italics his). He quotes this from Davies, *Death, Burial, and Rebirth in the Religions of Antiquity*, 34. For further discussion to understand what Egypt, Canaan, Mesopotamia, and Persia believed about the resurrection, Davies's book is pivotal.

[55] Wright, *Resurrection of God*, 47–48.

[56] Ibid., 49.

[57] Along with Wright, who documents this, numerous scholars note this, including these: James Barr, *The Garden of Eden and the Hope of Immortality* (London: SCM Press, 1992); John J. Collins, *Daniel: A Commentary on the Book of Daniel* Hermeneia: A Critical and Historical Commentary on the Bible, ed. Frank Moore Cross (Minneapolis: Fortress Press, 1993); Christian Grappe, "Naissance de l'idée de résurrection dans le Judaïsme," in *Résurrection: L'aprè-mort dans le monde ancien at el Nouveau Testament*,

ed. Odette Mainville and Daniel Marguerat (Geneva and Montreal: Labor et Fides and Médiaspaul, 2001); Leonard Greenspoon, "The Origin of the Idea of Resurrection," in *Traditions in Transformation: Turning Points in Biblical Faith*, ed. Baruch Halpern and Jon D. Levenson (Winona Lake, IN: Eisenbrauns, 1981); Philip S. Johnston, *Shades of Sheol: Death and Afterlife in the Old Testament* (Downers Grove, IL: InterVarsity Press, 2002); Matthias Krieg, *Todesbilder im Alten Testament, oder, "Wie die Alten den Tod gebildet,"* Abhandlungen zur Theologie des Alten und Neuen Testaments, vol. 73 (Zürich: Theologischer Verlag, 1988); Tryggve N. D. Mettinger, *The Riddle of Resurrection: "Dying and Rising Gods" in the Ancient Near East*, Coniectanea biblica. Old Testament series vol. 50 (Stockholm: Almqvist & Wiksell International, 2001); Ben C. Ollenburger, "If Mortals Die, Will They Live Again? The Old Testament and Resurrection.," *Ex Auditu* 9 (1993); Emile Puech, *La croyance des Esséniens en la vie future: immortalité, résurrection, vie éternelle? Histoire d'une croyance dans le judaïsme ancien*, 2 vols., Etudes bibliques, 21–22 (Paris: J. Gabalda, 1993); Alan F. Segal, "Life After Death: the Social Sources," in *The Resurrection: An Interdisciplinary Symposium on the Resurrection of Jesus*, ed. Stephen T. Davis, Daniel Kendall, and Gerald O'Collins (Oxford: Oxford University Press, 1997); Klaas Spronk, *Beatific Afterlife in Ancient Israel and in the Ancient Near East*, Alter Orient und Altes Testament 219. (Kevelaer: Butzon & Bercker, 1986; reprint, Neukirchen-Vluyn: Neukircherner Verlag); Nicholas J. Tromp, *Primitive Conceptions of Death and the Nether World in the Old Testament*, Biblica et orientalia 21 (Rome: Pontifical Biblical Institute, 1969); Wright, *Resurrection of God*, 85 n. 4.

[58] Wright, *Resurrection of God*, 86.

[59] Bock and Wallace, *Dethroning Jesus*, 209. For an interpretation of Romans 8:18–30 see René A. Lopez, *Romans Unlocked: Power to Deliver* (Springfield, MO: 21st Century Press, 2005), 175–82.

[60] Ben Witherington III, *Jesus, Paul and the End of the World* (Downers Grove, IL: InterVarsity Press, 1992), 185.

[61] Wright says, "It is of course true that the third position, explicit belief in resurrection, is only one of several strands in the range of biblical belief about death and what happens afterwards, and that this belief developed markedly in the post-biblical period. In particular, the third, though clearly cutting across the first in certain ways, joins the first in affirming the goodness and vital importance of the present created order, which is to be renewed by YHWH, not abandoned. For both, the substance of hope lies within creation, not beyond it" (*Resurrection of God*, 86).

[62] Ibid., 87.

[63] See Psalms 30:9; 88:3–7, 10–12; Isaiah 38:10–18; Job 3:13–19; 7:7–10; 14:1–14; 16:22; Jeremiah 51:39, 57. Even using poetic license, like that of Isaiah 14:9–11, descriptive of a scene of a king arriving in the depths of

sheol, the point made is that such a tyrant's power is now ineffective. For further discussion on how most of the OT emphasizes the point that "to die is to be forgotten for good" see Wright, *Resurrection of God,* 92–99.

64 Ibid., 91. See Ecclesiastes 2:24; 3:12–22; 5:18–20; 6:3–6; 8:15; 9:7–10; 11:9; 12:1–8.

65 See Ecclesiastes 1:3, 9, 14; 2:11, 17–20, 22; 3:16; 4:1, 3, 7, 15; 5:13, 18; 6:1, 12; 8:9; 9:3, 6, 9, 11, 13; 10:5.

66 Once the LXX translations came to the fore many ambiguous passages were made clearer (Margaret Williams, "The Contribution of Jewish Inscriptions to the Study of Judaism," in *The Cambridge History of Judaism,* ed. William Horbury, W. D. Davies, and John Sturdy, vol. 3 [Cambridge: Cambridge University Press, 1999], 60). Wright suggest, "That possibility (of an early Christian reading in support of a christological belief) may cautiously be explored in a relation to a few prophecies of a coming king... any early Christian reading 2 Samuel 7.12, *kai anasteso to sperma sou,* would have had no difficulty identifying who the *sperma* was. So too the various messianic promises in Jeremiah and Ezekiel could easily have been taken, and were perhaps intended by their LXX translator(s) to be taken, as indicating the resurrection through which God's leader(s) would 'arise' in the age to come. God will 'raise up' shepherds, and especially a righteous Branch, to rule over Israel and the world. 'I will raise up one shepherd over them, my servant David,' declares YHWH: *kai anasteso ep' autous pimena hena, ton doulon mou Dauid.* We should be wary of reading too much into these verses like this; equally, we should be just as wary of reading too little" (*Resurrection of God,* 149).

67 These promise passages were well known to OT Jews. Hence Wright suggests "they must be recalled here in case any impression be given that the absence, for most ancient Israelites, of any statement of human life beyond the grave meant that they were without a living and vibrant hope" (*Resurrection of God,* 102).

68 Derek Kidner says, "The assurance that Isaac as well as Abraham would *come again* from the sacrifice was no empty phrase: it was Abraham's full conviction, on the ground that 'in Isaac shall thy seed be called' (21:12). Hebrews 11:17–19 reveals that he was expecting Isaac to be resurrected; henceforth he would regard him as given back from the dead" (*Genesis: An Introduction and Commentary,* Tyndale Old Testament Commentaries, ed. D. J. Wiseman, vol. 1 [Downers Grove, IL: InterVarsity Press, 1967], 143).

69 Numerous passages seem have a temporal earthly emphasis instead of eternal bodily resurrection in mind (Ps. 116; Prov. 12:28; 14:32; 15:24; 23:14).

70 Collins, *Daniel,* 391–92.

71 Wright, *Resurrection of God,* 129. That the Pharisees believed in the bodily resurrection and the Sadducees did not is well known (Matt. 22:23; Mark 12:18; Luke 20:27; Acts 23:7–9). But according to Wright because Sadducees followed such a strict interpretation of the OT they saw life simply

existing no further than earth. Thus life and blessings for them were seen as enjoyed by their relationship to God here on earth. In fact, "the contemporary instinct to see the Sadducees as radicals, because they denied the resurrection, is 180 degrees wide of the mark. They denied it because they were conservatives" (ibid., 131).

[72] Ibid., 130.

[73] See Sirach 11:26–28; 14:16–19; 17:27–32; 38:21–23; 41:4.

[74] Why would such a wealthy group not want to believe in any form of existence after death since many wealthy advocates of the past desired to take their present riches with them to the after life? It seems that this would benefit them in another way. For example, "Powerful groups have sometimes advocated a strong post-mortem hope as a way of stopping the poor and powerless grumbling about their lot in the present life. And, where 'resurrection' has become an official dogma within a powerful system, it has had the capacity to become simply another instrument to keep ordinary people in line. It goes against such sociological assumptions to see first-century Jewish aristocrats staunchly denying any future life." The Sadducees denied this for several reasons. They did not find any such passages supporting resurrection in the Torah (Law), their primary source of interpretation, or the Former Prophets (the historical books from Joshua to Kings). Also an unduly interest in the dead, like pagan cults, came close to violating the Law (Lev. 11:31–32; 19:28; 21:1, 11; Num. 6:6; 19:11, 18; Deut. 18:11) (Wright, *Resurrection of God*, 137). Since the teaching of Daniel 12:2–3, Isaiah 26:19, and Ezekiel 37:1–14 were not part of the Pentateuch, they simple discounted it. Wright points out other passages that seem to argue for the absence of any future life (1 Macc. 2:49–70; Tob. 4:10; 12:9; 13:2, 5; 14:10; 1 Baruch 2:27). However, the same can be said about these texts that were said of the OT perspective on life. That Sadducees and other groups may have misinterpreted and used them wrongly to defend their belief, and others used them to show how this belief arose, does not make this interpretation correct, since nothing in these texts argues definitively that resurrection was impossible. In fact other passages argue just the opposite in a clear and forceful way. Wright does not believe the silence of any direct resurrection statement "is not as weak as is sometimes supposed" (ibid., 139).

[75] Ibid., 142-43.

[76] Ibid., 144.

[77] Wright notes a number of scholars who agree on this point (ibid., 144 n. 57). Two of these are Peder Borgen, "Philo of Alexandria," in *Compendia Rerum Iudaicarum as Novum Testamentum, Section Two: The Literature of Jewish People in the Period of the Second Temple and the Talmud*, ed. Michael E. Stone, Jewish Writings of Second Temple Period: Apocrypha, Pseudepigrapha, Qumran Sectarian Writings, Philo, Josephus. 2 vols. (Philadelphia: Fortress Press, 1984), 233–82; John M. Dillon, *The Middle Platonists, 80 B.C. to A.D.*

220 rev. 2nd ed. (Ithaca, NY: Cornell University Press, 1996), 139–83. For example Philo says in the following statements: "The death of the good is the beginning of another life; for life is a twofold thing, one life being in the body, corruptible; the other without the body, incorruptible" (*Quaestiones* Gen 1.16). "What does it mean of, 'But thou shalt go to thy fathers in peace, being nourished in a fair old age?'" (*Quaestiones* Gen. 3.11). He here clearly indicates the incorruptibility of the soul. "Whatever else you may choose to call this concrete animal; but rather the purest and most unalloyed mind, which, while contained in the city of the body and of the mortal life is cramped and confined, and like a man who is bound in a prison confesses plainly that he is unable to relish the free air" (*De Ebrietate* 26, 101). "For it is not possible for one who dwells in the body and belongs to the race of mortals to be united with God, but he alone can be so whom God delivers from that prison house of the body" (*Legum* 3.14, 42). See also *De Migratione* 2 (9); *Quod Deterius* 22 (80). This, by no means is an exhaustive list.

78 All passages from the Apocrypha are from *New Revised Standard Version* (New York: American Bible Society, 1989).

79 Bock makes a similar observation in *Dethroning Jesus*, 209.

80 Whether we agree with Judas's theological conclusion is not the point here but whether belief in a bodily resurrection was part of the culture. A reading of 2 Maccabees makes this clear. "Resurrection belief, throughout 2 Maccabees, means new bodily life, a life which comes after the 'life after death' that dead people currently experience. And the whole book is introduced with the reported prayer, from the time of Nehemiah, that God would gather the scattered people of Israel, punish the Gentiles for their arrogance and oppression, and plant his people in the holy place [2 Macc. 1:24–9]. Resurrection, in other words, is both the personal hope of the righteous individual and the national hope for faithful Israel" (Wright, *Resurrection of God*, 153). For a contrary view of 2 Maccabees see Stanley E. Porter, "Resurrection, the Greeks and the New Testament," in *Resurrection*, ed. Stanley E. Porter, Michael A. Hayes, and David Tombs, Journal for the Study of the New Testament. Supplement series, vol. 186 (Sheffield: Sheffield Academic Press, 1999), 59. See 4 Macc. 8–17.

81 *1 Enoch* 1:8; 25–27; 37–71 does not make it clear, although in various places it mentions a future world to come where the righteous will dwell. This would imply physical resurrection since the future world is analogous in form, without the sin element, with the present world.

82 The translation is accessed from OakTree Software: Accordance 7.4, electronic book R. H. Charles, "Old Testament Pseudepigrapha," (Oxford: The Clarendon Press, 1913).

83 Wright points this out but did not include Dan. 7:13 (*Resurrection of God*, 155).

84 For the highly debatable Wisdom of Solomon passages that may or may not

refer to physical resurrection see Ibid., 162–74.

[85] On another occasion the question asked how a person can live again since in death he turns to dust. In *bSanh* 90b–91a it is answered, "*Queen Cleopatra asked R. Meir, saying, 'I know that the dead will live, for it is written, 'And [the righteous] shall blossom forth out of your city like the grass of the earth'* [Psa. 72:16]. 'But when they rise, will they rise naked or in their clothing?' He said to her, 'It is an argument a fortiori based on the grain of wheat.' 'Now if a grain of wheat, which is buried naked, comes forth in many garments, the righteous, who are buried in their garments, all the more so [will rise in many garments]!' *Caesar said to Rabban Gamaliel, 'You maintain that the dead will live. But they are dust, and can the dust live?' His daughter said to him, "Allow me to answer him:* 'There are two potters in our town, one who works with water, the other who works with clay. Which is the more impressive?' He said to her, 'The one who works with water.' She said to him, 'If he works with water, will he not create even more out of clay?' *A Tannaite authority of the house of R. Ishmael [taught],* '[Resurrection] is a matter of an argument a fortiori based on the case of a glass utensil.' 'Now if glassware, which is the work of the breath of a mortal man, when broken, can be repaired, 'A mortal man, who is made by the breath of the Holy One, blessed be he, how much the more so [that he can be repaired, in the resurrection of the dead]'" (italics original).

[86] In these quotations the word Sadducees appears in some manuscript. See Efraim E. Urbach, *The Sages, Their Concepts and Beliefs*, trans. Israel Abrahams, World and Wisdom of the Rabbis of the Talmud (Cambridge, MA: Harvard University Press, 1987), 652; Wright, *Resurrection of God*, 135 n. 17–19. Perhaps these texts should be understood as a rabbinic polemic against the Sadducee notion that any form of resurrection was impossible.

[87] Wright mentions *mBerakhot* 4:1–5:5 and records the translation of the prayer from S. Singer, *The Authorized Daily Prayer Book of the Hebrew Congregations of the British Commonwealth of Nations* (London: Eyre and Spottiswood, 1962), 46–47 (*Resurrection of God*, 146).

[88] Wright, *Resurrection of God*, 177, see also 178–81. See also N. T. Wright, *The New Testament and the People of God*, vol. 1 (Minneapolis: Fortress Press, 1992), 324–27. Wright points out in numerous places the common Pharisaic belief in the resurrection that was obviously also Paul's since he was a Pharisee (Josephus, *The Jewish War* 2.163; Josephus, *The Antiquities of the Jews* 18:14).

[89] Wright reaches this conclusion after investigating the following passages: Josephus, *The Jewish War* 2.151; 153 [compare with 2 Macc. 7:11, 29]; 154–8; Josephus, *The Antiquities of the Jews* 18.18 (*Resurrection of God*, 185-86).

[90] Puech, *La croyance des Esséniens en la vie future*. This was noted by Wright (*Resurrection of God*, 186).

[91] Paragraphs two and three are translated by Geza Vermes and appear in Wright, *Resurrection of God*, 186. Where brackets and ellipsis appear, the text is missing and the probable words that fit the context are added.

[92] The translation of paragraphs four and five are from the electronic version of Accordance 7.4 Michael O. Wise, Jr. Martin G. Abegg, and Edward M. Cook, "The Dead Sea Scrolls: A New English Translation," (New York: HarperCollins Publishers, 1996).

[93] Philip Jenkins, *Hidden Gospels: How the Search for Jesus Lost Its Way* (Oxford: Oxford University Press, 2001), 80. See Scrolls 1QSa, 1Q28a, and the complete 4Q521 in Wise, Martin G. Abegg, and Cook, "The Dead Sea Scrolls: A New English Translation."

[94] Wright, *Resurrection of God*, 189. See also Puech, *La croyance des Esséniens en la vie future*, 791–92; Wright, *New Testament and the People of God*, 203–9.

[95] Levy Yitzhak Rahmani, *A Catalogue of Jewish Ossuaries in the Collections of the State of Israel*, ed. Ayala Sussmann and Peter Schertz (Jerusalem: Israel Antiquities Authority, 1994), 53. Rachael Hachlili also says, "One of the main Jewish burial rites characterizing the Second Temple period is the *Ossilegium*, a deliberate procedure of gathering the skeletal remains of an individual after the decay of flesh and placing them in a special container, an ossuary, while retaining this individual burial within the family tomb to await the individual's physical resurrection" (*Jewish Funerary Customs Practices and Rites in the Second Temple Period*, Supplements to the Journal for the Study of Judaism, ed. John J. Collins, vol. 94 [Leiden: E. J. Brill, 2005], 483).

[96] Wright, *Resurrection of God*, 147.

[97] I am indebted to Wright for this observation. See the *Gospel of Thomas* sayings 11; 21; 29; 37; 51; 71; 87; 112; The *Book of Thomas the Contender* 138:39–139:30; 141:16–19; 142:10–144:19; 145:8–16; The *Epistle to Rheginos* [also known as *Treatise on Resurrection*] 44:13–38; 45:32–46:2; 46:16–47:27; 48:6–16, 34-8; The *Gospel of Philip* 68:31-7 ["true flesh"?]; 56:15–57:8; 59:9–22; 73:1–8. In agreement with Wright, we cannot be sure exactly what the *Gospel of Philip* wanted to say since it is too obscure, but an attempt to harmonize the Jewish concept of bodily resurrection with the Hellenistic belief of a returning soul may be intended, as argued by J. E. Menard, "La notion de résurrection dans l'épître à Rheginos," in *Essays on the Nag Hammadi Texts in Honor of Pahor Labib*, ed. M. Krause (Leiden: E. J. Brill, 1975). See also the *Apocalypse of Peter* 83:6–84:6; the *Apocryphon of James* 7:35–8:84; 14:32–6; *1 Apocalypse of James* 29:16–19; the *Letter of Peter to Philip* 133:15–17; the *Letter of Philip* 134:9–19; 137:6–9; the *Exegesis of the Soul* 134:6–29; the *Gospel of the Savior* 100:7.1–6.

[98] *Epistle to Rheginos* 47:2–27; 49:14–24. This is a different rising that occurs to believers as Paul mentions in Romans 6:1–23 and 8:10–13 See Wright, *Resurrection of God*, 540.

99 See chapter 3 for a discussion of Gnostic literature.

100 Wright, *Resurrection of God*, 548.

101 This has been the argument of various scholars today. They seek to smuggle Gnostic books back into the first century by dating them earlier than they actually are and push the NT books into the second century by dating them later than they actually are. This creates an illusion as if orthodoxy and Gnosticism are competing views that coequally existed in the same period. Philip Jenkins says, "As in the case of the 'other gospels,' assertions about the independent authority of the Gnostic tradition rely on misleading claims about the dates of key documents. Basically, the orthodox position is thoroughly spelled out in texts from the first century onward, while the documents which Pagels, King, and others cite to illustrate rival Gnostic concepts are far later, and in many cases assume a knowledge of one or more of the four canonical gospels" (*Hidden Gospels*, 116). See Karen L. King, *The Gospel of Mary Magdala: Jesus and the First Woman Apostle* (Santa Rosa, CA: Polebridge Press, 2003); Elaine Pagels, *The Gnostic Gospels* (New York: Random House, 1979). Gregory Riley argues from the *Gospel of Thomas* that early Christianity denied the bodily resurrection (*Resurrection Reconsidered: Thomas and John in Controversy* [Minneapolis: Fortress Press, 1995], 133–56).

102 Jenkins, *Hidden Gospels*, 116.

103 Ibid., 118.

104 This translation is from the electronic version of Accordance 7.4, Michael William Holmes, ed., *The Apostolic Fathers: Greek Texts and English Translations*, trans. J. B. Lightfoot and J. R. Harmer, 2nd ed. (Grand Rapids: Baker Books, 1992).

105 Wright, *Resurrection of God*, 481–3.

106 See how the phrase "enter His kingdom" also appears in *2 Clement* 11:7.

107 Holmes, ed., *Apostolic Fathers*, 293. This is just one of the suggested dates, but no one knows for sure.

108 Wright says, "This [passage] could, at a stretch, be understood to be compatible with, say, 2 Corinthians 4 and 5; but it seems more natural to take it as a moderate Platonic statement, not seeing an incorruptible body as a gift from heaven but seeing the immortal soul awaiting a complete immortality, away from the corruptible material world, as a gift which will be enjoyed in heaven itself. Diognetus thus probably articulates the view of personal eschatology which many western Christians still assume to be that of the New Testament." He also acknowledges in a footnote that Hill "suggests, more positively, that though the work does not clearly refer to the resurrection, there is no evidence that the author doubted it" (*Resurrection of God*, 494 n. 78). See Charles E. Hill, *Regnum Caelorum: Patterns of Millennial Thought in Early Christianity*, 2 ed. (Grand Rapids: Wm. B. Erdmans Publishing, 2001), 103.

[109] See the Koran, *Surah* 56:60–61.

[110] Caroline Walker Bynum, *The Resurrection of the Body in Western Christianity, 200–1336* (1995), 54, 57–58.

[111] Wright, *Resurrection of God*, 147. See also Williams, "Contribution of Jewish Inscriptions to the Study of Judaism," 91, as quoted by Wright.

Chapter Four

[1] Hugh J. Schonfield, *The Passover Plot: New Light on the History of Jesus* (New York: Random House, 1965), 163–65.

[2] John 1:29, 32; see also Genesis 3:15; Psalm 22; and Isaiah 53:1–12.

[3] Hugh J. Schonfield is a British Bible scholar with a doctorate from the University of Glasgow who has written over forty books. See also Hugh J. Schonfield, *After the Cross* (London: Tantivity Press, 1981).

[4] Gary G. Cohen, "The Passover Plot: Verdict, Not Guilty," *Grace Theological Journal* 13 (winter 1972): 33–45; Gary R. Habermas, *The Historical Jesus: Ancient Evidence for the Life of Christ* (Joplin, MO: College Press Publishing, 1996), 69–99.

[5] Elmar R. Gruber, *The Jesus Conspiracy: The Turin Shroud and the Truth about the Resurrection*, trans. Holger Kersten and Elmar R. Gruber (Munich: Langen and Verlag, 1992; reprint, Rockport, MA: Element, 1994), 249–50.

[6] Michael Baigent, *The Jesus Papers: Exposing the Greatest Cover-Up in History* (San Francisco: HarperSanFrancisco, 2006), 126. In summary the more popular views today are wide ranging: "Jesus never died on the cross; he was connected with the Qumran community; someone else changed his message to fit their own desires; he traveled to various parts of the world during the so-called 'silent years' or even after the crucifixion" Habermas, *Historical Jesus*, 69.

[7] The Greek word for "beat," κολαφίζω, means "to strike with a fist" and/or "to cause physical impairment." This is much more severe than to "slap," which is a different Greek word ῥάπισμα, meaning "a blow on the face with someone's hand" (Walter Bauer et al., *A Greek English Lexicon of the New Testament and Other Early Christian Literature*, rev. and ed. Frederick William Danker, 3rd ed. [Chicago: University of Chicago Press, 2000], 555, 904).

[8] R. Bucklin, "The Legal and Medical Aspects of the Trial and Death of Christ," *Science Law* 10 (1970): 14–26, quoted in John Ankerberg and Dillon Burroughs, *What's the Big Deal about Jesus?* (Eugene, OR: Harvest House Publishers, 2007), 135. Roman soldier deserters were also flogged.

[9] John P. Mattingly, "Crucifixion: Its Origin and Application to Christ" (Th.M. thesis, Dallas Theological Seminary, 1961), 21. Mayo Foundation holds the copyright for the pictures in this chapter. All rights to these pictures appear in the following article, which belong solely to Mayo Foundations and are used by permission of Mayo Foundation for Medical Education

and Research: William D. Edwards, Wesley J. Gabel, and Floyd E. Hosmer, "On the Physical Death of Jesus Christ," *Journal of the American Medical Association* 255 (March 21, 1986): 1455–63.

10 See http://the-crucifixion.org/scourging.htm#2. Interested researchers are encouraged to visit the site in order to see other documentations regarding the quote.

11 Mattingly, "Crucifixion: Its Origin and Application to Christ," 36.

12 Norman L. Geisler and Ronald M. Brooks, *When Skeptics Ask* (Grand Rapids: Baker Books, 1990), 120–30.

13 Nails of this size driven into the wrist "would crush or server the rather large sensorimotor median nerve. The stimulated nerve would produce excruciating bolts of fiery pain in both arms" (Edwards, Gabel, and Hosmer, "On the Physical Death of Jesus Christ," 1460).

14 Gary R. Habermas and Michael R. Licona, *The Case for the Resurrection of Jesus* (Grand Rapids: Kregel Publications, 2004), 102. He notes, "The many physicians who have studied crucifixion over the years have invariably concluded that the major problem faced by victims of crucifixion was breathing, or more precisely—asphyxiation. Once on the cross, the victim would want to take the pressure off his nailed feet. To do this, he would allow the weight of his body to be held up by his nailed hands. However, in this 'down' position, certain muscles would be in the inhalation position, making it difficult to exhale. Thus, the victim would have to push up on his pierced feet in order to exhale. However, the first several times he did this would cause intense pain, since it would cause the nail to tear through the flesh in the feet until it enlodged itself against one of the bones. Thus, the crucifixion victim would be seen pushing up quite often and retuning to the down position. Sever muscle cramps and spasms would also make breathing all the more difficult and painful" (ibid., 101) See also Edwards, Gabel, and Hosmer, "On the Physical Death of Jesus Christ," 1461.

15 Gruber, *Jesus Conspiracy*, 249.

16 *BDAG*, 682–3.

17 Edwards, Gabel, and Hosmer, "On the Physical Death of Jesus Christ," 1463.

18 Josh McDowell, *Evidence That Demands a Verdict: Historical Evidences for the Christian Faith*, vol. 1 (San Bernardino, CA: Here's Life Publishers, 1972), 198–99.

19 Habermas, *Historical Jesus*, 73. See David F. Strauss, *A New Life of Jesus*, vol. 2 (London: Williams and Norgate, 1865), 408–12.

20 Wilbur M. Smith, *Therefore Stand: Christian Apologetics* (Grand Rapids: Baker Book House, 1965), 370–71.

21 John Ankerberg and John Weldon, *The Passion and the Empty Tomb* (Eugene, OR: Harvest House Publishers, 2005), 42–43.

22 Josephus, *The Jewish Wars* 4:51; Cicero *Against Verres* 2.5.64 cited by Gerard

S. Sloyan, *The Crucifixion of Jesus: History, Myth, Faith* (Minneapolis: Fortress Press, 1977), 13. See also Martin Hengel, *Crucifixion* (Philadelphia: Fortress Press, 1977), 8.

[23] See Hengel, *Crucifixion*, 8–9.

[24] Josephus, *The Antiquities of the Jews* 18:64 (18.3.3.64) taken from Accordance 7.4 of the electronic volume, Flavius Josephus, *The Works of Josephus: Complete and Unabridged,* trans. William Whiston, New Updated ed. (Peabody, MA: Hendrickson Publishers, 1987).

[25] Tacitus, *Annals* 15.44 (A.D. 115), cited in Habermas and Licona, *Case for the Resurrection of Jesus*, 59.

[26] Lucian of Samosata, *The Death of Peregrine*, 11–13 (A.D. 150–175) cited in ibid.

[27] This translation is in Alexander Roberts, James Donaldson, and A.C. Coxe, eds., *The Ante-Nicene Christian Library: Translations of the Writings of the Fathers Down to A.D. 325*, trans. A. Roberts, J. Donaldson, and A.C. Coxe (Oak Harbor, OR: Logos Research Systems, 1997), cited in Habermas and Licona, *Case for the Resurrection of Jesus*, 59.

[28] *bSanhedrin* 43a (6.2.1e) translation from Accordance 7.4 electronic volume Jacob Neusner, *The Babylonian Talmud: A Translation and Commentary* (Peabody, MA: Hendrickson Publishers, 2005).

[29] John D. Crossan, *Jesus: A Revolutionary Biography* (San Francisco: Harper SanFrancisco, 1994), 145, see also 154–55, 196, 201.

[30] Gerd Lüdemann, *The Resurrection of Christ: A Historical Inquiry* (Amherst, NY: Prometheus Books, 2004), 50.

[31] James D. Tabor, *The Jesus Dynasty: The Hidden History of Jesus, His Royal Family and the Birth of Christianity* (New York: Simon & Schuster, 2006), 230 (italics his). Hence Habermas concludes, "Such strange 'twists' to the swoon theory have been virtually ignored by scholars with good reason, for serious problems invalidate each of these theses" (*Historical Jesus*, 93).

[32] Smith, *Therefore Stand*, 373–74.

[33] These eight points are taken from William Lane Craig, *The Son Rises: The Historical Evidence for the Resurrection of Jesus* (Chicago: Moody Press, 1981), 45–90; and *idem, Reasonable Faith: Christian Truth and Apologetics*, rev. ed. (Chicago: Moody Press, 1984; reprint, Wheaton, IL: Crossway Books, 1994), 272–78.

[34] Craig, *Reasonable Faith*, 272.

[35] N. T. Wright, *The Resurrection of God*, Christian Origins and the Question of God, vol. 3 (London: SPCK, 2003), 321, see also n. 21. Craig says, "Second, the expression 'on the third day' implies the empty tomb. Since no one actually saw Jesus rise from the dead, why did the early disciples proclaim that he had been raised 'on the third day'? The most likely answer is that it was on the third day that the women discovered the tomb of Jesus empty; and so naturally, the resurrection itself came to be dated on that day.

In this case, the expression 'on the third day' is a time-indicator pointing to the discovery of the empty tomb" (*Reasonable Faith*, 274).

[36] The date one picks depends on how one dates Jesus' death. See Harold W. Hohner, *Chronological Aspects of the Life of Christ* (Grand Rapids: Zondervan Publishing House, 1977), 37.

[37] Habermas and Licona, *Case for the Resurrection of Jesus*, 52–53, see also n. 25. See also Craig, *The Son Rises*, 47–51; Habermas, *Historical Jesus*, 29–30, 143–44.

[38] Habermas and Licona, *Case for the Resurrection of Jesus*, 53.

[39] Craig, *Reasonable Faith*, 274.

[40] Craig, *The Son Rises*, 51–52; Craig, *Reasonable Faith*, 274–75.

[41] Craig, *Reasonable Faith*, 275.

[42] *The Gospel of Peter* 8:28; 9:34–35; 10:38. Christian Maurer, "The Gospel of Peter," in *New Testament Apocrypha*, ed. Wilhelm Schneemelcher, trans. E. McL. Wilson, vol. 1 (Tübingen: J. C. B. Mohr (Paul Siebeck), 1990; reprint, Louisville: John Knox Press, 1991), 224–25.

[43] Craig, *Reasonable Faith*, 275–76.

[44] Matthew 28:1–8; Mark 16:1–8; Luke 24:1–10; John 20:1–8.

[45] Accordance 7.4 electronic volume Josephus.

[46] Accordance 7.4 electronic volume Neusner, "The Babylonian Talmud: A Translation and Commentary."

[47] Gary R. Habermas, *The Secret of the Talpiot Tomb: Unravelling the Mystery of the Jesus Family Tomb* (Nashville: Broadman & Holman Publishing, 2007), 72.

[48] Gaius Suetonius, *The Twelve Caesars*, trans. Robert Graves, Augustus 44 (New York: Penguin, 1989), 80, cited in Habermas and Licona, *Case for the Resurrection of Jesus*, 73.

[49] Habermas and Licona, *Case for the Resurrection of Jesus*, 73 (italics his). See also Craig, *The Son Rises*, 77–78.

[50] Craig, *Reasonable Faith*, 277.

[51] Mark 14:30, 47 [John 18:10], 50–51, 66–72.

[52] Louis A. Jr. Barbieri, "Matthew," in *The Bible Knowledge Commentary, New Testament*, ed. John F. Walvoord and Roy B. Zuck, vol. 2 (Wheaton, IL: Victor Books, 1983; reprint, Colorado Springs: Cook Communications, 1996), 93.

[53] Craig, *Reasonable Faith*, 277–78.

Chapter Five

[1] Williams Milligan, *The Resurrection of Our Lord* (New York: Macmillian Company, 1927), 71.

[2] Electronic, "Dictionary," (Apple Computer, 2005).

[3] Accordance 7.4 version electronic sources: Walter Bauer et al., *A Greek English Lexicon of the New Testament and Other Early Christian Literature*, rev.

and ed. Frederick William Danker, 3rd ed. (Chicago: University of Chicago Press, 2000); Ludwig Koëhler and Walter Baumgartner, *The Hebrew and Aramaic Lexicon of the Old Testament*, trans. M. E. J. Richardson, rev. Walter Baumgartner and Johann Jakob Stamm ed., ed. M. E. J. Richardson, vol. 2 (Leiden: E. J. Brill, 2001).

[4] Craig R. Koester acknowledged that even if the stories in Kings refer to resuscitation since those in the stories would die again, those involved (like Isaac's deliverance from being sacrificed in Gen. 22) foreshadow the future final resurrection (*Hebrews: A New Translation with Introduction and Commentary*, Anchor Bible, ed. Williams F. Albright and David N. Freedman, vol. 36 [New York: Doubleday, 2001], 514). This was also noted by N. T. Wright, *The Resurrection of God*, Christian Origins and the Question of God, vol. 3 (London: SPCK, 2003), 458 n. 18.

[5] D. J. Wiseman, *1 & 2 Kings: An Introduction and Commentary*, Tyndale Old Testament Commentaries, ed. D. J. Wiseman, vol. 9 (Downers Grove, IL: InterVarsity Press, 1993), 205.

[6] Wright, *Resurrection of God*, 96.

[7] Marvin H. Pope says, "This verse is notoriously difficult. The ancient versions all differ and no reliance can be placed in any of them. Various emendations have been proposed, but are scarcely worth discussing. Many Christian interpreters since Origen have tried to read here an affirmation of immortality or resurrection, but without success: Chrysostom quite correctly refuted this interpretation with the citation of xiv 12ff. If one sticks to the text as received, the given translation appears to fit the context as well as any, though many problems persist" (*Job*, Anchor Bible, ed. William Foxwell Albright and David Noel Freedman, vol. 15 [Garden City, NY: Doubleday & Company, 1965], 135). For a good bibliography and various view points on this passage see Wright, *Resurrection of God*, 98 n. 63.

[8] Bold type is added for emphasis.

[9] T. J. Meek, "Job 19:25–27," *Vetus Testamentum* 6 (January 1956): 100–3.

[10] Roy B. Zuck, "Job," in *The Bible Knowledge Commentary, Old Testament*, ed. John F. Walvoord and Roy B. Zuck, vol. 1 (Wheaton, IL: Victor Books, 1985; reprint, Colorado Springs: Cook Communications, 1996), 742.

[11] F. Delitzsch said, "The hope of a resurrection as a settled principle in a creed of Israel is certainly more recent than the Solomonic period. Therefore by far the majority of modern expositors have decided that Job does not indeed here avow the hope of the resurrection, but the hope of a future spiritual beholding of God, and therefore of a future life; and thus the popular idea of Hades, which elsewhere has sway over him, breaks out.... This rendering ... does not exhaust the meaning of Job's confession" (*The Book of Job*, trans. Francis Bolton, Commentary on the Old Testament in Ten Volumes, ed. C. F. Keil and F. Delitzsch, vol. 4 [reprint, Grand Rapids: Wm. B. Eerdmans Publishing, 1980], 360).

[12] Wright, *Resurrection of God*, 98 n. 63. In another place Wright says regarding Job 19:25–26. "Finally, one of the most blatant denials of the resurrection to be found in the Old Testament, that in Job 14.12, has been altered in the Targum, as in the LXX, so that it only denies the future life of the wicked, leaving the way clear for a resurrection of the righteous—which may indeed be mentioned in the Targum on Job 19.25–26, though this passage, like its Masoretic original, is obscure. As with the main rabbinic writings themselves, so with the Targumim; there is no question but that they insist, again and again, on interpreting scripture in the direction of bodily resurrection" (ibid., 199).

[13] For this view see Isaiah 26:19 in Edward J. Kissane, *The Book of Isaiah*, trans. Edward J. Kissane (Dublin: Richview Press, 1941–43).

[14] Wright says, "But those who seek YHWH in distress find themselves in pangs like a woman giving birth; and when birth comes it turns to be a new birth of the dead themselves (26:16–19)" (*Resurrection of God*, 117).

[15] J. Alec Motyer, *Isaiah: An Introduction and Commentary*, Tyndale Old Testament Commentaries, ed. D. J. Wiseman, vol. 18 (Downers Grove, IL: InterVarsity Press, 1999), 178 (italics his). Others who interpret this as referring to literal bodily resurrection are Arthur S. Herbert, *The Book of the Prophet Isaiah, Chapters 1–39* (Cambridge: University Press, 1973); Kissane, *Isaiah*; John A. Martin, "Isaiah," in *The Bible Knowledge Commentary, Old Testament*, ed. John F. Walvoord and Roy B. Zuck, vol. 1 (Wheaton, IL: Victor Books, 1985; reprint, Colorado Springs: Cook Communications, 1996), 1075; Harold H. Rowley, *The Faith of Israel: Aspects of Old Testament Thought* (London: SCM Press, 1956), 1160; John Skinner, *The Book of the Prophet Isaiah: Revised Version, with Introduction and Notes*, rev. ed. (Cambridge: University Press, 1915–17).

[16] Wright, *Resurrection of God*, 117; see n. 140 for the names of other scholars. Motyer makes an interesting observation. "The evolutionary supposition that OT thought progressed from poor beginnings to brilliant endings has led to the conclusion that this doctrine of death and resurrection must be late. How insubstantial is all this! The Egyptians had an intricate theology of life after death centuries before Isaiah. Even Canaanite religion, for all its brutishness, depended on the annual triumph of Baal over death. In the name of all logic, how could Israel, with its foundational belief in the living God lack, within revealed religion, what others arrived at by wishful thinking and natural religion?" (*Isaiah*, 178 n. 2). While Motyer is correct in some sense, one must be careful in fully attributing to Israel the "life after death" beliefs of their pagan neighbors since Israel's belief in bodily resurrection was not the same. See Edwin M. Yamauchi, "Tammuz and the Bible," *Journal of Biblical Literature* 84 (September 1965): 283 –90.

[17] Some have tried using this passage to prove Ezekiel teaches literal bodily resurrection, and others that it teaches spiritual regeneration. The symbolic

two sticks have also been incorrectly interpreted as British Israelites and have also been used to refute them. See John B. Taylor, *Ezekiel: An Introduction and Commentary*, Tyndale Old Testament Commentaries, ed. D. J. Wiseman, vol. 20 (Downers Grove, IL: InterVarsity Press, 1969), 234.

[18] The Qumran community interpreted Ezekiel 37 as metaphor and literal resurrection: "[And I said, 'O LORD,] I have seen many from Israel who have loved Your name and have walked in the ways[of Your heart. So,] when will [th]ese things come to pass? And how will their faithfulness be rewarded?' And the LORD said to me, 'I see the Children of Israel, and they shall know that I am the LORD.' (vacat) [And He said,] 'Son of man, prophecy over these bones, and say, "Come together, bone to its bone and joint [to its joint."' And it wa]s s[o.] And He said a second time, 'Prophecy, and let sinews come upon them and let skin cover [them.' And it was so.] And He s[ai]d, 'Again prophecy to the four winds of the heavens, and a let them blow a wind [upon the slain.' And it was so.] And a great many people [revi]ved (Ezekiel 37:4–10). And they blessed the LORD of hosts wh[o] [had revived them. (vacat) And] I said, 'O LORD, when will [th] ese things come to pass?' And the LORD said to [me, 'Until']" (4Q385 f2:2–9; see also 4Q386 f1:1–10; 4Q388 f8:4–7). This translation comes from the electronic version of Accordance 7.4 Michael O. Wise, Jr. Martin G. Abegg, and Edward M. Cook, "The Dead Sea Scrolls: A New English Translation" (New York: HarperCollins Publishers, 1996). Wright also notes this (*Resurrection of God*, 188–89).

[19] In the following OT passages "sleep" refers to "death": 2 Kgs. 4:31; 13:21; Job 13:13; 14:12; Ps. 13:3; Jer. 51:39, 57; Nah. 3:18. The word "dust" also refers to where the dead will end: Gen. 3:19; Job 19:9; 34:15; Ps. 104:29; Eccl. 3:20; 12:7; Isa. 26:19.

[20] J. Dwight Pentecost makes this point. ("Daniel," in *The Bible Knowledge Commentary, Old Testament*, ed. John F. Walvoord and Roy B. Zuck, vol. 1 [Wheaton, IL: Victor Books, 1985; reprint, Colorado Springs: Cook Communications, 1996], 1372).

[21] Gleason L. Archer, Jr., "Daniel," in *The Expositor's Bible Commentary with the New International Version: Daniel and the Minor Prophets*, ed. F. E. Gaebelein, vol. 7 (Grand Rapids: Zondervan Publishing House, 1985), 152.

[22] Wright, *Resurrection of God*, 110.

[23] Ibid.

[24] The NET Bible recorded in a note on Daniel 12:2, "This verse is the only undisputed reference to a literal resurrection found in the Hebrew Bible" (*The NET Bible: New English Translation*, [Dallas], TX: Biblical Studies Press, 2001], 1608 n.10).

[25] Wright, *Resurrection of God*, 109.

[26] John J. Collins, *Daniel, with an Introduction to Apocalyptic Literature* (Grand Rapids: Wm. B. Eerdmans Publishing, 1984), 391.

[27] Describing one of the parallel accounts (Mark 5:21–43; Luke 8:40–56) will be enough to illustrate the point.

[28] *mKetubot* 4:4 mentions, "R. Judah says, 'Even the poorest man in Israel should not hire fewer than two flutes and one professional wailing woman.'"

[29] David F. Strauss notes that Paulus, Schleiermacher, and Olshausen believe the girl was not dead but asleep (*The Life of Jesus Critically Examined*, trans. Geroge Eliot, Life of Jesus Series, ed. Peter C. Hodgson [Philadelphia: Fortress Press, 1972], 478–79 n. 10).

[30] *BDAG*, 490.

[31] Louis A. Jr. Barbieri, "Matthew," in *The Bible Knowledge Commentary, New Testament*, ed. John F. Walvoord and Roy B. Zuck, vol. 2 (Wheaton, IL: Victor Books, 1985; reprint, Colorado Springs: Cook Communications, 1996), 40.

[32] D. A. Carson, "Matthew," in *The Expositor's Bible Commentary: with The New International Version of the Holy Bible*, ed. Frank E. Gaebelein, vol. 8 (Grand Rapids: Zondervan Publishing House, 1984), 581–82.

[33] It appears that Jesus ascended after forty days according to Acts 1:3 instead of fifty days, as Glasscock suggests. Kenneth Barker argues, however, "The number 'forty' in Scripture means a full period of time, a rounded-out period; it does not necessarily mean literally forty calendar days. In this context, then, it means that Jesus appeared to his disciples regularly for a period and then left them permanently" ("Jesus Ascended Into Heaven," in *Fundamentals of Catholicism*, vol. 1 [San Francisco: Ignatius Press, 1995], 78). Without any markers telling us otherwise, it is bets to interpret forty days literally as the actual time when Jesus ascended after rising bodily.

[34] Ed Glasscock, *Matthew*, Moody Gospel Commentary (Chicago: Moody Press, 1997), 541.

[35] Darrell L. Bock, *Acts*, Baker Exegetical Commentary on the New Testament, ed. Robert W. Yarbrough and Robert H. Stein (Grand Rapids: Baker Academics, 2007), 68.

[36] Ibid., 378.

[37] Robert L. Thomas, *Revelation 8–22: An Exegetical Commentary* (Chicago: Moody Press, 1995), 96.

Chapter Six

[1] Clark Pinnock, "A Dialogue on Christ's Resurrection," *Christianity Today*, April 12, 1968, 11.

[3] For a chronological chart pinpointing these appearances see Louis A. Barbieri, Jr., "Matthew," in *The Bible Knowledge Commentary, New Testament*, ed. John F. Walvoord and Roy B. Zuck (Wheaton, IL: Victor Books, 1983; reprint, Colorado Springs: Cook Communications, 1996), 91. Twelve appearances rather than 10 may be counted if one includes Paul's vision of Jesus on the road to Damascus in Acts 9:1–9 and the witness of the 500 believers (1 Cor.

15:6). See John Ankerberg and John Weldon, *The Passion and the Empty Tomb* (Eugene, OR: Harvest House Publishers, 2005), 64–65.

[4] For an orderly account of how these events progressed see J. Dwight Pentecost, *The Words and Works of Jesus Christ: A Study of the Life of Christ* (Grand Rapids: Zondervan Publishing House, 1981), 496–97.

[5] See the discussion in chapter 4.

[6] Pentecost, *Words and Works of Jesus Christ*, 496.

[7] J. Carl Laney, *John*, Moody Gospel Commentary, ed. Paul Enns (Chicago: Moody Press, 1992), 360–61.

[8] Raymond E. Brown, *The Gospel According to John (XII–XXI)*, Anchor Bible, ed. W. F. Albright and D. N. Freedman (New York, NY: Doubleday, 1969), 987.

[9] Pentecost, *Words and Works of Jesus Christ*, 496.

[10] Scholars debate whether Mark 16:9–20 was originally part of the Gospel or whether it was added later. Even if one accepts that it was added later, that does not mean it was not part of the original Gospel at one point. Since all Bibles carry the longer ending and that is what people continue to read, I assume its inclusion since it serves (whether or not it belongs here) to show the common first-century belief in Jesus' physical resurrection. However for further studies see William R. Farmer, *The Last Twelve Verses of Mark* (Cambridge: Cambridge University Press, 1974); Kelly R. Iverson, "A Further Word on Final Γάρ," *Catholic Biblical Quarterly* 68 (January 2006): 79–94; J. Carl Laney, *Answers to Tough Questions From Every Book of the Bible: A Survey of Problem Passages* (Grand Rapids: Kregel Publications, 1997), 217; Bruce M. Metzger, *A Textual Commentary on the Greek New Testament*, 2d ed. (Stuttgart: Biblia-Druck, 1994), 102–7.

[11] See chapter 4.

[12] Walter Bauer et al., *A Greek English Lexicon of the New Testament and Other Early Christian Literature*, rev. and ed. Frederick William Danker, 3rd ed. (Chicago: University of Chicago Press, 2000), 272–73.

[13] Joel B. Green sees a similar contrast between Jesus and Philip's disappearance (*The Gospel of Luke*, New International Commentary on the New Testament, ed. Gordon D. Fee [Grand Rapids: Wm. B. Eerdmans Publishing, 1997], 850).

[14] See my explanation of Romans 1:4 of Jesus' glorified state in René A. Lopez, *Romans Unlocked: Power to Deliver* (Springfield, MO: 21st Century Press, 2005), 32-33. Of course, this in itself does not disprove He was not spiritually resurrected, since angels are spirits that can materialize and dematerialize; but it does not prove that Jesus was spiritually resurrected either, especially when considering all of the evidence in the Gospel accounts and background research which points to bodily resurrection as the best option. See chapter 9.

[15] Darrell L. Bock, *Luke 9:51—24:53*, Baker Exegetical Commentary on the

New Testament (Grand Rapids: Baker Books, 1996), 1933. See chapter 4.

[16] Ibid., 1934.

[17] Ibid.

[18] Ibid., 1935.

[19] C. K. Barrett, *The Gospel According to John: An Introduction with Commentary and Notes on the Greek Text*, 2 ed. (Philadelphia, PA: Westminster Press, 1955; reprint, 1978), 572. Tabor, however, argues that Jesus' body can be viewed like that of angels materializing. See chapter 9

[20] Frederick L. Godet correctly interprets the point of the section. "That Jesus intended, however, to teach some lesson of dependence on His wisdom and guidance as related to the future work of the apostles, and as, in some sense, preparatory for what was to be said to Peter, is to be regarded as probable" (*Commentary on the Gospel of John: Vol. 2 John 6 to End*, trans. Timothy Dwight, Classic Commentary Library [n.p.: Funk & Wagnalls, 1893; reprint, Grand Rapids: Zondervan Publishing House, n.d.], 538).

[21] Ed Glasscock, *Matthew*, Moody Gospel Commentary (Chicago: Moody Press, 1997), 552.

[22] BDAG, 252.

[23] Craig L. Blomberg, *Matthew*, The New American Commentary: An Exegetical and Theological Exposition of Holy Scripture, ed. David S. Dockery (Nashville: Broadman Press, 1992), 430; I. P. Ellis, "But Some Doubted," *New Testament Studies* 14 (July 1968): 574–80. Ankerberg sees Jesus appearing to the 500 witnesses as a separate event (*Passion and the Empty Tomb*, 65).

[24] N. T. Wright, *The Resurrection of God*, Christian Origins and the Question of God, vol. 3 (London: SPCK, 2003), 560 n. 22.

[25] Because of time, space and limited scope of this book, I have chosen to deal only with the crucial and most used passage to defend the spiritual resurrection view. For a comprehensive treatment covering other passages (e.g., 2 Cor. 4–5:10), which do not contradict the exegesis and conclusions arrived here, see ibid., 209–309, 361–72.

[26] See Otto Pfleiderer, *Paulinism: A Contribution to the History of Primitive Christian theology*, trans. Edward Peters, vol. 1 (London: Williams and Norgate, 1877), 201; Johannes Weiss, *Earliest Christianity: A History of the Period A.D. 30-150*, trans. Frederick C. Grant, vol. 2 (New York: Harper Collins, 1959), 535. "Startling, since all exegetical, theological, and lexicographical evidence is against it, Louw and Nida astonish us by placing 15:44 almost alone in a short sub-category under the heading 'pertaining to not being physical'" (Anthony C. Thiselton, *The First Epistle to the Corinthians: A Commentary on the Greek Text*, New International Greek Testament Commentary, ed. I. Howard Marshall and Donald A. Hagner [Grand Rapids: Wm. B. Eerdmans Publishing, 2000], 1277). See J. P. Louw and E. A. Nida, *Lexical Semantics of the Greek New Testament: A Supplement*

to the Greek-English Lexicon of the New Testament Based on Semantic Domains, vol. 1 (Atlanta: Scholars Press, 1992), 694, sect. 79–3.

[27] Darrell L. Bock and Daniel B. Wallace, *Dethroning Jesus: Exposing Popular Culture's Quest to Unseat the Biblical Christ* (Nashville: Thomas Nelson, 2007), 211 (italics theirs).

[28] See chapter 10. Wright makes this point that creation was redeemed by the new bodily resurrection (*Resurrection of God,* 313–14). See also Ben Witherington III, *Jesus, Paul and the End of the World* (Downers Grove, IL: InterVarsity Press, 1992), 185.

[29] "Philosophers made distinctions between different kinds of substance, but they did not draw the line in the same place that modern western thought has done, between 'physical' and 'non-physical'" (Wright, *Resurrection of God,* 348–49).

[30] Thiselton, *1 Corinthians,* 1276. He notes, "This is confirmed by... the generally accepted modal use of ἐάν in the sets of contrasts."

[31] Wright, *Resurrection of God,* 347.

[32] In fact, Thiselton observes, "On rare (always non-Pauline) occasions in the New Testament, πνεῦμα may denote a ghost or spirit being (almost exclusively Mark 14:26; Luke 24:37; Acts 23:8), but such a use is generally avoided because of its association with evil spirits (Mark 9:25; cf. Mark 1:34, δαίμων)" (*1 Corinthians,* 1276).

[33] Charles L. Quarles also notes, "In other contexts it is clear that they do not refer to persons or objects as either made of matter or spirit. In 1 Corinthians 2:14–15, for example, the terms refer respectively to people influenced by human drives versus people under the control of the Spirit. It is likely that Paul's use in 1 Corinthians 15:44 is related to this earlier use" (*Buried Hopes or Risen Savior: Is the Talpiot Tomb the Burial Place of Jesus of Nazareth?* (online:https://www.lacollege.edu/ifl/jesus_tomb.pdf, March 4, 2007, accessed October 18, 2007), 12.

[34] Paul used *pneumatikos* ten times in 1 Corinthians (2:13, 15; 3:1; 9:11; 10:3; 12:1; 14:1, 37; 15:44, 46).

[35] Elsewhere in the letter Paul contrasted believers to unbelievers as they are controlled by carnal desires and thus act like unbelievers. See René A. López, "Does the Vice List in 1 Corinthians 6:9-10 Describe Believers or Unbelievers?," *Bibliotheca sacra* 164 (January-March 2007): 59–73. "The overall structure and logic of the chapter thus confirms what we would have guessed from the direction in which the rest of the letter points: that this is intended by Paul as a long argument in favour of a future *bodily* resurrection.... Paul repeatedly indicates earlier in the letter that Christian behaviour in the present life is predicated upon continuity between this life and the future one. It would be surprising if now, addressing the issue head on at last, he were to undermine what he said all along. There was, in any case, no indication in Judaism either before or after Paul that 'resurrection'

could mean anything other than 'bodily'; if Paul was going to argue for something so oxymoronic as a '*non*-bodily resurrection' he would have done better not to structure his argument in such a way as to give the appearance of articulating a Pharisaic, indeed biblical, worldview in which the goodness of the present creation is reaffirmed in the age to come. Since that is the kind of argument he has composed, at the conclusion of a letter which constantly points this way, no question should remain. When Paul said 'resurrection,' he meant 'bodily resurrection'" (Wright, *Resurrection of God*, 314).

[36] A similar observation is made by Quarles, *Buried Hopes or Risen Savior: Is the Talpiot Tomb the Burial Place of Jesus of Nazareth?* (accessed), 12; and Thiselton, *1 Corinthians*, 1276.

[37] Thiselton clarifies the difference between both of these adjectives. "The widely accepted (although not decisive) lexicographical distinction between –ινος endings, which often, perhaps regularly, denote composition, in distinction from –ικος endings, which regularly denote modes of being or characteristics" (*1 Corinthians*, 1276). See also Quarles, *Buried Hopes or Risen Savior: Is the Talpiot Tomb the Burial Place of Jesus of Nazareth?* (accessed), 12.

[38] Thiselton, *1 Corinthians*, 1277. See also Eduard Schweizer, "πνευματικός," in *Theological Dictionary of the New Testament*, ed. Gerhard Friedrich and Geoffrey W. Bromiley, trans. Geoffrey W. Bromiley, vol. 6 (Grand Rapids: Wm. B. Eerdmans Publishing, 1968; reprint, 1999), 389–455.

[39] Thiselton, *1 Corinthians*, 1276 (iltalics his).

[40] F. F. Bruce, *1 & 2 Corinthians*, Life Application Bible Commentary, ed. Grant R. Osborne (Wheaton, IL: Tyndale House, 1999), 152.

[41] C. K. Barrett, *A Commentary on the First Epistle to the Corinthians*, Harper's New Testament commentaries. (New York: Harper & Row, 1968), 372.

[42] See David E. Garland, *1 Corinthians*, Baker Exegetical Commentary on the New Testament, ed. Robert W. Yarbrough and Robert H. Stein (Grand Rapids: Baker Academic, 2003), 734.

[43] For an explanation of the "new man" in all regenerate Christians see Lopez, *Romans Unlocked*, 129–31.

[44] "Body, therefore, affirms the biblical tradition of a positive attitude toward physicality as a condition for experiencing life in its fullness, but also assimilates, subsumes, and transcends the role of the physical in the public domain of the earthly life. Hence it would be appropriate to conceive of the raised body as a form or mode of existence of the whole person including every level of intersubjective communicative experience that guarantees both the continuity of personal identity and enhanced experience of community which facilitates intimate union with God in Christ and with differentiated 'others' who also share this union" (Thiselton, *1 Corinthians*, 1278).

[45] Schweizer also makes a similar observation based on the context. "The idea that σῶμα as a form represents the continuum which simply exchanges

the carnal substance for the spiritual substance is also quite untenable. The true concern of Paul may be seen in the fact that ψυχικός (v. 44) on the one side is interpreted by φθορά (v.[sic] 42, 50), ἀσθένεια and ἀτιμία (v. 43; cf. Phil. 3:21 ταπείνωσις), and πνευματικός on the other side is interpreted by ἀφθαρσία (v. [sic] 42, 50), δύναμις and δόξα (v. 43; Phil. 3:21). Behind the form of thinking in terms of substance there thus lies the OT distinction between weakness and power. Man is referred to the creative power of his Lord, who will raise him up. Continuity between the earthly and the heavenly body rests on a miracle. The same is to be seen in v. 47, where the first clause with γῆ denotes that stuff from which the first man is made, while the second clause characterises [sic] the second man, not by the substance of which he consists but by his origin. Thus the σῶμα πνευματικόν of either Redeemer or believer is to be understood, not as one which consists of πνεῦμα, but as one which is controlled by the πνεῦμα" ("πνευματικός," 6:421).

[46] Thiselton, *1 Corinthians*, 1277.

[47] Hence Bock concludes, "In experiential form, this is what Paul discusses conceptually in 1 Cor. 15:35–49, especially 15:41–44.... Paul's point is that another force is the key to the resurrection body; it is a 'spiritual' body as opposed to a 'soulish' body. This is why it is more than flesh and bone and can be immortal." Then he points out that the resurrection bodies of believers will be similar in that of Jesus' body. "The resurrection body is flesh and bone transformed into a form that is able to move through material matter.... There is no way to distinguish the person of Jesus from the risen Christ except that his existence now takes place at an additional dimension of reality. They are basically one and the same. A spirit has not taken his place, nor is he just a spirit. The person buried in the tomb is raised and transformed, but Jesus is sufficiently distinct in appearance that he is not always immediately recognizable. In his resurrected state, he clearly is transformed, though in a way that still leaves traces of his former existence (e.g., the nail prints in his hands and feet)" (Darrell L. Bock, *Luke 9:51—24:53*, Baker Exegetical Commentary on the New Testament [Grand Rapids: Baker Books, 1996], 1933–34). Paul Lampe also said, "For him, the term 'spiritual' emphasizes that God's Spirit is the *only* force that creates the new body. The creation of this new body is totally *beyond* all the possibilities of the present nature and creation. That is all that Paul wants to convey with this term. Therefore I do not see how the natural sciences could help us to understand the totally different 'nature' of this future body—unless natural science were able to transcend the nature of this universe. Paul asserts that our spiritual body will be very similar, even 'conformed' (*symmorphon*), to that of the resurrected Christ (Phil. 3:21). But he refrains from giving further details, which later evangelicals pretend to 'know' by describing the resurrected Christ. The apostle only affirms that

our spiritual body 'in heaven' will be a 'body of glory' as opposed to the 'body of lowliness' in which we now live (Phil. 3:20–21)" ("Paul's Concept of a Spiritual Body," in *Resurrection: Theological and Scientific Assessments:*, ed. Ted Peters, Robert John Russel, and Michael Welker [Grand Rapids: Wm. B. Eerdmans Publishing, 2002], 109 [italics his]).

Chapter Seven

[1] Quote by Josh McDowell, *Evidence That Demands a Verdict: Historical Evidences for the Christian Faith*, vol. 1 (San Bernardino, CA: Here's Life Publishers, 1972), 167.

[2] Josh D. McDowell, *The New Evidence that Demands a Verdict* (Nashville: Thomas Nelson, 1999), 168.

[3] Ibid., 144, 167.

[4] Ibid., 167.

[5] Numerous views exist in how to interpret Ps. 16:8–11: the ancient views, hermeneutical error view, *sensus plenior* view, canonical approach view, typological view, single message view, direct prophecy view. For a thorough description of all these views see Gregory Vance Trull, "Peter's Use of Psalm 16:8–11 in Acts 2:25–32" (Ph.D. diss., Dallas Theological Seminary, 2002), 13–59.

[6] Ibid., 133.

[7] For a complete analysis of Psalm 16:10 see Gregory Vance Trull, "An Exegesis of Psalm 16:10," *Bibliotheca sacra* 161 (July–September 2004): 304–21.

[8] Gregory Vance Trull, "Peter's Interpretation of Psalm 16:8–11 in Acts 2:25–32," *Bibliotheca sacra* 161 (October–December 2004): 447. Peter, however, acknowledges David's meaning of the shift from the first person pronoun of himself to refer to the third person pronoun as a referent of Messiah, Jesus, by himself inserting the third person pronoun instead of the Hebrew second person pronoun. Δαυὶδ γὰρ λέγει εἰς αὐτόν ("For David says of Him," Acts 2:25). See also Gregory Vance Trull, "Views on Peter's Use of Psalm 16:8–11 in Acts 2:25–32," *Bibliotheca sacra* 161 (April–June 2004) 194–214.

[9] Darrell L. Bock, *Proclamation from Prophecy and Pattern*, Journal for the Study of the New Testament Supplement Series (Sheffield: Sheffield Academic, 1987), 175–76; *idem, Acts*, Baker Exegetical Commentary on the New Testament, ed. Robert W. Yarbrough and Robert H. Stein (Grand Rapids: Baker Academics, 2007), 124–25; Trull, "Peter's Interpretation of Psalm 16:8–11 in Acts 2:25–32," 435; Trull, "Psalm 16:8–11 in Acts 2:25–32," 179 n 13.

[10] Trull said, "The likelihood of ancient Near Eastern religious serving as the source of the Old Testament belief in resurrection seems questionable.... However, the above evidence demonstrates the rich afterlife views of cultures surrounding Israel. Therefore, expressions of physical immortality, perhaps

even resurrection ought not be surprising in the Old Testament" ("Psalm 16:8–11 in Acts 2:25–32," 148).

11 Bock, *Acts*, 125.

12 Bock says, "Peter's reading presses all the language here in a very literal direction. The text is not about premature death but about not being left in hades. The status of the flesh is part of the text's promise as well. It is Jesus' σάρξ (*sarx*) that does not see corruption; this stresses the bodily nature of his resurrection" (ibid., 126).

13 The Babylonian Talmud *Baba Bathra* 1.11 mentions David's tomb being in Jerusalem that was moved there because an underground brook was constantly removing the uncleanness. Herod tried raiding the tomb for money at the time of Antiochus VII (135–34 B.C.), which actions were stopped by fire that killed two guards. "This also led Herod to build a marble memorial to the tomb, and so it was an impressive site in Peter's day. The location was 'probably on the south side of the southeast hill of Jerusalem near the pool of Siloam" (ibid., 126–27). See also I. Howard Marshall, *The Book of Acts: An Introduction and Commentary*, Tyndale New Testament Commentaries, ed. Leon Morris (Grand Rapids: Wm. B. Eerdmans Publishing, 1980; reprint, 2002), 76.

14 Trull, "Psalm 16:8–11 in Acts 2:25–32," 246–52. I. Howard Marshall also says "it seems likely that *thy Holy One* was understood as a reference to the Messiah (*cf.* 13:35 where the same Psalm is quoted)" (*Acts*, 76). Derek Kidner further notes, "Admittedly some commentators see here [Ps. 16:9–10] no more than recovery from an illness (*cf.* Is. 38:9–22); but the contrast in Psalms 49 and 73 between the end of the wicked and that of the righteous supports a bolder view. And at its full value, as both Peter and Paul insisted (Acts 2:29ff.; 13:34–37), this language is too strong even for David's hope of his own resurrection. Only 'he whom God raised up saw no corruption'" (*Psalms 1–72: An Introduction and Commentary*, Tyndale Old Testament Commentaries, ed. D. J. Wiseman, vol. 14a [Downers Grove, IL: InterVarsity Press, 1973], 86).

15 Trull, "An Exegesis of Psalm 16:10," 307.

16 Trull, "Peter's Interpretation of Psalm 16:8–11 in Acts 2:25–32," 448.

17 Enemies of Jesus' resurrection were not denying that He rose bodily but that He rose then instead of in the anticipated future resurrection when everyone would rise.

18 John N. Oswalt, *The Book of Isaiah Chapters 40-66*, New International Commentary on the Old Testament, ed. Jr. Robert L. Hubbard (Grand Rapids: Wm. B. Eerdmans Publishing, 1998), 403.

19 N. T. Wright, *The Resurrection of God*, Christian Origins and the Question of God, vol. 3 (London: SPCK, 2003), 164. A similar argument can be made in Psalm 22 but it seems to be a bit more ambiguous than Isaiah 53:1–12, which refers to the suffering servant that fits the person of Jesus

of Nazareth.

[20] William Lane Craig, *Assessing the New Testament Evidence for the Historicity of the Resurrection of Jesus*, Studies in the Bible and Early Christianity, vol. 16 (Lewiston, NY: Edwin Mellen Press, 1989), 9–13.

[21] Though some may say this servant is Cyrus (cf. Isa 44:28), Israel, or a prophet, Oswalt explains it best. "It means exactly what has been talked about throughout the book, but particularly from ch. 49. This man, *my Servant*, is the Anointed of God to restore sinful Israel to himself, just as Cyrus was to the anointed to restore exiled Israel to her land. In contrast to Cyrus, this man's servanthood is redemptive. It finds it [*sic*] true fulfillment in th realization of what the whole sacrificial system prefigured. When an offerer accepted and carried out the provision of God for his guilt as stated in the manual of sacrifice (Lev. 1–11), he could be clean in the sight of God. But that cleansing was only symbolic, because an animal life is no substitute for a human one. Now a human life, yet obviously more than just a human life (he will make 'many' righteous), has been freely given, and the symbol is a reality. Fellowship with God is possible. As the body can come home to the land, so the heart can come home to its God. No prophet could do this for Israel, much less the world, and neither Israel as a whole nor any segment of Israel could do it either. Whoever he is, the Servant stands in the place of God pronouncing a pardon that the Sinless One alone can offer (51:4–6)" (*The Book of Isaiah Chapters 40-66*, 404–5 [italics his]).

[22] Romans 4:24–25 says, "but also for us. It shall be imputed to us who believe in Him who raised up Jesus our Lord from the dead, who was delivered up because of our offenses, and was raised because of our justification." J. Alec Motyer says that because the "Servant's work is successful" (i.e., the sacrificial atonement), the Lord's prolongation of the Servant's life mentioned in Isaiah 53:10 reflects the "resurrection" in Romans 4:25 (*Isaiah: An Introduction and Commentary*, Tyndale Old Testament Commentaries, ed. D. J. Wiseman, vol. 18 [Downers Grove, IL: InterVarsity Press, 1999], 338).

[23] Merrill C. Tenney, *The Reality of the Resurrection* (Chicago: Moody Press, 1963), 39.

[24] John A. Martin, "Isaiah," in *The Bible Knowledge Commentary, Old Testament*, ed. John F. Walvoord and Roy B. Zuck, vol. 1 (Wheaton, IL: Victor Books, 1985; reprint, Colorado Springs: Cook Communications, 1996), 1109.

[25] G. W. Grogan, "Isaiah," in *The Expositor's Bible Commentary with the New International Version: Isaiah, Jeremiah, Lamentation, Ezekiel*, ed. F. E. Gaebelein, vol. 6. (Grand Rapids: Zondervan Publishing House, 1986), 304.

[26] Norman L. Geisler and Ronald M. Brooks, *When Skeptics Ask* (Grand Rapids: Baker Books, 1990), 119.

[27] See chapters 10–11.

[28] See Genesis 5:21–24; Genesis 22:5; Deuteronomy 32:39; 1 Samuel 2:6;

Job 19:25–27; Psalms 17; 22; 49; 73. Trull views these as either having an implicit or explicit view of physical resurrection. ("Psalm 16:8–11 in Acts 2:25–32," 148–65).

Chapter Eight

[1] Josh McDowell, *A Ready Defense* (San Bernardino, CA: Here's Life Publishers, 1990), 231.

[2] Ibid.

[3] James B. Conant, *Science and Common Sense* (New Haven, CT: Yale University Press, 1951), 25.

[4] Josh McDowell, *The Resurrection Factor: Does the Historical Evidence Support the Resurrection of Jesus Christ?* (San Bernardino, CA: Here's Life Publishers, 1981), 21 (italics added).

[5] Josh McDowell, *More Than a Carpenter* (Wheaton, IL: Tyndale House Publishers, 1977), 38–39. See also John Ankerberg and John Weldon, *The Passion and the Empty Tomb* (Eugene, OR: Harvest House Publishers, 2005), 97–113.

[6] N. T. Wright, "The Resurrection: Historical Event or Theological Explanation? A Dialogue," in *The Resurrection of Jesus: John Dominic Crossan and N. T. Wright in Dialogue*, ed. Robert B. Stewart (Minneapolis: Fortress Press, 2006), 23.

[7] For an excellent scholarly discussion on numerous scientific-based arguments and the resurrection see Ted Peters et al., eds., *Resurrection: Theological and Scientific Assessments* (Grand Rapids: Wm. B. Eerdmans Publishing, 2002).

[8] McDowell, *A Ready Defense*, 231.

[9] Norman L. Geisler and Ronald M. Brooks, *When Skeptics Ask* (Grand Rapids: Baker Books, 1990), 124.

[10] John R. W. Stott, *Basic Christianity* (Downers Grove, IL: InterVarsity Press, 1971), 51.

[11] A. T. Robertson, *The Gospel According to Matthew*, Word Pictures in the New Testament, vol. 4 (Grand Rapids: Baker Book House, 1931), 239.

[12] McDowell, *A Ready Defense*, 230.

[13] Robertson, *Matthew*, 239.

[14] McDowell, *A Ready Defense*, 233.

[15] The information in this section is from John Foxe, *The New Foxe's Book of Martyrs*, rewritten and updated by Harold J. Chadwick ed. (Gainesville, FL: Bridge-Logos Publishers, 2001), 3–10. Of this list we only possess reliable evidence of martyrs 1. Stephen, 2. James the son of Zebedee, 4. James the less (who was killed in A.D. 62 not in A.D. 66), 8. Peter, and 9. Paul. All of the rest of the accounts are based on legendary hagiography. Foxe's list is used because of its popularity. For a better list of authentic martyr accounts see Herbert A. Musurillo, *The Acts of the Christian Martyrs* (Oxford: Clarendon Press, 1972). I am indebted to

Edwin M. Yamauchi who pointed this out.

[16] Gary R. Habermas and Michael R. Licona, *The Case for the Resurrection of Jesus* (Grand Rapids: Kregel Publications, 2004), 59. "A skeptic may reply, 'How do you know they *willingly* died for their beliefs? What if they were arrested and executed against their will and perhaps even recanted under torture before they died?' This is a fair question. From the early martyrdoms of Stephen and James the brother of John as well as the imprisonments and sufferings of Peter, Paul, and others, the disciples became well aware that publicly proclaiming Jesus as risen Lord in certain times and places made sufferings and, perhaps, martyrdom inevitable. Therefore, to continue on this path, fully aware of the probable outcome, was to demonstrate a *willingness* to endure suffering and martyrdom, regardless of whether these were actually experienced. Furthermore, the primary purpose of getting someone to recant under torture is to gain evidence by which to discourage others publicly. Recantation under torture would not necessarily indicate a change in the victim's mind. Nevertheless, there is no evidence of a recantation being announced. Instead, all the reports testify to steadfast courage during suffering. If the news spread that several of the original disciples had recanted, we could expect that Christianity would have been dealt a severe blow. If those in management of a publicly traded company are bailing out, the workers are not going to dump their life savings into the company stock. And yet we find early Christians willingly suffering and dying for their beliefs" (ibid., 59–60 [italics theirs]).

[17] Romans; 1 Corinthians; 2 Corinthians; Galatians; Ephesians; Philippians; Colossians; 1 Thessalonians; 2 Thessalonians; 1 Timothy; 2 Timothy; Titus; Philemon. Though many regard Hebrews as Pauline, I prefer not to include it. And though others believe the pastoral letters (1 and 2 Tim. and Titus, and perhaps others) are not Pauline I have chosen to include these traditionally accepted Pauline Epistles.

[18] Habermas and Licona, *Case for the Resurrection of Jesus*, 65.

[19] Elias Andrews, in *The Encyclopaedia Britannica*, vol. 17 (Chicago: William Benton Publisher, 1970), 469; Archibald MacBride, *Chamber's Encyclopedia*, vol. 10 (London: Pergamon Press, 1966), 516, quoted in McDowell, *More Than a Carpenter*, 86.

[20] Norval Geldenhuys, *Commentary on the Gospel of Luke*, The New International Commentary on the New Testament, ed. F. F. Bruce (Grand Rapids: Wm. B. Eerdmans Publishing, 1951), 628.

[21] For a good discussion of the early martyrs see http://www.letusreason.org/Doct13.htm.

[22] This testimony in a revised form appeared in René A. López, "Change: Not Mission Impossible," *Kindred Spirit*, Summer 2005, 1–2. It also appears online in http://scriptureunlocked.com/pdfs/Change-Its-Not-A-Mission-Impossible.pdf.

Chapter Nine

[1] Simcha Jacobovici and Charles Pellegrino, *The Jesus Family Tomb: The Evidence Behind the Discovery No One Wanted to Find* (San Francisco, CA: HarperOne, 2007), 213–34.

[2] Ibid., 220.

[3] See chapter 10 for a discussion on this point.

[4] Jacobovici and Pellegrino, *Jesus Family Tomb Revised and Updated*, 221–22.

[5] See chapters 1 and 9 for further discussion of this point.

[6] Jacobovici and Pellegrino, *Jesus Family Tomb Revised and Updated*, 222.

[7] See chapter 3.

[8] Jacobovici and Pellegrino, *Jesus Family Tomb Revised and Updated*, 222–23.

[9] Ibid., 223.

[10] Levy Yitzhak Rahmani, *A Catalogue of Jewish Ossuaries in the Collections of the State of Israel*, ed. Ayala Sussmann and Peter Schertz (Jerusalem: Israel Antiquities Authority, 1994), 17. See chapter 9 for further discussion.

[11] Jacobovici and Pellegrino, *Jesus Family Tomb Revised and Updated*, 223.

[12] Ibid., 224–25, see also pages 232–33.

[13] James D. Tabor, *The Jesus Dynasty: The Hidden History of Jesus, His Royal Family and the Birth of Christianity* (New York: Simon & Schuster, 2006), 4.

[14] Jacobovici and Pellegrino, *Jesus Family Tomb Revised and Updated*, 226.

[15] Ibid.

[16] See chapter 4 for further discussion of this point.

[17] Jacobovici and Pellegrino, *Jesus Family Tomb Revised and Updated*, 226.

[18] See his technical article online: http://www.ingermanson.com/jesus/art/tomb/Ingerman sonTombComments.pdf.

[19] See chapter 7.

[20] For a summary of these points see http://www.ingermanson.com/jesus/art/stats3.php.

SELECTED BIBLIOGRAPHY

Ankerberg, John, and Dillon Burroughs. *What's the Big Deal about Jesus?* Eugene, OR: Harvest House Publishers, 2007.

Ankerberg, John, and John Weldon. *The Passion and the Empty Tomb*. Eugene, OR: Harvest House Publishers, 2005.

Bauckham, Richard. *Jesus and the Eyewitnesses: The Gospels as Eyewitness Testimony*. Grand Rapids: Wm. B. Eerdmans Publishing, 2006.

Blomberg, Craig L. "Where Do We Start Studying Jesus?" In *Jesus Under Fire: Modern Scholarship Reinvents the Historical Jesus*, ed. Michael J. Wilkins and J. P. Moreland, 17-50. Grand Rapids: Zondervan Publishing House, 1995.

Bock, Darrell L. *Can I Trust the Bible?* Norcross, GA: Ravi Zacharias International Ministries, 2001.

Bock, Darrell L. *Breaking the Da Vinci Code: Answers to Questions Everyone's Asking*. Nashville: Thomas Nelson, 2004.

Bock, Darrell L. *The Missing Gospels: Unearthing the Truth Behind Alternative Christianities*. Nashville: Thomas Nelson, 2006.

Bock, Darrell L., and Daniel B. Wallace. *Dethroning Jesus: Exposing Popular Culture's Quest to Unseat the Biblical Christ*. Nashville: Thomas Nelson, 2007.

Boyd, Gregory A. *Jesus Under Siege*. Wheaton, IL: Victor Books, 1995.

Burroughs, Dillon. *The Jesus Family Tomb Controversy: How the Evidence Falls Short*. Ann Arbor, MI: Nimble Books LCC, 2007.

Bynum, Caroline Walker. *The Resurrection of the Body in Western Christianity, 200–1336*, 1995.

Crossan, John Dominic, and Jonathan L. Reed. *Excavating Jesus: Beneath the Stones, Behind the Texts: Revised and Updated*. 1st ed. San Francisco: HarperSanFrancisco, 2001.

Evans, Craig A. *Jesus and the Ossuaries*. Waco, TX: Baylor University Press, 2003.

Evans, Craig A. *Fabricating Jesus: How Modern Scholars Distort the Gospels*. Downers Grove, IL: InterVarsity Press, 2006.

Farnell, F. David. "Philosophical and Theological Bent of Historical Criticism." In *The Jesus Crisis: The Inroads of Historical Criticism into Evangelical Scholarship*, ed. Robert L. Thomas and F. David Farnell, 85-131.

Grand Rapids: Kregel Publications, 1998.

Habermas, Gary R. *The Historical Jesus: Ancient Evidence for the Life of Christ.* Joplin, MO: College Press Publishing, 1996.

Habermas, Gary R. *The Secret of the Talpiot Tomb: Unravelling the Mystery of the Jesus Family Tomb.* Nashville: Broadman & Holman Publishing, 2007.

Habermas, Gary R., and Michael R. Licona. *The Case for the Resurrection of Jesus.* Grand Rapids: Kregel Publications, 2004.

Hachlili, Rachael. "Hebrew Names, Personal Names, Family Names and Nicknames of Jews in the Second Temple Period." In *Families and Family Relations: As Presented in Early Judaisms and Early Christianities: Texts and Fictions,* ed. Jan Willem Van Henten and Athalya Brenner. Studies in Theology and Religion, vol. 2, 83–115. Netherlands: Deo Publishing, 2000.

Hachlili, Rachael. *Jewish Funerary Customs Practices and Rites in the Second Temple Period.* Supplements to the Journal for the Study of Judaism, ed. John J. Collins, vol. 94. Leiden: E. J. Brill, 2005.

Jenkins, Philip. *Hidden Gospels: How the Search for Jesus Lost Its Way.* Oxford: Oxford University Press, 2001.

Quarles, Chales L., ed. *Buried Hope or Risen Savior: The Search for the Jesus Tomb.* Nashville, TN: Broadman & Holman Publishing, 2008.

Sausa, Don. *The Jesus Tomb: Is It Fact or Fiction? Scholars Chime In,* ed. Jeffrey Clark. Fort Myers, FL: Vision Press, 2007.

Witherington III, Ben. *The Gospel Code: Novel Claims about Jesus, Mary Magdalene and Da Vinci.* Downers Grove, IL: InterVarsity Press, 2004.

Witherington III, Ben. *What Have They Done with Jesus? Beyond Strange Theories and Bad History—Why We Can Trust the Bible.* San Francisco: HarperSanFrancisco, 2006.

Wright, N. T. *The Resurrection of God.* Christian Origins and the Question of God, vol. 3. London: SPCK, 2003.

Yamauchi, Edwin M. "Tammuz and the Bible." *Journal of Biblical Literature* 84 (September 1965): 283–90.